D1234121

PRINCIPLES AND PRACTICE
OF TRIAL CONSULTATION

PRINCIPLES AND PRACTICE OF TRIAL CONSULTATION

STANLEY L. BRODSKY

THE GUILFORD PRESS
New York   London

© 2009 The Guilford Press
A Division of Guilford Publications, Inc.
72 Spring Street, New York, NY 10012
www.guilford.com

Printed in the United States of America

This book is printed on acid-free paper.

Last digit is print number: 9 8 7 6 5 4 3 2 1

Library of Congress Cataloging-in-Publication Data

Brodsky, Stanley L., 1939–
  Principles and practice of trial consultation / Stanley L. Brodsky.
    p. cm.
  Includes bibliographical references and index.
  ISBN 978-1-60623-173-9 (hardcover : alk. paper)
  1. Trial practice—United States. 2. Witnesses—United States. 3. Jury selection—
United States. 4. Consultants—United States. I. Title.
  KF8915.B664 2009
  347.73′75—dc22
                                                                    2009006663

ABOUT THE AUTHOR

Stanley L. Brodsky, PhD, is Professor of Psychology at The University of Alabama in Tuscaloosa, where he coordinates the Psychology–Law PhD concentration. He is the author of 12 books and over 200 articles and chapters. His most recent books are *Testifying in Court*, a bestseller; *The Expert Expert Witness*; and *Coping with Cross-Examination*. Dr. Brodsky received the 2006 Distinguished Contributions to Psychology and Law Award from the American Psychology–Law Society, an award given on only seven other occasions. Previous recipients include former U.S. Attorney General Janet Reno and Supreme Court Justice Harry Blackmun. He was also the 1996 recipient of the Distinguished Contributions to Forensic Psychology Award from the American Academy of Forensic Psychology. Dr. Brodsky maintains an independent practice in trial consultation and forensic psychology.

ACKNOWLEDGMENTS

Tess M. S. Neal was especially helpful in preparation of the manuscript. She looked over more than half of the chapters, made suggestions for rephrasing sentences, and did the spade work to locate missing references and content. Diane Wyzga read through Chapter 2 and offered constructive suggestions about discussion of the Story Spine. Jim Nageotte of The Guilford Press encouraged me from the beginning and assisted in thinking through many thorny issues. Finally, The University of Alabama generously granted me a sabbatical leave that gave me the time to complete this book.

CONTENTS

PRINCIPLES AND PRACTICE
OF TRIAL CONSULTATION

Part I

❖

ESSENTIAL ISSUES IN
TRIAL CONSULTATION

The Runaway Jury (1996), a bestseller by John Grisham, and the film that followed it (*Runaway Jury*) paint an unflattering portrait of trial consultation. The plot lines in the book and film are similar. A juror with a personal agenda negotiates with the trial consultant for the defense to help sway the verdict. In the book the suit has been filed against a tobacco company and in the film the suit has been filed against a firearms manufacturer.

In the film Gene Hackman portrays the trial consultant as a man without scruples. In the conventional and more believable component of his role, Hackman led a trial team that gathered a great deal of personal information on each juror. In the unlikely component, Hackman, while secreted in the back room of a closed costume shop, delegated assistants to photograph, spy on, blackmail, and bribe jurors. The only thing that mattered to him was the verdict, as he had no moral or ethical boundaries.

In the end, the trial consultant and culpable defendant both get a proper comeuppance. What matters for us is how trial consultants are portrayed in the film and often perceived by the public as unscrupulous and malevolent men and women who manipulate the workings of juries and the justice system in unfair and venal ways.

The first three chapters invite readers to enter the applied world of trial consultation, starting with a description of trial consultation, moving next to practices within the profession, and then to the tools of the profession. One aspect of the popular view from *Runaway Jury* and other sources is correct and will be examined: Trial consultants are not impartial participants in the justice process. Judges, juries, and expert witnesses are expected to be neutral and objective. Trial consultants are not. Instead, consultants are best understood as allied with attorneys, avidly pursuing the objectives of the side that has retained them. Fairness is not the goal; that is up the courts and juries. Making the strongest case, as part of the adversarial process, is the goal.

More than a million attorneys (the ABA estimated 1,143,000 in 2007) in the United States are governed by specific and strict guidelines regarding professional and ethical standards, licensure, continuing education, and rules that define the boundaries of acceptable professional behavior. However, even though a set of ethical guidelines for trial consultants has been published, they are largely toothless since a consultant does not have to be a member of the American Society of Trial Consultants to practice. Chapter 1 discusses these ethical and licensure issues in the context of examining the role and aims of the profession.

One marker of a profession is how it conceptualizes its tasks. Even in a field committed to applied outcomes, a conceptual frame of reference underlies how practitioners think and act. Chapter 2 describes these conceptualizations, including the role of story and narrative in helping cases unfold in the courtroom, both on the part of the storytellers, that is, the attorneys, and the audience, or the jury. One specific formulation of the narrative, the Story Spine, is described in depth. The nature of focus groups and shadow juries is also explained.

Like medicine and psychotherapy, trial consultation is both an art and a science. Although techniques and methods are sometimes constructed intuitively and sometimes on an ad hoc basis, some methods are also drawn from an existing pool of scales, instruments, and sources. In Chapter 3, these methods, which describe the type and nature of specific constructs related to jury selection and the voir dire process, are presented through the handbooks in which they are found. Constructs such as authoritarianism and need for cognition are discussed in detail because of their logical link to types of jurors and how jurors process information.

Chapter 1

INTRODUCTION TO TRIAL CONSULTATION

THE CONSULTANT AS COACH: AN ORIENTING METAPHOR

Given how much attention is paid to trial consulting, including the widely publicized cases in which consultants are involved, and to jury selection and the outcomes of the trials themselves, it is sometimes startling how little is known about trial consultants. The media and the public think of trial consultants as pervasively influential (Tooher, 2005). More power, responsibility, and influence are attributed to consultants than they merit, and, occasionally, excessive blame is attributed as well.

There is a modest literature about trial consultation. Nobody knows how many trial consultants there are because they are not required to register in any jurisdiction. They are not regulated. They are not licensed. No particular credentials are needed to be a trial consultant. Although there is a U.S. organization of these practitioners, the American Society of Trial Consultants (ASTC) membership is optional for trial consultants. No professional or scholarly journal is published. At the same time, this is a profession with defined methods, with professional pride and collegiality, a profession that has a visible and profound influence on the perception of justice in the nation.

Trial consulting is like coaching a team sport. A relatively small number of people are actually playing and a much smaller number yet serve as coaches, whereas a great many people are invested emotionally or financially in the competition, in what occurs on the playing field, and especially in the outcome—who wins and who loses.

It is more apt to compare trial consultants to coaches than to the players, who are the attorneys who try the cases (as well as their clients and witnesses who also are participants). The trial consultants help to think of ways to proceed, diagram how the presentation of evidence and the arguments during the trial are going to unfold, think about home team advantages and disadvantages, and help select the jurors.

Of course, if one examines the trial consulting-as-coaching metaphor closely enough, the metaphor breaks down. Coaches in team sports more clearly make decisions about plays, and coaches take (or are given) the blame when things go badly, processes that are not necessarily true of trial consultants. A relevant example is former Alabama football coach Paul W. (Bear) Bryant from the University of Alabama, who explicitly took responsibility and was seen as bigger than life. In his book about Alabama football fans, St. John (2004) described how Bear Bryant always and excessively took responsibility for losses.

I agree with St. John that the players are heavily responsible for successes or failures. The talent of the players (up to a certain point) usually trumps coaching skill. Similarly, the talent of the attorneys and the strength of the evidence usually trump the skill of the consultants. When the attorneys are inexperienced, unprepared, or just barely adequate and the evidence supporting their side is weak, even the best trial consultants cannot win a favorable verdict. In the same sense, with savvy attorneys and strong evidence, it is not clear whether consultants add to the likelihood of a favorable verdict or settlement. Trial consultants may make the most difference when the attorneys are more or less matched in ability and the evidence is sufficiently equivocal that it can be read as favoring either side.

THE NATURE OF TRIAL CONSULTANTS AND CONSULTATION

Although this book is about the tasks and work of trial consultants, I want to comment first about what they are like as people. Being boring is the last thing that trial consultants are ever accused of, as people or as professionals. They are, by and large, an animated, charming, intelligent group of people who energize the cases in which they are involved. Furthermore, trial consultants are hardly alike. There are some consultants who take on small cases in a limited scope of work, and there are other consultants who work on civil actions filed against large corporations in which hundreds of millions of dollars are at stake.

A marked unfolding and exposition of the work of trial consultants has occurred in the last few years. In a field in which relative little had been written, an emerging body of knowledge is becoming available to other consultants, to social scientists, and to the public. The books by Kressel and Kressel (2002), Posey and Wrightsman (2005), and Lieberman and Sales (2007) have made a difference in making public what had been private and sometimes proprietary and guarded.

The specific content areas in which trial consultants work include the general tasks of assisting in developing the theory of cases and how to present the theory, especially in opening statements and closing arguments. The work that trial consultants prepare for attorneys encompasses broad approaches to the various cases, as well as narrowly defined conceptualizations of key issues. The broad approaches begin with legal theory and concepts; the narrower focus is typically drawn from social science frames of references. These differences are elaborated further in Table 2.1 in Chapter 2.

Some trial consultants specialize in surveys, particularly of community attitudes and predispositions, as well as those that are used as parts of motions for changes of venue. Other trial consultants specialize in preparation of witnesses to testify, including expert witnesses, and in assisting attorneys in developing their examinations of witnesses. A number of trial consultants address the technical aspects of trials, including the preparation of graphic or video presentations. Others work with voir dire questions and jury selection. Leading focus groups and conducting other small-group research related to the trial issues are also frequent tasks. Almost no trial consultants perform all of these tasks. Still, most trial consultants take on multiple roles. Furthermore, almost all consultants are engaged in marketing or advertising their work.

An astute observer of the nature of trial consultation is Franklin Strier, a professor of law at the California State University at Dominguez Hills. As a scholar in business law, Strier (1999, 2004) observed that the practice of trial consultation is tied as closely to the field of marketing as it is to its behavioral psychology and legal roots. He wrote, "In essence, the trial consultant performs a marketing function in two basic ways. First, a target audience is identified—that is, those who will be most receptive to the client's case—in much the same way marketing experts would test public receptivity to new consumer products. Then, a strategy is devised to help persuade the jury *qua* consumers to 'buy' the client's product by emphasizing those case-specific factors having the most appeal to the particular individuals on the jury" (1999, p. 95). Strier also pointed out a fundamental irony in how trial consultation has evolved. When it began in the 1970s, trial consulting served either poor and indigent criminal defendants or defendants who typically were being prosecuted for antiwar protests against the Vietnam War. The majority of contemporary clients are the well-to-do and the privileged, the celebrities, the leaders of corporate America, and the insurance companies and corporations themselves.

TRIAL CONSULTATION AND FAIRNESS

The criticisms of trial consultation have been fierce. The critics argue that trial consultants stack the deck unfairly for the side that can afford to retain trial consultants, thus adding further unfairness to a system of civil and criminal trials in which much injustice is already present. Many critics have argued that the dice are already loaded against the poor and underprivileged. This issue of fairness is important to address. When I proposed to write this book, some reviewers outside the field of trial consultation raised the issue of whether it was even right to publish a book that would assist despicable people in getting acquitted. Do consultants help people who have committed contemptible acts get off? The answer is that the question is a non sequitur; what trial consultants do is help attorneys do their jobs better. Are there injustices in trial outcomes? Yes, there are. Is it the responsibility of trial consultants to ensure that justice is done? Not once they have agreed to consult on a particular case. Justice is what the courts decide. Promoting a good adversarial position is what attorneys and trial consultants do. Nevertheless, one of the prized values of the ASTC is to offer pro bono services to the needy and underserved.

At the most basic level, the question raised about trial consultants stacking the deck has to be asked generally about the system of justice. Should one assume that our system works well enough? Does the adversarial presentation of evidence and arguments as assessed by impartial juries or judges usually succeed in producing a fair and just verdict? There is no simple answer to those questions.

Recently, the graduate students in our psychology–law PhD concentration were listening to a series of speakers on the topic of occupational socialization in the law. Several of the speakers were defense attorneys, most of whom were asked by the students about the ethics of their profession. Each answered in a different way, but the underlying theme was that they each believed that the justice system was inherently good and it would serve justice well if all the players put their best efforts into their work. That is, even though some of the clients these defense attorneys were defending may have committed the offenses they were charged with, the defense attorneys believed they should do everything possible to defend a client. In the same way, the prosecuting attorneys do all they can to promote justice as they prosecute this person. The overarching belief among these speakers was that if everyone did his or her job well, justice would be served, and that injustices particularly occur when some parties don't do their jobs well. The case can be made that wide use of trial consulting would similarly allow both sides to be more effective in trials, and it has the potential to help improve their chances.

In this same spirit, Myers and Arena (2001) noted that the work of a trial consultant may indeed place one side at a disadvantage, but that the same is true of the role of everyone else involved in the trial: "Attorneys, witnesses, experts, and judges all differ from case to case and allow for variations in the 'justice' associated with a judgment" (p. 389). They further argue that consultants actually serve to restore balance to the scales of justice. For instance, many jurors believe that if defendants are charged, they are likely to be guilty (Kassin & Wrightsman, 1983; Skitka & Houston, 2001) and that it is the defendants' job to prove their innocence. Trial consultants can help identify potential jurors with these and other biases that would preclude their serving impartially and working from a presumption of innocence.

Lieberman and Sales (2007) examined these fairness issues and they concluded:

> The practice of hiring consultants is legally permissible, and one could even argue inherently important for attorneys to do, if they are going to represent clients to the best of their abilities by using all the tools at their disposal. Any imbalance in the courtroom created by the disparate wealth between individuals or corporations involved in litigation would be present regardless of whether jury selection consultants were used. Indeed, as fairness is an important component of trials, it is worth considering steps that can be taken to increase the availability of scientific jury selection to a greater number of people or small businesses. (p. 200)

WORKING ASSUMPTIONS

Let us move to my basic working understandings about trial consultation in this book.

1. *Impossible cases are truly impossible to win.* No magic or arcane knowledge allows trial consultants or attorneys to win with lost causes; difficult cases are difficult to win. When the overwhelming weight of evidence is on one side or another, it is an uphill battle and expectations about the contributions of trial consultants should be modest, at best. At the same time, cases can be "won" in indirect ways. Sometimes a defendant is found guilty of a lesser included charge rather than the primary charge. A plea or settlement may be negotiated by both parties for a less risky or odious outcome than that which may emerge from a trial.

2. *Close cases offer the most potential.* It has been demonstrated that evidence is the major foundation of jury verdicts (e.g., Kalven & Zeizel, 1966; Fulero & Penrod, 1990). When the evidence is equivocal or hovers around the legal standard of preponderance of evidence or beyond reason-

able doubt, then consultation can make its best contribution. In close cases, a small edge matters. Kerr and Huang (1986) have observed that juror personality variables and demographic factors may account for as little as 5–15% of the variance, but enough to make a meaningful difference in many cases.

3. *Jury selection has an uncertain payoff in trial consultation.* The research on effectiveness of consultants in scientific jury selection has yielded mixed results. This specific application is especially attractive to attorneys, despite the uncertain payoffs. The research on jury selection has been summarized in the thoughtful review by Lieberman and Sales (2007), and we discuss this literature in various chapters throughout the book.

4. *Jury selection by attorneys typically is demographic, simplistic, and ill developed from a social science perspective.* Many attorneys are ill prepared to do careful and meaningful jury selection. Going back to the rules developed by Clarence Darrow in the 1930s, it has been common for defense attorneys in criminal cases and plaintiff attorneys in personal injury litigation to use their peremptory strikes to eliminate potential jurors who are Republican, rigid, right-wing, conservatively dressed, middle-class or wealthy, as well as being employed in occupations seen as impersonal, such as accountants and engineers (Darrow, 1936/1981). Prosecuting attorneys in criminal cases and defense attorneys in civil cases often use similar stereotypes as they strike Democrats, liberals, casually dressed, working or lower-class, apparently empathic persons who are employed in occupations seen as caring or helping, such as social workers, school counselors, and union organizers.

5. *Case conceptualization is seen as a desirable professional path.* The term *case conceptualization* refers to the patterns and theories used to organize the central issues in a forthcoming trial. The case conceptualization usually draws from social science thinking merged with legal concepts and trial advocacy. The resulting concepts are applications of knowledge and theory to case issues. A useful aspect of conceptualization is the focus in depth on central constructs and strategies; it is known by different names. For example, trial conceptualization has been called the *operating generalization* by Strier (1999), referring to the organizing themes around which the consultant's plans and attorney's decisions are made. The concept of constructs around which understandings and perceptions are organized and anticipated may be traced in part to George Kelly's personal construct theory (1955). Kelly wrote that all individuals have personal organizing constructs such as safe–dangerous, good–bad, or happy–unhappy.[1] Individuals

---

[1]Kelly's writings helped to found cognitive psychotherapy and actively continue to influence authors of articles in the journals, *Personal Construct Theory and Practice* and the *Journal of Constructivist Psychology.*

use them to cope, either successfully or poorly. Kelly described humans as informal scientists, always testing and modifying their core constructs. In trial consultation the Kelly ideas are part of a conceptual frame of reference that links case content with constructs about how people process evidence and make decisions.

6. *Focused preparation can make both expert witnesses and lay witnesses more persuasive.* Much of witness preparation consists of attorneys meeting informally with witnesses and simply discussing the content of what will be presented on the stand. There tends to be little attention to the style of the testimony in terms of persuasion mechanisms and the general believability of the witnesses. Within trial consultation and related disciplines, a literature has emerged about the process of preparing witnesses to be more effective.[2] Witness preparation, training in the form of practicing testimony, and directive feedback about what works well or poorly can improve the effectiveness of testimony. Witnesses can learn to be more lucid, more responsive to questions, and better communicators with the jury.

7. *Social science research can sometimes be extrapolated to trial issues.* The key word is *extrapolated*, which means going beyond actual findings to anticipated applications. Thoughtful consultants stay acutely aware of the limitations of going from laboratory research, often conducted with undergraduate students, to actual trials and jurors. Changes of venue and jury selection consultations, in particular, often draw on these empirical foundations. In addition, when consultants conduct telephone surveys about how much pretrial publicity has influenced or contaminated a community, in preparation for change of venue motions, they typically utilize reliable and known methods.

8. *Thoughtful attorneys choose trial consultants with care. Thoughtful trial consultants accept cases with care.* Trial consultants are highly diverse in their backgrounds, experience, skills, and methods. Careful, detailed, focused approaches characterize the best consultants. Most attorneys select trial consultants via word-of-mouth recommendations; they rarely believe the glowing testimonials on consultants' websites or in their brochures, which are marketing tools. In turn, trial consultants encounter cases in which they may choose not to work because of the nature of the case issues or their own limits of competence. That is, some consultants choose not to work on issues involving sex crimes because of their own personal discomfort with the alleged offenses. Other trial consultants decline a case when they are approached by firms defending or suing for, say, industrial injuries because the case topic is in an area in which these consultants have no training or

---

[2]My books *Testifying in Court* (1991), *The Expert Expert Witness* (1999), and *Coping with Cross-Examination* (2004) are part of this literature.

experience. In other words, consultants sometimes decline a request because the allegations have to do with behaviors that are personally offensive, or they decline because they simply do not know enough to do a good job.

THE OBVIOUS AND BEYOND THE OBVIOUS

One of the ways trial consultants approach their work is to identify the obvious and then go beyond the obvious. For example, in jury selection two obvious juror characteristics to discern and weigh are juror occupation and appearance. Both lead to easy-to-draw but weak conclusions taken from a combination of stereotypes, personal experience, and shared understandings. The conclusions are obvious in the sense that they appear valid on their face to attorneys, but are usually drawn without knowledge of research into how specific occupations or grooming habits are related to trial predispositions.

A rich history of anecdotes and observations in our lives and culture supports the quick and superficial interpretation of appearance. There is a widely accepted belief that people are their appearances, and their appearances are who they are. In their analysis of questionnaire data from 10,000 men and women who had participated in HurryDate (a form of speed dating), Kurzban and Weeden (2005) reported that most of the judgments could have been made in 3 seconds, as opposed to the allocated 3 minutes. Men used relative thinness of women as a factor for judgments. Women used several elements of men's appearance, including shoulders tapering to narrower waists. Thus, appearance surely does matter in social approval, and the so-called beauty bias clearly shapes many judgments (Berry, 2007). It also influences inaccurate judgments in the courtroom that arise from the deceptively obvious.[3] That is, attorneys sometimes look at jurors and depend to some degree on their own subjective feelings of liking or disliking; such personal social judgments are not necessarily related in any way to predispositions or opinions that might be related to the case issues.

IS TRIAL CONSULTATION A PROFESSION?

The term *profession* is typically defined as an occupation in which there is a professed knowledge of a field or science, or as an occupation that involves both lengthy training and a formal test of qualification to practice (Cruess, Johnston, & Cruess, 2004). In his landmark book on professions,

---

[3]The book *Beauty Bias* by Bonnie Berry (2007) develops the full range of knowledge and influence of attractiveness and appearance on social influence and consequences.

Freidson (1953) observed that a profession is composed all at once of a body of knowledge, work activities, and occupational organization. However, he also wrote, "Virtually all self-conscious occupational groups apply it to themselves at one time or another either to flatter themselves or to try to persuade others of their importance" (pp. 3–4). If trial consultation is a profession, should it be regulated like medicine, psychology, and cosmetology?

The case for licensing trial consultation as a profession is dependent on how one thinks of the consultation work and what one concludes needs to be done to protect the public. Franklin Strier (2004) made a compelling case, first, that such consultation does influence the outcome of a trial and, second, that trial consultants are wholly unregulated—an accurate assertion—and nobody who retains a trial consultant can be assured that minimal training, knowledge of ethical practices, or relevant education have been attained. He wrote, "The trial consulting industry is completely unregulated; anyone can hold himself or herself out and practice as a trial consultant. There are no state licensing requirements, nor is there any binding or meaningful code of professional ethics" (p. 70). In an earlier review, Strier (1999) asserted that the practice of trial consultation is fraught with potential problems, not the least of which is how trial consultants may compromise the public perception of fairness in trial proceedings and outcomes.

In contrast to Strier's conclusion about there being no meaningful code of professional ethics, the ASTC (2008) does indeed maintain an ethical code. The code covers each of the major areas in which trial consultants work: change of venue assessments, witness preparation, jury selection, small-group research, and posttrial juror interviews. The following excerpts and paraphrases describe the ethical code in each major area of work:

> "In witness preparation, trial consultants do not script specific answers or censor appropriate and relevant answers based solely on the expected harmful effect on case outcome."
> In venue surveys, "trial consultants shall not participate in, sponsor, or conduct surveys known as 'push polls,' that are primarily designed to influence survey respondents' opinions by presenting systematically biased information."
> "In witness preparation, trial consultants in their professional capacity shall not intentionally communicate or have contact with persons summoned for jury duty or seated jurors except as permitted by the trial court."
> "When reporting small-group research (focus group) results, trial consultants shall present the results accurately and draw inferences and make interpretations consistent with the research findings."

"In posttrial juror interviews, trial consultants should avoid offering excessive or inappropriate financial or other inducements for interview participants if such inducements are intended to unduly influence or coerce participation."

The ASTC code itself is ambivalent about how enforceable the standards are. At once it declares, "The code provides enforceable standards" and that the standards include "rules enforceable by the Society." At the same time it states, "Although Ethical Principles and Practice Guidelines are not enforceable rules, they should be considered by trial consultants in choosing courses of action."

An additional concern presented by Strier was licensure. If trial consultants were licensed, then at least minimal educational, knowledge, or experience standards would govern entry into the profession. Consultants who were inept or who acted unethically then could be disciplined, expelled, or have their licenses to practice revoked. Attorneys, physicians, social workers, and psychologists are all required to meet continuing education requirements to ensure that they have stayed current with professional and ethical knowledge. No such requirement is in effect among trial consultants. In contrast, Gary Moran (2004) observed that the successful origins of the profession of psychology came about in the absence of regulation. Moran held that the influence of trial consultants is greatly overstated, both by consultants themselves in the marketing of their services and by the general public. In place of licensure, with its restriction on offering services, he argued that consumers of such services need to be better informed about the nature and limitations of trial consultants.

DIFFERENCES BETWEEN JURISDICTIONS

This book describes the nature of trial consultation in general. I have tried to bring together practices and knowledge that are common across the country. Yet I recognize that there are major differences across jurisdictions in jury selection, in the use of supplemental jury questionnaires (SJQs),[4] in voir dire, and in access to the trial process by consultants. In the southeastern United States, where I work, it is not unusual for state courts to set aside an hour or so at most for the voir dire questioning and to deny use of SJQs in all but some capital murder trials, trials of major public figures, and a few large civil suits. The trials themselves usually last less than a week. In important cases in some California jurisdictions in which I have been involved, the

---

[4]A supplemental questionnaire is defined as structured questions added to the standard and limited questionnaires routinely used by the courts.

jury selection may go on for a week and the trial for many months. Take the voir dire. In a capital murder trial I watched last month, it took 90 minutes. Angela Dodge (personal communication, May 9, 2007) wrote how different it is where she practices:

> Trial consultants in the Pacific Northwest, beginning with the good work of Joyce Tsongas and Karen Lisko, have had a tremendous influence on the voir dire practices of judges in the Ninth Circuit. Not in all states, but in several, voir dire is for "as long as needed and remains productive," voir dire is staggered between plaintiff and defendant (i.e., each side gets several rounds of anywhere from 30 to 45 minutes), many judges allow and encourage SJQs (which often ask if there is any item on the questionnaire that the potential juror would prefer to speak about in private, and this is honored by in camera questioning), trial consultants are accepted/acknowledged by judges and often sit at counsel table, judges allow time for attorneys to confer with their trial consultants before strikes are exercised, the struck method is used, and it is not unusual for jury selection to take the better part of the first day. Let me say again that is not the case in every state.

According to a survey of jury improvement efforts in the states, South Carolina had an average of 30 minutes for voir dire in felony cases, and a median length of 1 hour was reported for Alabama, Delaware, Maine, New Hampshire, and Virginia (Mize, Hannaford-Agor, & Waters, 2007). At the other end of the continuum, Connecticut had a median length of 10 hours and New York 5 hours. In civil trials South Carolina again anchored the low point with a half hour, and Connecticut anchored the high end with an average of 16 hours.

One measure of how likely jurors are to be free of social conformity effects that may compromise honesty is whether they are questioned privately, that is, at sidebar or in chambers. The Mize et al. (2007) report indicated a wide range of practices among states. Rhode Island and Connecticut, for example, had 66.1 and 63.7%, respectively, of respondents indicating that jurors were questioned out of hearing of other jurors. At the other extreme, North Carolina had 2.4% of respondents indicating that jurors were questioned privately; Oregon had 4.8% reporting private questioning.

These statistics just touch the surface of the differences between jurisdictions. Much of what is true in jury selection and trial procedures in Connecticut is not true in other states. As you read about the procedures of trial consultation, there may be occasions when you, as a knowledgeable reader, say, "Yes, but that is not so in my state." No single book can cover the differences between states on every dimension of trial consulting, so this volume has aimed at commonalities and at jurisdictions with which I am most familiar, with the clear awareness that there will be exceptions in some jurisdictions. With that caution in mind, let us move now to the structure of this book.

CASE BUT NOT OUTCOME DRIVEN

This book is case driven. That is, the principles and issues I discuss are seated in actual consultation experiences. I describe cases and trials to illustrate how consultants work, as well as the practices and research that follow the natural contours of these cases.

When I started to write this book, I included information about how the cases or trials ended. That emphasis nudged me toward writing about cases that were successful because such cases seemed to be examples of what worked well. However, there are problems in being outcome driven.

In his data-based review of trial consultations, Selzer (2006) did not offer data about whether cases were won or lost. Among other reasons, Selzer pointed out that a member of a defense team sometimes "wings it" at the last moment and ignores advice from the trial consultant. Sometimes clients settle or plea bargain. Sometimes a client is convicted, but the verdict or award is more or less favorable than anticipated. He concluded that it is not clear how to interpret pleas, settlements, and other dispositions.

I would add another reservation. When one thinks of the outcome as the essential worth of the consultation, it diverts attention from the consultation activities themselves and the intrinsic nature and value of the work and information. As a result, I have not included most information about verdicts, pleas, settlements, and awards. In this way *res ipsa loquitor:* The methods and knowledge speak for themselves.

HOW THIS BOOK IS ORGANIZED

Chapter 2 deals with the concept of the case conceptualization in trial consulting, with a special emphasis on the story model and the qualitative small-group research that takes the form of focus groups and shadow juries. Chapter 3 follows with a presentation of the consultant's toolbox: the books, instruments, and measures that are useful tools. Chapters 4, 5, and 6 address witness preparation: preparing lay witnesses, preparing expert witnesses, helping witnesses cope with cross-examination, and research on the topics from the Witness Research Lab. Then Chapters 7, 8, 9, and 10 address jury selection and consider case-driven understandings of how to approach jury selection in terms of what to do and what one must know.

Chapters 11 and 12 discuss aspects of change of venue evaluations, followed by Chapters 13 and 14, in which case applications are used to illustrate an overall synthesis of consultation knowledge and case demands. Finally, the book concludes with Chapter 15 on the future of trial consultation, including the major challenges and imminent changes in the study and practice of trial consultation.

Chapter 2

—◆—

THE CASE
CONCEPTUALIZATION

In our examination of trial consultation, one unifying theme we will use is the case conceptualization, which is defined as an organizing construct in approaching trial consultation. Case conceptualizations come from three sources: (1) a theoretical understanding of what transpires in the courtroom, (2) social science scholarship, some produced specifically for the case at hand and some drawn from the existing body of knowledge, and (3) practical knowledge of what information and understandings make a difference in particular trial situations. Case conceptualizations can be applied to almost every trial and legal proceeding. They make the most difference when applied to the essential aspects of cases. Why use them at all? The answer is that they permit a theoretical and applied schema for consultation. In this chapter we look at how to identify and apply case conceptualizations, examining in particular the use of narrative and small-group research.

INTRODUCTION TO CASE
CONCEPTUALIZATIONS

Like the adjustment of the lens on a camera, good consultation brings the blurred and vague into sharp focus. There are blurred, diffuse, and indistinct elements in most cases. Some attorneys recognize these elements readily. However, for many attorneys with whom consultants work, an early task is to identify the parts of the case that stand out, those that need to be clarified, and those that call for applying social science knowledge and perspectives. Some attorneys are psychologically minded in their work; most others think primarily about legal issues and precedents, procedural concerns, motions, and evidence. Yet every case is psychological in part; it is psychological in how the defendant, state, or plaintiff thinks and feels about what is happening. It is psychological as each side weighs the relative strength of its argument. It is psychological as strategies of persuasion are planned.

It is in regard to the nonobvious psychological elements that consultants can make a difference. When the case is conceptualized, attorneys are limited by the nature and number of constructs they use. Consultation on a case can give good results when enough constructs are developed in a way that is meaningful for the particular case. That is, trial consultation can bring clarity and sharp, explicit, well-defined perspectives about what to do.

In discussing this approach to trial consultation, we describe different conceptual frames of reference as we address the tasks and methods of trial consultation. A general goal is to identify the most important concepts for the case. Throughout this book, the nature and application of case conceptualizations appear, with accompanying explanations of how they are developed and applied.

CASE CONCEPTUALIZATIONS IN PSYCHOTHERAPY

Trial consultants, like psychotherapists, stay alert for central, defining elements in the content presented to them, so they can use the central elements as an organizing principle around which many other issues may be engaged. Psychotherapists write of noting the moment of change, the awareness or shift that permits clients to move toward resolving the problems that led them to therapy (Miller, 2004). Trial consultants can serve a parallel function, in the sense that they seek an organizing and essential theme that not only rings true, but also is connected to other main topics and issues, and that promotes a change in how the case is managed.

In therapy the client's change may arise from a central insight, in which murky and muddled content becomes clear. It can also be something simpler, a process, perhaps labeled, that can be recognized when it recurs. An example of such labeling is to call a person with repeated dysfunctional behaviors with others "Prince Charming" or an "emotional distancer" because they represent engaging but arguably shallow ways of relating. In consulting, the conceptual issues sometimes can have simple labels, but the contribution of trial consultants often consists of identifying a compelling but not obvious construct around which the case can be structured. Later in the book, some of these conceptualizations are described in detail, including the impact of photographs of bloody victims, the ways in which jurors may react to sexual language, and other complex issues.

TRIAL CONSULTANTS, ATTORNEYS, AND SOCIAL SCIENTISTS

Trial consultation is a young field in which working constructs are in the process of being identified. However, because of the applied nature of the work, few trial consultants engage in the academic exercise of developing theoretical constructs they prepare as part of applied work in cases. Trial consultants are doers, individuals who are faced with immediate demands to make a difference in a case. Think of trial consultants as being much more like trial attorneys than behavioral scientists, in the sense that attorneys need to find a way of thinking that resolves the case in their favor. Behavioral scientists have the leisure to think through, plan, carry out, and examine the results of formal and controlled experiments to answer their questions. Few trial consultants have such opportunity;[1] what they do, instead, is apply their best working knowledge, and when such knowledge is scant, extrapolate from what they do know.

The differences between lawyers and social scientists have been described by Ralph Slovenko (1973, 2002) in his books on psychiatry and law. Three of his distinguishing features that help differentiate attorneys from social scientists also have implications for the roles of trial consultants:[2]

1. The art of being theatrical or acting within a role is common in a trial attorney. Although good legal scholarship may precede the trial and be the foundation of motions, the actual trial itself goes beyond evidence. How the evidence is presented makes a difference. The sense of bonding with, or at least promoting a liking of the attorneys and their clients by the jury, is assumed to make a difference. Persuasive opening and closing statements infused with emotionality are common. A prosecuting attorney I have observed always becomes teary eyed during his closing arguments. In contrast, social scientists value authenticity and detachment. Researchers

---

[1] A significant portion of the behavioral science research related to trial consultation has been reported in doctoral dissertations. However, few of these dissertations make their way into the published scholarly literature.

[2] This differentiation between trial consultants and social scientists does not apply to all trial consultants. A small number are employed in academia, studying consultation issues. Most of these consultants have a primary appointment in a psychology or communications department. Others have studied theater or graphic design. Nevertheless, these features do distinguish the majority of practitioners of trial consultation.

are expected to report their results in full and to be impersonal and objective. It is not by accident that many more novels are written and movies are made of trials and courtroom dramatics than of social scientists at work. Trial consultants often help develop dramatic or effective presentation of evidence and may draw from social science knowledge.

2. There can be (but does not have to be) a winner and a loser in a trial. Few cases do go to trial, and settlements, plea bargains, and mistrials are exceptions to thinking in absolute terms about winners and losers. However, trial attorneys understand the common all-or-nothing nature of jury trials. One party may leave the courtroom feeling like a victor and the other party may feel defeated. In scientific work, the opposite process holds. With the occasional exception of laboratories that compete to bring out radically new findings of great significance, in the sciences there are no comparable winners or losers. Social and physical scientists engage in collaborative efforts in which no one is defeated. We should add that sometimes settlements and plea bargains also leave a sense of mutual satisfaction or dissatisfaction. Trial consultants are clearly allied with attorneys in this respect. When attorneys feel that they have lost or not done as well as hoped, often so do their trial consultants.

3. Trials seek to bring forth justice and are primarily practical. Justice means what is right or fair, as determined under clearly specified rules. Because of rules that govern admissibility of evidence and procedures in the courtroom, information that might lead to a more truthful outcome often is not admitted. Thus, when investigators have conducted illegal searches or when defendants have not been given full warnings of their rights, the products of searches or confessions may be excluded. Social science is interested in truth and theory. Both quantitative and the more subjective qualitative approaches to research are used. Wherever good knowledge can be found, it can be embraced. Once again trial consultants are constrained by what limits attorneys, but they do draw on research knowledge that is usually freely accessible.

Here I emphasize caution: Looking for a single, consistent theory of trial consultation is illusory. Most of the content in books, journal articles, and conference talks in this field is applied, how-to-do-it material. What kind of theory is present in trial consultation? It is best described as fragments of theory that have specific applications. As we move to comparing case conceptualizations to narrative theory and to other organizing structures within trial consultation, it is best to think of these outlooks as related to grounded theory (Charmaz, 2006), seated within the specific contexts of cases and trials and often drawn inductively from those sources. Both case conceptualizations and grounded theory examine notes, field events, or case information and seek to discover essential variables and how they relate to each other.

STORY AND NARRATIVE

Information and concepts are often understood and used by jurors to construct a story. Pennington and Hastie (1992) have been central figures in asserting that jurors seek to organize evidence and attorney arguments into a narrative story organization. Thus, jurors evaluate evidence and reach decisions in large part depending on how evidence and the verdict fits with their constructed story. More specifically, jurors also fold in their own world knowledge about similar events and about story structures to construct the story. Verdicts come about from matching the story they have accepted with the instructions they receive about the law and their understandings of categories of possible verdicts. Pennington and Hastie put it this way: "This constructive mental activity results in one or more *interpretations* of the evidence that have a narrative story form" (p. 189, emphasis in original).

In a series of studies Pennington and Hastie (1992) found support for the story model. They reported that story organization of evidence influenced jurors' decisions and their evaluations of the credibility of evidence. Furthermore, when causal stories were connected to the case materials, the evaluation of evidence shifted in the direction of the story. The overall conclusions were that a narrative story sequence was effective in leading to sense of proof in juror judgments.

When we add to the story model the ideas of trial consultants Jill Schmid (2007) and Diane Wyzga (2007), we may be reasonably reassured that jurors want to hear a story unfold that will put the case into a familiar and understandable framework. Such stories engage the listener and make the facts of the case emotionally meaningful. Schmid (2007) and Walter Fisher (1989) have written about a narrative paradigm, an often illogical process in which rational thought is secondary to a series of stories that help us make sense of our lives. They suggest that stories shape how human beings think about things. The questions that Schmid and Fisher raise are, How compelling is the story, how well does the story fit into our values, how coherent is the story, and how much narrative fidelity does it have; that is, how much does it ring true? From this perspective, jurors look for a verdict that makes a statement about what they value and believe. In contrast to some attorneys' tendencies to put everything about a case on the table and let it speak for itself, narrative theory holds that there is one story that will resonate best with jurors, and that story has a foreseeable beginning, a middle, and an ending that satisfies our values.

In Steven Hartwell's (2002) analysis, storytelling and narrative help human beings appreciate time and memories and, more than that, give order, coherence, and meaning to life events such as trials. He goes on to assert that narratives are true to life only when they appear reliable, when they are based on visible common sense, and when they move us emotionally. In contrast to the typical courtroom understanding of ascertaining truthfulness as a cognitive process, the use of narrative addresses how coherence and true-to-life qualities make courtroom content believable. Attorney and provocateur Gerry Spence, while addressing the deficiencies in law school preparation, has observed, "The trial of a case, in its simplest form, is telling a story jurors can understand. Yet most lawyers are taught little, if anything, about communicating with others" (Spence, 2008, p. 2). The role of the trial consultant is often to help construct the story.

This perspective applies first to opening statements, because they are made at a point when neither evidence nor the law has been presented. Instead, the opening narrative seeks to resonate with the values and feelings of the jurors. In closing arguments, the narratives often become more complex and nuanced. Still, the overall goal is to move the jurors' understandings into and then past cognitive appraisals of truths and falsehoods and into stories that meet emotional needs as well as cognitive demands, along with being profoundly meaningful.

Diane Wyzga (2007) expands further on the story as a frame of reference. She states that all legal stories are really stories about ourselves, in which universal elements of plot and experiences are developed. In her presentations, Wyzga tells stories from her own life that have such universal elements. When I have listened to her stories, I have been emotionally touched—for the same reasons that jurors are moved when listening to meaningful stories. The stories she elicits are full of sensory details, so that in a hospital story she addresses how hospitals smell, what they sound like and look like, and what it feels like as a patient to be confined in a hospital.

How do trial consultants as storytellers develop such universal stories that enter into the sensory experiences of the audience? Wyzga suggests that the best way of first eliciting and then defining the story is by using an exercise that comes out of improvisation theater, with a method called the *Story Spine*. It works this way. The attorney and consultant collaboratively seek to fill in the story by completing the following beginnings of sentences:

Once upon a time
And every day
But one day
And because of this [can be repeated up to three times]
And because of that
Until finally
So that forevermore

To illustrate how this works, we examine a Story Spine describing a civil case alleging racial harassment:

1. *Once upon a time:* A large company with more than 1,000 employees assigned many African American workers to skilled work positions. There were white supervisors at every station.

2. *And every day:* The African American employees saw nooses hung from the ceilings of rooms, the letter *J* crossed out on the jigger machines and replaced with the letter *N*, and racial insults painted on the walls of the restrooms.

3. *But one day:* Several African American workers were criticized and demeaned more than usual. They received disciplinary reports and demotions for doing ordinary things that white workers did without consequences.

4. *And because of this [can be repeated up to three times]:* (a) *And because of this:* The African American workers stayed in their cars as long as they could before going to work; these workers felt resentment and anxiety when they were unfairly criticized; (b) *And because of this:* The employers punished these recalcitrant workers by holding back privileges; (c) *And because of this:* The African American workers were not assigned to the most desirable jobs or given promotions.

5. *And because of that:* These workers experienced major emotional distress and difficulties in their nonwork lives.

6. *Until finally:* The racial hostility and work conditions became intolerable, and they filed a racial harassment class action.

7. *So that forevermore:* African American workers at this company would not be insulted, would not be subjected to prejudice and discrimination, would be treated fairly, and the company would be taught a memorable lesson for permitting these conditions to occur.

The Story Spine illustrates how the events unfolded in sequence, with some events causing other consequences. It begins with the essential element in every familiar fairy tale, "once upon a time." It progresses to the background with the phrase "and every day." Next, the sentence stem "but one day" identifies a precipitating event. After that, the repeated phrases "and because of this" and "and because of that" identify causes and effects. Ultimately, the story is brought up to date with "until finally," and the moral lesson in justice is identified with "so that forevermore."

Now we examine the Story Spine in a criminal case:

1. *Once upon a time:* The adult son of an affluent couple went through a long period of arrests for minor crimes while developing a psychiatric disorder.

2. *And every day:* He drank too much and feared that terrorists were out to get him.
3. *But one day:* He became actively psychotic.
4. *And because of this [can be repeated up to three times]:* (a) *And because of this:* the son was psychiatrically hospitalized for a while; (b) *And because of this:* He came to believe that his parents and doctors were plotting against him; (c): *And because of this:* His parents became the main focus of his delusions.
5. *And because of that:* He yelled at his parents, threatened them, demanded money from them, hit them, and then would weep uncontrollably.
6. *Until finally:* The son shot his father in his sleep and killed him.
7. *So that forevermore:* This son will not forgive himself and will be anguished about what he has done, through all hospital or prison treatment.

These two stories illustrate a way of organizing and making meaningful to jurors the nature of cases that come to trial. But how are trial consultation frames of reference and case conceptualizations different from *narrative* and *story?* Trial consultation is broad in nature, encompassing multiple elements, characters, causes, and consequences. Case conceptualizations are narrow, targeted components within consultation that address key events or understandings from which many other elements arise. Stories are the ways of organizing the events, perceptions, and experiences of the litigants in a descriptive and chronological pattern. Table 2.1 illustrates these differences.

Case conceptualization begins with developing and explaining the underlying theory in each case or issue. How does it add to consultation knowledge? The case conceptualization perspective starts with a general overview; then (and sometimes in this order) the specifics of the case are applied to hypothesis development, methods, rating scales, and witness preparation. This conceptualization also aids in developing items for jury questionnaires and for the questioning of potential jurors in court, a process known as the voir dire—originally meaning "to see, to speak."

In this book we examine cases in which trial consultation approaches have used organizing constructs with tasks faced by trial attorneys. That is, specific principles and case data explain how, for example, to move toward good witness preparation and how to assist attorneys in developing substantive challenges during cross-examination. In the same sense, case conceptualizations assist in thinking through the content of survey questions as part of change of venue questions. Case conceptualizations do not belong to any one profession, but serve as pathways for the productive working together

TABLE 2.1. Conceptualizations, Story, and Narrative

	Approaches to trial consultation	Case conceptualization	Story and narrative
Directed at	Attorney	Attorney	Jurors
Time at which used	Early in trial preparation	Early and middle of trial preparation	During the trial
Breadth	Very broad, covering one or two general issues	Narrow, addressing one or several key targets or issues	Follows the contours of the events, and breadth reflects the chronology
Theory	Legal theory comes first and then psychological theory	Mini-social science theories about central themes, such as grounded theory	Storytelling and narrative
Example	Understandings of discrimination and racism influence how whites and blacks see what is just.	Different types of individuals assign responsibility for racist acts in the organization.	Once upon a time, 200 black workers were racially insulted and then had major personal problems.

of attorneys and social scientists. Two applications of case conceptualizations are their use with focus groups and with shadow juries.

FOCUS GROUPS AND SHADOW JURIES

Important activities within trial consultation are focus groups and shadow juries, both of which fall under the larger rubric of small-group inquiries and research.

Focus Groups

Focus groups are a central part of qualitative research in sociology and related social science disciplines. Generally speaking, they seek to bring together individuals representative of a population of interest—such as a community from which a panel of jurors will be selected. Leaders of the focus groups used in trial consultation define in advance the topics to be discussed, how open-ended the inquiries will be, and the nature of the options for responding by the participants. In some cases the participants give simple evaluative responses to the trial issues. In other cases the participants are encouraged to offer wide-ranging and emotional or personal subjective reactions. Thus, the individual participants and the group working as a whole offer solicited opinions, attitudes, and reactions to the topics under study. In many focus groups a structured interview is used to elicit attitudes toward, say, crime, disease, poverty, stigma, or other social problems. As an integral part of qualitative research, focus groups have a substantial accompanying methodological literature. For example, Keller (1995) has described how to plan and implement focus groups and how to use them in marketing research, organizational consulting, and jury selection. Focus groups directed toward trial and jury issues have distinct components in the form of practical and goal-directed aids to trial consultation. Focus groups of persons who are similar to actual jurors are commonly used to learn how, in what direction, and with what intensity, typical citizens react to case issues, arguments, and strategies.

Utilizing focus groups in general and for purposes of trial consultation relies partly on skill of leadership, partly on professionalism, and partly on science. Leaders usually are trained to maintain a clear detachment from their own preexisting opinions, attitudes, and emotions, so that the content comes from the participants. Because focus groups depend on the often unpredictable personal responses and comments of participants, leaders look to them for new insights, often following up on what appear at first to be idiosyncratic or slightly off-task remarks. Indeed, the less predictable the responses are, the more value they may be to the leaders. Within trial consulting, the focus group offers an opportunity for a dry run for testing out alternate approaches, as well as a potentially fertile ground for discovering how jurors may think and respond. A survey by Posey and Wrightsman (2005) reported that focus groups and mock trials made up 32% of the practice of trial consultants and constituted the single most common professional activity.

Focus group members must be selected carefully. The less members are representative of the target jurors, the less reliable and useful will be their results. Many trial consultants depend on market research companies to select a representative sample and offer a good venue for running the group, because sample selection and site selection are important.

It is important that leaders of focus groups be objective, be clear about the goals and methods of the particular focus group, draw on representative samples when possible, and use meaningful samples of participants in all instances. Some experimental evidence exists to support the assumption that the products of focus groups may reflect trial outcomes. Thus, O'Connor (2006) simulated jury deliberations with a focus group methodology. She reported that punitive damage judgments were reduced when the participants were exposed to messages that advocated against the worth of excessive civil litigation.[3]

One of the primary reasons focus groups in trial consultation (and shadow juries, as well) are not given more attention in this book is that the scholarly literature about them is modest. As noted in Chapter 1, the material in the book is case driven, utilizing published cases and my own experiences.[4] In the area of focus groups, my own experiences are limited.

Shadow Juries

Sometimes a carefully selected and reasonably representative group of individuals are employed to attend the actual or simulated proceedings in a trial. In the simulations, the group listens to selected arguments, evidence, or testimony anticipated from either side, presented by the attorneys or consultants. If the group attends an actual trial, then it is often labeled "a shadow jury." These shadow jurors convene after the jury workday to critique what they heard. The shadow jurors comment about what the attorneys did, what evidence was effective and what was not, how the attorneys for both sides were coming across, and to what extent they had come to accept or reject the various arguments. Unlike trial attorneys, who come in with a strong adversarial perspective that may serve as blinders, trial consultants need to remain sufficiently objective in order to bring out the negatives in the trial arguments and presentation, every bit as much as the positives. Shadow juries, like focus groups, are at their best for trial consultants when the strategies the attorneys are pursuing in court to develop a case have problems or may not be effective. If what the trial attorneys are doing is already very effective, relatively little more may be needed or of value.

Readers interested in more information about focus groups and other small-group research in trial consultation should look at Chapter 4 in Posey and Wrightsman (2005). The areas of witness preparation, jury selection, and changes of venue are identified and developed in more detail in later chapters.

---

[3]This introduction to focus groups does not capture the richness of experiences elicited, nor does it describe how much the groups are valued. The published information on focus groups has appeared primarily in articles and books by sociologists who have used the small-group process both as a source of ethnographic data and as a link to grounded theory. For example, Lichtenstein (2005) has used focus groups as a means of learning about the sexually transmitted disease (STD) stigma and about barriers to seeking medical care for HIV/AIDS and other STDs. In the same sense, Hyde, Howlett, Brady, and Drennen (2005) used focus groups as a vehicle for inquiring into sensitive areas of sexual health among adolescents.

[4]It would have been a long reach to offer professional and scholarly opinions and perspectives, given that my own published reports and direct involvement and experience have been in other areas of trial consultation.

CONCLUSION

Case conceptualizations represent applied theorizing about trial issues as well as a way of homing in on essential components of events central to a trial. Trial consultation draws in part on social science knowledge, theory, and practical applications. What is in focus in the social sciences often is blurred in legal settings, owing in large part to how information is gathered, processed, and judged in legal contexts. As case conceptualizations apply social science knowledge to the law, key variables are generated from experience in a number of trials.

A related theory is that of narrative. This theory holds that storytelling is a fundamental part of the human experience. When the narrative presentations of case perspectives succeed, they do so because of how meaningful, coherent, and true to life they are for the jurors.

The development of case conceptualizations and narrative stories emerges often from early meetings with attorneys and then from focus groups. In these settings, the trial consultant initially gains a sense of the implicit constructs that run through a case and how they "play," with individuals who have characteristics in common with actual jurors for the case. The scholarly literature is modest in the instances of focus groups and shadow juries in trial consultation, although a robust body of scholarly knowledge is present for focus groups and mock juries in general. Now that they have been introduced, these elements of case conceptualizations are revisited regularly in this book.

Chapter 3

— ✦ —

TOOLBOX FOR
TRIAL CONSULTANTS

My favorite home repair book is the *Reader's Digest New Fix-It-Yourself Manual* (1996). It has cutaway and colorful illustrations for virtually all home repairs, and it begins by showing and explaining uses for the common tools one needs for repairs. This knowledge of tools allows those of us who do not make a living with our hands to undertake, for example, fixing spout drips from a leaky ball faucet or checking the functioning of a pump assembly in a dishwasher. So it goes with trial consultation. The tools of the profession are always selectively applied to the case and task at hand, but just as surely as with home repairs, having the right tools available gets us off to a good start. Of course, it takes training and skill to use tools well to repair leaky faucets and, arguably, considerably different skills to be an effective trial consultant. This chapter is about the tools.

Many trial consultants use no tools. Dimitrius and Mazzerella (1999) and others explain that they depend on their intuition and experience. They define intuition as "nearly always the surfacing of a submerged memory, a barely noticed event, or some combination of the two" (p. 227). Instruction in intuition is beyond the reach and aims of this book. Experience may help particularly when there is directed feedback after one's efforts, because feedback can make the experience a learning process.[1] Aside from intuition

---

[1] I suggest this use of experience cautiously because Garb (1989), Faust et al. (1988), and Wedding and Faust (1989) have presented compelling research implying that experience does not assist diagnostic accuracy in neuropsychology and related fields.

and experience, consulting tools based on data can offer an improved work product as well as generalizable knowledge. Furthermore, when clinical judgments are made explicit and are placed in actuarial formulas, they have the potential for being more accurate and effective than intuition and experience.

Broadly speaking, the tools I discuss here are assessment scales. Social-psychological scales used in trial consultation work are the opposite of intuition. Intuition depends on subjective judgments, on feelings, hunches, and ideas that are not accountable or replicable. It is also idiosyncratic: It emerges from a complex set of personal skills and reactions that are unique to the intuitive individual. One person's intuition is another person's mystery. In contrast to the idiosyncratic nature of intuition, a number of scales exist that are available to anyone and are applicable to many court issues.

There are five cogent reasons to use scales:

1. They are usually constructed according to established principles of scale development. That is, a good scale is the product of a systematic process of gathering of items, followed by a sorting out of the items and their relation to each other and the overall scale, to form a logical and empirical cluster.
2. Scales are usually known quantities, in the sense that the user can gain access to what a scale measures and how much individual items contribute to the scale. The latter contribution of items is sometimes important, as decisions are made about submitting individual voir dire questions that will be acceptable to the court or that fit with concepts that emerge from the consultation.
3. Scales usually have been standardized, and norms are available for particular populations. Although the norms may apply to college students,[2] the norms also may apply to the specific audience or group the trial issues seek to address.
4. Scales have research data about their reliability and validity. In the resources discussed in the following section, most of the scales have data available about their internal reliability and some have data about equivalent form reliability or reliability over time. Many of the scales have validity data, including discriminant validity.
5. I consider the informed use of scales to be an important component of good trial consultation. The use of known or standardized scales means that the trial consultant does not have to start from point zero, but rather builds on an existing knowledge base.

---

[2]Bornstein (1999) has reviewed 20 years of research on students as mock jurors and concluded that the results have a moderate degree of generalizability to actual jurors.

It is preferable to use all of the items in scales because the developmental and research data apply to the complete scales. However, often only selected scale items are used because of court limitations, or time or space constraints in jury questionnaires, in preparing the voir dire, or in assessing pretrial bias in a venue. This issue of limitations and constraints is explored in depth in Chapter 9, "No Questions but Deselection Questions." With supplemental jury questionnaires (SJQs), the judge typically considers the items submitted by both sets of attorneys and decides whether to permit the questions. Both sets of attorneys have an opportunity to object to questions prepared by opposing counsel. Active judges may screen out most items aggressively. Judges inclined to let attorneys manage juror questionnaires themselves may permit most or all items. In the voir dire process in federal court, the judges themselves typically ask all or some of the questions prepared by the attorneys; furthermore, federal judges are selective. I have been in a trial in which several dozen voir dire questions had been prepared by both sets of attorneys and the federal judge decided that only 2 questions of 70 submitted were to be asked. In many state courts the attorneys are often given relatively free rein during the voir dire; most states allow for both attorneys and judges to conduct voir dire questioning, and at the judge's discretion the decision is made as to who will question the prospective jurors. In four states only attorneys conduct the voir dire, in which judges do not participate; these states are Connecticut, North Carolina, Texas, and Wyoming (Rottman et al., 2000). Other states designate judges to conduct the voir dire questioning, and sometimes attorneys are not permitted to participate; these states include Arizona, California, Delaware, Illinois, Massachusetts, New Hampshire, and New Jersey[3] (Rottman et al., 2000). Nevertheless, what happens is that if the attorneys are conducting the voir dire, they are limited to posing questions that are fairly obviously related to the evidentiary or prejudicial issues at hand.

With these introductory perspectives in place, let us now examine books that are collections of scales and that have some application in trial consultation.

BOOKS OF SCALES

Volume 1. Measures of social psychological attitudes: Measures of personality and social psychological attitudes. (1991). Edited by John P. Robinson, Phillip R. Shaver, and Lawrence S. Wrightsman. (753 pages)

---

[3]California, Illinois, and Massachusetts *may* allow attorneys to participate in voir dire (Rottman et al., 2000).

In 12 chapters contributed by separate authors, scales of personality functioning and social attitudes are presented in full, along with comments about variables studied by each scale, the normative sample, reliability and validity data, the results of research, and the citation for the original article in which the scale appeared. This book is the single premier source for good content in trial consultation because of its breadth of inclusion of so many attitude scales. Still, as with all of these books, some of the chapters are of little help for trial consultation.

One chapter entitled "Interpersonal Trust and Attitudes toward Human Nature" is authored by Lawrence Wrightsman. It opens with a good presentation of Machiavellianism and presents three Machiavellianism scales. The construct itself is defined as representing cool detachment. A factor analysis yielded factors of duplicity, negativism, and distrust of people. Wrightsman also reviewed his own thoughtful Philosophies of Human Nature Scale, as well as the Rotter Interpersonal Trust Scale with items like "The judiciary is a place where we can all get unbiased treatment" and "Most people answer public opinion polls honestly." Of course, if potential jurors answer this latter question "false," we should wonder about their own honesty in responding to the scale items at hand.

A chapter on locus of control describes the construct and presents 21 scales, many of which are little known but nicely developed. *Locus of control* refers to how people attribute happenings in the world around them; people with an internal locus of control attribute things that go on in their lives to aspects of themselves, whereas people with an external locus of control attribute these things to external forces—influences outside their control. On the occasions when locus of control is an organizing concept in trial work, these scales are worthwhile.

Perhaps the most useful chapter is the one by Richard Christie, "Authoritarianism and Related Constructs." It opens with an enlightening and cogent review of the construct of authoritarianism and how the measures came to be developed historically and psychometrically. The 16 scales include a variety of iterations of the F scale, versions counterbalanced for acquiescent response bias, and the Rokeach Dogmatism Scale. Christie particularly praises the Right-Wing Authoritarianism Scale. He also describes the Four-Item F Scale as "the best short form of the F scale currently available for use in large cross-sectional studies of the population." Two items are "What young people need most of all is strict discipline by their parents" and "A few strong leaders could make this country better than all the laws and talk."

Other chapters in this book may have applications in trial consultations. The chapter on values covers much conceptual territory. The other chapters of interest cover scales that assess alienation and anomie, subjective well-being, self-esteem, social anxiety, and, for cases in which sexual discrimination or harassment is at issue, scales of masculinity, femininity, and androgyny.

Handbook of sexuality-related measures. (1998). Edited by Clive M. Davis, William L. Barber, Robert Bauserman, George Schreer, and Sandra L. Davis. (591 pages)

This collection has 226 scales that fall into 86 categories. The majority of the scales are reproduced in full in the book. The review of each of the scales is organized by introduction, then description, response mode and timing, then scoring, reliability, validity, other information, and, finally, references. Unlike most of the other resources described here, this book includes references to multiple published articles in which a scale has been used, a helpful addition.

The largest number of scales are about HIV/AIDS; 19 scales are presented. The AIDS attitude scales have potential applications in litigation, and the best of the group in terms of content (but not psychometric qualities) is the Meharry Questionnaire: The Measurement of Attitudes toward AIDS-Related Issues. This quickly administered 13-item scale has highly evaluative and evocative items, such as "AIDS is the result of God's punishment" and "People with AIDS have gotten what they deserve."

The 14 scales about homosexuality include gay identity scales that have selected uses in forensic contexts. The carefully developed Heterosexual Attitudes toward Homosexuality Scale by Larsen has solid reliability and validity. The equally reliable and valid Attitudes toward Lesbians and Gay Men Scale by Herek has the advantage of separate subscales for attitudes toward lesbians and attitudes toward gay men. An item from the former subscale is "Female homosexuality is bad for society because it breaks down the natural divisions between the sexes" and from the latter subscale is "Male homosexual couples should be allowed to adopt children the same as heterosexual couples."

Of the eight scales that measure sexual attitudes, the only one that has good psychometric qualities and many items useful for trial work is the Valois Sexual Attitude Scale. It has items such as "Sexual intercourse should only occur between married partners" and "Sex education should not be taught in the schools."

Other scales also measure knowledge about sex, sexual beliefs, attitudes about sexual abuse, and other related topics. These scales may be a good resource in cases involving sexual harassment allegations, pornography, sexual abuse, and personal injury claims in which sexual dysfunction is at issue.

Measures for clinical practice: A sourcebook (3rd ed.): *Volume 2. Adults* (2000). By Kevin Corcoran and Joel Fischer. (900 pages)

As compared with its companion volume (described in the following entry), also by Fischer and Corcoran, this book of measures for adults has more scales for use in trial consultation. It has 220 scales presented in full. The scale descriptions are organized around categories of purpose, description, norms, scoring, reliability, validity, primary reference, and availability. The measures are mostly intended for use in clinical practice and research by mental health professionals. Nevertheless, there are enough scales that tap broad areas of possible juror predispositions to make it a useful addition to a trial consultant's library. A paradoxical note is present in both books. A few scales that are presented in full also have the warning "This scale cannot be reproduced or copied in any manner," which is peculiar, given that Corcoran and Fischer have reproduced them in their books.[4] In any case, specific information is given about whom to contact for permission to use or for purchase of the measures.

From this volume of adult measures, seven areas are thoroughly covered:

- Anxiety and fear (24 scales)
- Depression and grief (13 scales)
- Health issues (21 scales)
- Interpersonal behavior (17 scales)
- Locus of control (12 scales)
- Psychopathology and psychiatric symptoms (16 scales)
- Substance abuse (13 scales)

Because alcohol or drug use is a common element in criminal and civil trials, the substance abuse scales are likely to be of interest in trial consultation. Most of these scales are designed to be administered to clinical populations who are substance abusers and, as a consequence, often need rephrasing to be used in jury selection.

Because authoritarianism is a construct considered in jury selection, the Patrick Heaven Authoritarianism Scale (revised F Scale) presents a reasonably reliable 35-item measure of authoritarianism. It has the disadvantage (to American users) of being normed on an Australian sample. However, the items are consistent with other measures of authoritarianism, including, "Does the idea of being a leader appeal to you?" and "Do you tend to domi-

---

[4]Items I have included are drawn only from scales for which permission to reproduce is not required.

nate the conversation?" Another Australian scale that assesses this construct is the Authority Behavior Inventory, a 24-item measure of the tendency to defer or submit to authority.

Many court proceedings drag on with periods in which little happens that is dramatic, interesting, or visibly relevant to the issues being litigated. Thus, the Boredom Proneness Scale by Richard Famer and Norman Sundberg has logical applications to trial work. This 28-item scale was designed to measure predisposition to boredom. It has good internal consistency and validity. Two items from this scale are "In situations where I have to wait, such as a line or queue, I get very restless"[5] and "Time always seems to be passing slowly."

A measure included in this book of scales for adults addresses socially controlling behavior and was developed by Logan Wright and his colleagues in the form of the vaguely named Way of Life Scale. This 43-item scale has many neutral buffer items to disguise its purpose; the scale has good temporal reliability. This scale appears to be related to authoritarian measures. A sample item is "I like to monitor other people to make sure things are going the way they should be."

Measures in this book may have forensic utility in cases in which mental health, adjustment, or coping are at issue. Although not intended for court work, the breadth of scales in this and the volume next discussed present good resources for the attorney and trial consultant.

Measures for clinical practice: A sourcebook (4th ed.): *Volume 1. Couples, families and children* (2007). By Joel Fischer and Kevin Corcoran. (626 pages)

As its title indicates, the scales in this book are of use in issues related to family law, family functioning, couple relationships, parent–child relationships, and sexuality. Thirty-seven scales are included for family functioning alone. In the category of Boundary Ambiguity Scales (BAS), six subgroups are present, including the potentially useful ones assessing boundaries for Divorced Adults and for Caregivers of Patients with Dementia. The BAS for Divorced Adults has items such as "I still consider myself a wife/husband to my former spouse," and "I feel upset when I imagine my former spouse with another man/woman." The BAS for Caregivers of Patients with Dementia includes items such as "I feel guilty when I get out of the house to

---

[5]When I have asked college students in my classes about their restlessness when waiting in lines, there is almost a uniformly expressed impatience. They switch lines all the time at supermarkets and banks. I used to be that way when I was in college. Still, this does not mean they would be predictably bored and restless as jurors.

do something enjoyable while _____ remains at home" and " I often feel mixed up about how much I should be doing for _____." Other scales of family functioning include the Family Adaptability and Cohesion Evaluation Scale, the Family Distress Index, and the Healthy Family Parenting Inventory. When custody and parenting skills are issue, the reliable and valid Healthy Families Parenting Inventory may have utility. It includes items such as "I feel trapped by all the things I have to do for my child" and "I can remain calm when my child is upset."

Issues of abuse often make their way to the courts. This volume includes four interesting scales about abuse and other scales that assess violence in the family. Partner physical abuse scales and nonphysical abuse scales are specifically included. All four scales measure degree of perceived or reported abuse inflicted on or by a partner.

As in the other volume by Fischer and Corcoran, a number of scales deal with aspects of culture or ethnicity. The Scale of Racial Socialization for Adolescents is a 45-item measure of acceptance or understanding of African American family functioning and life experiences. A sample item is "Black parents need to teach their children how to live in two worlds: one black and one white." The commonly used Multigroup Ethnic Identity Measure is included and it applies to any ethnic group. The Youth Coping Index was designed to be ethnically sensitive to adjustment of African American youths. In addition, the highly reliable and valid Hawaiian Culture Scale— Adolescent is in this volume and is used for assessing how much Hawaiian beliefs and way of life are valued.

Handbook of scales for research in crime and delinquency (1983). By Stanley L. Brodsky and H. O'Neal Smitherman. (615 pages)[6]

This collection of reviews and listings of 380 scales in law, justice, crime, and delinquency includes the actual scale items and detailed reviews of almost half of the measures. From the eight groupings of reviewed scales, five groupings may be useful in trial consultation:

- Law enforcement and police, which include five measures of attitudes toward police.
- Courts and the law, which include eight scales of attitudes toward the law or legal system.
- Offenders, including two attitudes toward offenders or prisoners scales.

---

[6]All of the older books that are out of print are available through *www.abebooks.com*.

- Crime and criminality, including a number of measures of attitudes, views, opinions, and orientations.
- General measures, including scales of attitudes toward deviant behavior, toward government workers, and toward any institution. Despite its name, the latter measure holds promise in trial consultation.

The various measures of attitudes toward the police may be used in cases in which the actions of law enforcement officers are challenged. Thus, the Attitudes toward Police Scale has separate subscales of competency and hostility. A competency item is "Most cops are pretty good at their work." A hostility item is "Cops never believe you even when you're telling the truth." The other measures of attitudes toward police tap into areas of helpfulness, honesty, fairness, and intelligence of police.

The courts and the law section includes two scales that measure Attitude toward Capital Punishment (15 items) and the Capital Punishment Attitude Questionnaire (2 items). Neither scale has strong evidence of reliability or validity, but given that such constructs are often addressed in capital trials, these items may be considered for inclusion in a jury questionnaire. The attitudes toward the law measures have more systemic development and better psychometric characteristics. The Melvin Attitudes toward Prisoners Scale[7] has particularly good reliability and validity support and some normative data. Items from this scale include "Prisoners are just plain mean at heart" and "Most prisoners are victims of circumstances and deserve to be helped."

In addition to the attitudes scales in the crime and criminality section, two more specific scales should be noted: the Attitude toward Stealing Scale and Attitude toward Violence Scale. The general scales have a variety of measures that are indirectly related to crime and justice. For example, it may be assumed that a common element underlying defendant behavior in a variety of contexts is traditional or hegemonic masculinity. This section of the book includes the thoughtfully constructed Silverman and Dinitz Compulsive Masculinity Scale. Although developed in regard to delinquent youth, the items have broader application. Two of the items are "Nobody tells me what to do" and "I know how to hold my booze."

CONSTRUCTS AND MEASURES

The books described in the preceding section have collected measures that may be of use in trial consultation. This following discussion examines indi-

---

[7]This scale is discussed in depth in Chapter 9.

vidual measures themselves. Those presented here have these two characteristics:

- There is a conceptual frame of reference, so that the measure is seated in a theory or organized in a systematic way of approaching an issue.
- A body of research about the measure and its overarching construct have appeared in scholarly journals.

Need for Cognition

Some jurors during a trial appear to be mentally absent from the beginning of the proceedings. These jurors yawn, chew at their nails, fidget, tug at clothing, or have the unfocused gaze of people whose thoughts and minds are elsewhere. Some mentally absent jurors are preoccupied with family, work, or physical concerns. Others are part of a larger group that has a low need for cognition (NFC).

The motivating construct of NFC has a rich history in psychological research. NFC addresses the extent to which people like to process ideas deliberately and their ability to do so (Cacioppo, Petty, Feinstein, & Jarvis, 1996). Even when the issues may have little to do with them personally, people with high NFC like to think, to consider, and to deliberate. They are motivated to solve cognitive problems. Other individuals without naturally high NFC can be motivated to think deeply, especially when somebody communicates in a way that cogently draws them into the issues.

It is easy to assume that NFC is directly related to intelligence or ability. However, in their review article Cacioppo et al. (1996) observe that they see NFC as a cognitive motivation and not an intellectual ability. They draw an analogy to how individuals may be motivated to participate in physical endeavors and how the motivation is related to physical ability, but is not the same thing.

The application of NFC to the courtroom is straightforward. Individuals with a high NFC[8] are likely to work hard on the central and probative issues. They enjoy the challenge and are not satisfied until they have thoroughly examined the evidence, this way and that, top to bottom, from various perspectives, and weighed the nature and quality of what they have seen and heard. In contrast, individuals with a low NFC consider less content. They may process the various weak and strong points of evidence, but they make up their minds quickly based on peripheral information, such as the

---

[8]Even though NFC is discussed here in terms of people with high and low NFC, that dichotomy is simplistic and used for illustrating differences. In fact, NFC exists on a continuum and the motivation for deliberate thinking and central processing apparently falls on a normal distribution.

likeability of the attorneys and witnesses or which side takes the most time to present.

Low-NFC persons do not *explicitly* choose to not think through issues. It is simply who they are, which is persons who make decisions quickly and with minimal information. Are people with a low NFC good for some attorneys and in some trials? Yes, when the following trial goals are present:

1. Want jurors to respond well and lastingly to first impressions.
2. Look for jurors who are more likely to respond to emotional rather than rational arguments, to peripheral rather than central processing and cues.
3. Choose jurors who are less likely to attend to complex issues that require deep understanding.

Of course, the opposite considerations are present in preferring persons with a high NFC:

1. Choose jurors who will not be taken in by initial case descriptions, but will wait, as the law requires, until they have heard all evidence to make up their minds.
2. Have jurors who will see past emotional content and dramatic displays and flair by attorneys to the essential content.
3. Look for jurors who will have the disposition to stay with the complex, conflicting, and ambiguous evidence present in many trials.

Need for Cognition Scale[9]

In a series of studies Petty and his colleagues (Cacioppo & Petty, 1982; Cacioppo, Petty, & Kao, 1984) moved from an initial 45-item scale to a 34-item scale and eventually to the most current 18-item scale. The final scale was characterized by a single dominant factor and in 10 studies had high reliability in the form of Cronbach's alphas ranging from .81 to .97. In their summary of many studies, Cacioppo et al. (1996) also reported strong validity evidence, with NFC strongly related to intrinsic motivation and tolerance for ambiguity. Here the NFC scale is reproduced in full:

NFC INSTRUCTIONS

Indicate to what extent the statement is characteristic of you, using the following scale:

---

[9]In the literature the Need for Cognition Scale is typically abbreviated as NCS rather than my preferred acronym, NFC.

1   Extremely uncharacteristic or not at all like you
2   Somewhat uncharacteristic
3   Uncertain
4   Somewhat characteristic
5   Extremely characteristic of you (very much like you)

ITEMS

1. I would prefer complex to simple problems.
2. I like to have the responsibility of handling a situation that requires a lot of thinking.
3. Thinking is not my idea of fun.*
4. I would rather do something that requires little thought than something that is sure to challenge my thinking abilities.*
5. I try to anticipate and avoid situations where there is a likely chance I will have to think in depth about something.*
6. I find satisfaction in deliberating hard and for long hours.
7. I only think as hard as I have to.*
8. I prefer to think about small, daily projects than long-term ones.*
9. I like tasks that require little thought once I've learned them.*
10. The idea of relying on thought to make my way to the top appeals to me.
11. I really enjoy a task that involves coming up with solutions to problems.
12. Learning new ways to think doesn't excite me very much.*
13. I prefer my life to be filled with puzzles I must solve.
14. The notion of thinking abstractly is appealing to me.
15. I would prefer a task that is intellectual, difficult, and important to one that is somewhat important but does not require much thought.
16. I feel relief rather than satisfaction after completing a task that required a lot of mental effort.*
17. It is enough for me that something gets the job done; I don't care how or why it works.*
18. I usually end up deliberating about issues even when they do not affect me personally.

*Reverse scoring.
A high total score indicates high NFC.

Juror Bias

One of the most widely known constructs is juror bias, with its associated scale, the Juror Bias Scale (JBS), developed by Kassin and Wrightsman

(1983). Intended primarily for use in criminal cases, the JBS has two major components drawn from the developers' observations of likely importance in trials: the probability of commission of the crime by the defendant and the interpretation of what reasonable doubt actually means. Supplementing the face-valid nature of these two constructs, Kassin and Wrightsman (1983), Myers and Lecci (1998), and Lecci and Myers (2002) conducted research studies that provided an empirical foundation for understanding the JBS.

In the Kassin and Wrightsman scale development study, validity of the JBS was investigated. Mock jurors watched videotaped reconstructions of four different types of criminal trials or read transcripts of the trials. The mock pro-prosecution (as determined by the JBS) jurors were more likely to convict in assault, conspiracy, and auto theft cases than the mock pro-defense jurors. No difference was found in a rape case.

In the Lecci and Myers (2002) and Myers and Lecci (1998) studies, the reasonable doubt dimension was supported as a single strong factor. The probability of commission items did not hang together as a single factor. Indeed, the various studies point to the reasonable doubt component and items as being most predictive and useful. The JBS itself is presented and discussed in Chapter 9.

Punitiveness

In criminal trials in particular, but also to some extent in civil trials, a dimension of compelling interest is how punitive are the members of the venire. The term *punitiveness* refers to how oriented persons are toward inflicting or awarding punishment. It is possible to think of every trial as having some consideration of punishment.

Some of the resources already cited have scales that include an element of punitiveness. When the book *The Authoritarian Personality* was published in 1950 (Adorno, Frenkel-Brunswick, Levinson, & Sanford, 1950), punitiveness was seen as one of the defining characteristics of authoritarianism. Subsequent research (e.g., Garcia & Griffitt, 1978) failed to support the belief that authoritarianism was related to punitiveness. Ray (1984) posited the existence of a punitive personality, and he developed a 12-item scale of punitive attitudes toward criminals to assess this hypothesized trait.

The assumption is sometimes made that punitiveness is a single, coherent variable. Sprott (1999) used a simple measure of preferred sentencing for young persons found guilty of breaking and entering or assault. She concluded that punitiveness is complex, varies according to gender, and that simplistic notions should be discarded. In a study that brought together two of the concepts discussed in this chapter, Sargent (2004) used a 5-item scale of attitudes toward capital punishment for assessing punitiveness and the Cacioppo et al. (1996) 18-item Need for Cognition Scale. As would be expected, the two variables were negatively and significantly correlated, leading Sargent to conclude that less thought is associated with more punishment.

Some studies of punitive attitudes have drawn on other constructs. Thus, Philip (1973) employed the Hostility and Direction of Hostility Questionnaire (HDHQ). The HDHQ was also used by Tiller, Schmidt, Shireen, and Treasure (1995) to infer intropunitive and extrapunitive attitudes. Unlike many of the other measures discussed, the punitiveness scales discussed so far do not lend themselves readily to use in STQs. Some scales approach too closely to assessing what are ultimate legal conclusions, like sentencing. Other scales, like the HDHQ, seem a little tangential. The scale presented later in Chapter 9 is one that I developed by taking frequently occurring evaluative statements about prisoners that appeared in newspapers and discussions with attorneys and colleagues. Out of a larger pool of 16 statements, 8 statements have appeared useful in jury selection, mostly in capital murder trials. These 8 items were included because they yield a wide range of scores, because they lend themselves to defense use by soliciting only responses that are punitive in nature, and because 5 of the items specifically address the expectations of respondents as to what should happen to convicted offenders. A total score of degree of punitiveness is calculated by simply adding the number of agreement checkmarks.

CONCLUSION

The instruments and scales discussed here are best thought of as resources rather than solutions. They appear to offer better-formulated items than the improvised and untested items that are used in part of the routine practice of some trial attorneys. After all, we know something about the stimulus value and potential applications of these items and measures. We also know about their limitations.

Posey and Wrightsman (2005) put the limitations in perspective nicely when they reviewed two of these measures, the JBS and the Legal Attitudes Questionnaire. They wrote, "Individual items can serve as the bases for questions to individual prospective jurors during the voir dire, or if there is an opportunity to administer a supplemental juror questionnaire, prospective jurors can be asked to respond to all of the statements. But the trial consultant should always remember that general traits, as measured here, have a very limited relationship to verdicts in specific cases. They are better than nothing, and they are probably better than most people's intuitions, but their predictive accuracy is low when it comes to verdicts by individual jurors" (p. 169).

Part II

⧯⬥⧯

PREPARATION
OF WITNESSES
AND ATTORNEYS

I often ask participants in my expert witness workshops to send me in advance their descriptions of the worst experiences they have ever had on the witness stand. One person wrote about how she had reviewed thousands of pages of reports from psychosocial histories and medical records and occupational and family data. During her court testimony, she was asked about a piece of information referred to briefly in one sentence on one page and never mentioned again. She did not remember reading it. The opposing attorney made this one piece of information the entire focus of the cross-examination, so that the witness felt increasingly inept and frustrated.

Part of what trial consultants do is prepare lay and expert witnesses to make a positive impression, to speak well during direct examinations, and to manage themselves with ease during cross-examinations. Even though this one brief and arguably insignificant detail reported by the witness could not have been anticipated, the broader objective of preparing the witness could have made a difference so that she was more poised and able to handle the barrage of questions.

Trial consultants do not put words in the mouths of witnesses or permit lies or deceptions. The word *preparation* of witnesses means getting the best out of who the witnesses truly are. For some witnesses, preparation requires a mild tune-up, making sure that the machinery of testimony is running well. For others, preparation is more involved, such as working to improve poor posture, to slow down the pace of speaking, or to make answers more responsive.

The following three chapters address the nature of effective testimony and examine the ways in which witnesses present themselves so that they are credible. Much of a witness's credibility depends on nonverbal behaviors, a topic that is developed in Chapter 4. When there is a discrepancy between the content of what witnesses say and their physical bearing, nonverbal behavior, and voice quality, the jury will be less likely to believe them.

Chapter 5 delves into the role, preparation, and activities of the expert witness. Because expert witnesses are often regular visitors to the witness stand, they seek out guidance and feedback from trial consultants much more than lay witnesses do. Expert witnesses must meet specific requirements to be accepted as an expert, or one who is entitled to give professional or scientific opinions.

In the first part of this book, Chapters 1 and 2 on practices and principles were followed by Chapter 3, a research chapter. The same pattern is repeated in Part II: Two chapters on applications are followed by a chapter on research foundations. Thus, Chapter 6 reports on the research studies from my Witness Research Lab. After a brief history of how the lab started, the chapter examines the main research methods and investigations and the subsequent findings that have emerged from the studies.

Chapter 4

—✦—

WITNESS PREPARATION
FOR TESTIFYING
IN COURT

Juries and judges evaluate the credibility and worth of evidence in part according to the believability of the witnesses who present the evidence. Because attorneys cannot introduce evidence themselves, witnesses who speak effectively to what they have seen, heard, and know are essential to attorneys' presenting a winning case. Poor witnesses may contribute to cases being lost.

This chapter addresses what consultants do to prepare witnesses, the foundations of witness preparation, and preparation for cross-examination of other witnesses. For example, the bases of what trial consultants have learned about witness credibility go beyond the scope of consultations in which we personally prepare witnesses, and draw on the social psychology and legal literature and on other scientific and professional experiences. For me, part of these professional experiences includes regularly watching trials in our county courthouse. If I am not learning much or if the trial is bogged down in motions and sidebars, I slip out to the next trial down the hallway or up the stairs, often accompanied by friendly trial attorneys who share my interest in watching trials. What we see are some witnesses who are superb on the stand. One homicide investigator who testifies manages to be professional and poised and at the same time warm and thoroughly likeable. I have spoken to him after he testifies and have found him to be the same in personal conversations as he is on the stand: professional and likeable. He does not need or get much preparation.

This investigator is an exception. A distressed woman recently testified as a fact witness in the sentencing phase of a capital murder trial in which I was involved. She kept crying, apologizing to the judge, crying again, apologizing again, and eventually told of what a responsible person the defendant was, the impact of which was diminished by the distraction of her tears and apologies. She had not been prepared for the questions she was asked, and she had needed preparation for her testimony. A fundamental responsibility of trial attorneys is to invest the time and effort to ensure that what their witnesses have to say will be communicated effectively. Sometimes it takes a trial consultant to help bring out the best style of presentation on the witness stand.

This chapter addresses preparation of lay witnesses and then attorney preparation for examination of witnesses. Some of the preparation issues and examination methods overlap. We start with lay witnesses; their testimony is examined, especially with respect to what can be done by trial consultants, attorneys, and psychologists to prepare them.

HORSE-SHEDDING

Witness preparation has been called the dark secret of the legal profession. The ethics of witness preparation describe it as unethical to prepare misleading or fabricated testimony (Boccaccini, 2002). Long before the profession of trial consultation, attorneys sought to prepare their witnesses, sometimes in unduly directive ways. Boccaccini (2002) has reviewed the practice of horse-shedding in witness preparation, although the word "preparation" may be a somewhat kind term to describe the specific instructions that 19th-century U.S. attorneys gave to eyewitnesses and defendants. The term *horse-shedding* was first used by James Fenimore Cooper in his mid-19th-century novels, although the terms *wood-shedding* and *sandpapering* have also been used to describe the same process. *Horse-shedding* comes from attorneys taking their newly arrived witnesses into a nearby horse shed or stable before the trial opened or resumed. Once in the horse shed, the attorneys not only addressed demeanor and self-presentation. In addition, they told the witnesses the specific content that should be presented. These statements were often biased and one-sided reconstructions of events related to the charges. The attorneys instructed. The witnesses complied.

Do these unethical practices continue to the present day? It is impossible to know for certain, but if they do continue, they are much less blatant and decidedly more hidden. The attorneys with whom trial consultants work do not knowingly permit misrepresentation of facts by their witnesses or clients, nor do trial consultants. Indeed, one attorney I know gives a stern lecture to her clients about perjury and explains that she will withdraw as counsel if her clients lie at any time. Trial consultants set forth the same ground rules in the preparation of witnesses. They insist that defendants and other witnesses be truthful. At the same time, it is not always apparent as to whether a defendant's or plaintiff's story is truthful. Many stories are full of ambiguity and uncertainty.

WITNESS PREPARATION

Three aspects of witness preparation have been identified: witness education, attorney education, and modification of testimony delivery (Boccaccini, 2002). Witness education consists of reviewing facts and prior statements and orienting witnesses to trial proceedings and the physical nature of the witness stand and courtroom (Brodsky, 1991). Attorney education consists of the attorneys becoming thoroughly familiar with the anticipated testimony and knowing the strengths and weaknesses of the testimony. The third aspect is modification of testimony delivery, arguably the most important and most psychological of the three components. This component includes demeanor, style, confidence, and pace. In his article on witness preparation, Boccaccini (2002, p. 166) described the following fundamental testifying skills for witnesses:

When answering questions, witnesses should:

1. Always tell the truth.
2. Listen carefully to the question being asked, then pause, take a breath, and answer the question. This allows the witness to relax and, during cross-examination, gives the attorney a chance to object if necessary.
3. Answer only the question that is asked. If the attorney pauses, do not attempt to fill the resulting silence.
4. Avoid slang and jargon. Use language that everybody can understand.
5. Do not memorize answers to anticipated questions.
6. Speak loudly and clearly. Nervous witnesses ramble on and speak rapidly. Shy witnesses speak too softly.
7. Do not argue with opposing counsel about his or her line of questioning.
8. It is OK to ask an attorney to repeat or rephrase a question.
9. It is OK to say "no" and "I don't know." Do not guess on the witness stand.
10. Avoid qualifiers such as "I think" and "I guess." Also, avoid using hesitation words such as "uh" and "um."

Nonverbal behaviors that aid witness credibility:

1. Maintain good posture. Do not slouch, and try not to shift posture excessively or hastily.
2. Do not forget to look at the jury when testifying. Alternatively, do not stare at the jury.
3. Do not look to the attorney for answers. This behavior will imply that the attorney is giving instructions.
4. Use mannerisms and gestures, but do not use them excessively. Too many gestures may make the witness appear nervous or hyperactive.

An additional suggestion:

Ask the witnesses: "How do you know when a person is believable?" Then have them evaluate their testimony using their own internal norms for believability.

The research on effective witness testimony has indicated that specific verbal and nonverbal testimony characteristics are associated with believable testimony. The verbal characteristics include powerful and confident testimony, descriptive rather than fragmented (too brief) answers, and avoidance of overformal, hypercorrect speech (O'Barr, 1982; Boccaccini, 2002). Nonverbal characteristics of effective witnesses include relaxed postures, leaning forward slightly, good eye contact, and perceived authenticity of emotions.

PUBLIC FIGURES ON THE STAND

A path to understanding how lay witnesses perform in court is to examine public figures and celebrities on the stand. Even skilled public speakers can falter and struggle in court testimony. An example is the testimony of Tim Russert, former moderator of *Meet the Press* (until his sudden death in 2008), in the Lewis "Scooter" Libby[1] trial for perjury in January and February 2007. The *New York Times* reported how Russert's initially polished testimony during direct examination by the special prosecutor faltered during cross-examination by Libby's attorney (*New York Times*, February 8, 2007, pp. A1, A13).

---

[1]Libby had served as chief of staff for then Vice President Cheney.

Mr. Russert testified under a prosecutor's questioning that, contrary to Mr. Libby's sworn testimony, he never spoke with him about Valerie Wilson, the CIA officer.

Mr. Russert, the moderator of "Meet the Press," was unequivocal in his testimony that no such conversation occurred. But when Mr. Libby's chief defense lawyer, Theodore V. Wells, Jr., began his efforts to disparage Mr. Russert's reliability on cross-examination, Mr. Russert's confident demeanor changed abruptly.

Mr. Russert, whose appearance drew the largest crowd of spectators yet in the three-week-long trial, stopped speaking in the confident, complete sentences in which he had answered the prosecutor in his direct testimony. Instead, he became more deliberate and halting in his responses, frequently asking Mr. Wells to repeat the question or asking for time to examine the document about which he was being asked. "Say again?" he said frequently." (p. A13)

Three elements in the testimony of Mr. Russert are related to our examination of witness testimony.

1. During the direct examination Mr. Russert was a believable witness on the stand, speaking effectively and confidently.
2. During the cross-examination, Mr. Russert underwent a negative metamorphosis, shifting in style to an insecure speaker answering without confidence and speaking in fragmented thoughts.
3. In an effort to compensate for this fall from poise, Mr. Russert sought to gain time and composure by asking unnecessary questions, a ploy that served to reveal his feeling of inadequacy more than to show control and poise.

In the continuation of his testimony the next day,[2] Mr. Russert was confronted with the common situation in which witnesses are asked to give yes-or-no answers. He again attempted to gain control, as follows:

"Did you disclose in the affidavit to the court that you had already disclosed the contents of your conversation with Mr. Libby" Mr. Wells asked.

"As I said, sir ... , " Mr. Russert began.

"It's a yes or no question," Mr. Wells interrupted.

"I'd like to answer it to the best of my ability," Mr. Russert replied.

"This is a very simple question. Either it's in the affirmative or it's

---

[2]The *New York Times* the next day (February 9, 2007) reported that Mr. Russert was subdued during the 2 days of testimony, in contrast to his customary television persona, and went on to observe that he "seemed initially taken aback by the pace and ferocity of Mr. Wells' questions," but on the next day again was confident (p. A13).

not," Mr. Wells said. "Did you disclose to the court that you had already communicated to the F.B.I. the fact that you had communicated with Mr. Libby?"

"No," Mr. Russert said." (*New York Times*, February 9, 2007, p. A13)

Witnesses in his position would benefit from following these suggestions when answering yes-or-no questions. Simple and straightforward yes-or-no questions merit simple yes-or-no answers. When complex questions are accompanied by demands for yes-or-no answers, witnesses should consider answering:

"There is no simple yes-or-no answer to that question."
"It would be irresponsible of me to give a simplistic answer when an explanation is called for."

or even

"When I was sworn in, I took an oath to tell the whole truth, which I would not be doing if I gave a yes-or-no answer."

PREPARATION FOR CROSS-EXAMINATION OF LAY WITNESSES

There are both similarities and differences in the preparation of lay witnesses for direct examination and for cross-examination. A great latitude exists in examining lay witnesses. At the same time, many lay witnesses do not have the poise and protective experience of witnesses who are accustomed to being on the stand.

Our case study involves Althea, a woman who lost a struggle for custody of her 2-year-old son to her ex-lover. In a bitterly contested court hearing, the child's father had hired a skilled attorney and, perhaps unknowingly, the attorney drew on false reports by a coworker of Althea when Althea was cross-examined. Allegations were made during a first custody hearing that Althea had a serious psychological disorder, that she did not care about her son, that she had engaged in a variety of illegal activities, and that she was an inept mother. During the aggressive questioning and false allegations in this custody hearing, Althea froze, and out of anxiety and fear she was unable to hear or answer any questions clearly or well.

The first hearing left Althea shaken and anxious; she was distressed that she would not be able to have any visitation with her son. She sought assistance in preparing for the next custody hearing, which took place many months after the first one. She and I prepared a list of the most challenging and difficult questions she anticipated from the skilled opposing counsel. We role played her responses to each of these questions. I stopped the role-playing repeatedly to ask her what the truth actually was. When Althea got stuck, as she often did, I used what she told me earlier as I modeled positive replies. Her new answers to questions about her mental state, her prior marriage, and her parenting abilities were eventually given straightforwardly, honestly, and with appropriate display of feeling in our practice sessions.

When the next hearing came around, opposing counsel anticipated that Althea would continue as before—that is, speaking poorly and ineffectively and getting stuck. Instead, this time Althea was emotionally appropriate, in control, and able to speak to the essential issues in the case. What made the difference? Three components were influential: First, Althea got past the anxiety that had incapacitated her, as a result of rehearsal, reassurance, and understanding the cross-examination process. Second, she now anticipated the questions and was not frightened by the allegations. Third, Althea incorporated the considerable feedback about her manner, posture, and tone of voice, so she was able to speak authentically and effectively.

In criminal trials and occasionally in civil proceedings, I have worked with defendants, preparing them to testify. Some of the cases included the following modifications of the behaviors of defendants:

A woman who smiled relentlessly when talking about herself was trained to become aware of her smiling. She then learned to avoid smiling when talking about the accusations against her.

In a mock cross-examination a man who slouched in his seat seemed to try to make himself small when confronted with challenging questions. He was taught to thrust his lower back into the seat, to straighten his spine, and to answer questions with energy and conviction.

A man who was an immigrant with English language difficulties became confused and then passive or defensive during his first deposition. He learned to listen with care to questions, to clarify issues he did not follow, and to feel empowered enough to be assertive in the next deposition.

A woman started each of her answers to our practice questions well. However, she never sustained her good responses and would drift away into unrelated content in her narrative answers, so that listeners had difficulty in following her. In our meetings, she was not able to learn to maintain a consistent narrative line, so, instead, she was taught when and how to stop her answers after the initial successful part of her responses.

A man who was suffering from a manic disorder was simply unable to learn from witness preparation. A decision was made with his attorneys not to call him to testify, even though the case had aspects in which effective testimony would have made a difference.

WITNESS PREPARATION FOR RACE INQUIRIES

The following case was drawn in part from an article Virginia Sparrow, Marc Boaccaccini, and I wrote on racial inquiries in depositions and trials (Brodsky, Sparrow, & Boccaccini, 1998). The case involved allegations that racial discrimination was the basis of a termination of contract with a minority-owned business contact. The African American plaintiffs alleged that race was the single motivating factor in the actions of the white defendants. The consultation was with the attorneys for the defense. In this case, the trial consultation goals were to prepare the defendants for depositions and trial testimony and to assist the defendants' attorneys in preparing to question the plaintiffs in a manner that would serve the trial goals of the defense and would be respectful of the plaintiffs.

The first task was to prepare the three named defendants, all of whom were middle-aged white males raised in a rural, de facto segregated area with a history of overt racism. When asked what they most feared in depositions, the defendants feared being asked about their nonexistent friendships or close social relationships with African Americans and about their use of racist language while growing up. None of these issues related directly to the probative issues in the allegations and forthcoming trial. Three principles were taught in the context of repeated role playing about the likely questions the defendants would be asked during depositions and trials.

1. *Racist language.* The defendants anticipated that they would be asked to describe the specific incidents in which they had used the N-word in conversations. This question is broad and is designed to bring out explicit racist language and associated attitudes of racism by the defendants. The operating rule the defendants were taught was honesty first. The defendants were reminded that they would be under oath and that they had a legal and moral obligation to be honest. At the same time, they were told they did not have to describe what they could not remember about specific incidents.

2. *Racist behaviors.* In our conversations, the defendants were unequivocal in their denials of having acted in a discriminatory way in their business dealings. They were instructed to stay with facts and events of legal interest, to be dispassionate, and not to be defensive.

3. *Subtle racist attitudes:* One allegation was that some business decisions were made on the basis of race, but manifested in subtle and indirect patterns. The defendants were instructed not to try to read excessively into their actions or to acknowledge attitudes of which they were not aware or that they did not see as racist. Again, they were to stay with the factual

and accountable actions they took and to indicate the rationale for those actions.

In this trial consultation, part of the task was assisting retaining counsel in preparing questions that would be effective during the depositions of the plaintiffs. The operating rules that emerged were to be always respectful of the plaintiffs, especially when any race issues were raised, and to use the depositions as an opportunity to bring out any possibility that the plaintiffs held worldviews that saw most whites as being racist. Such worldviews, if found, would dilute the power of the specific allegations of the case because they would indicate that the plaintiffs saw and experienced discrimination against them by parties everywhere, rather than solely by the parties mentioned in the present allegations. For those reasons, the following sample questions were generated to prepare counsel to depose the plaintiffs.

The first questions about the general bases of the racial discrimination allegations were intended to elicit the breadth of racism and discrimination as perceived by the plaintiffs.

1. "To what extent is your city racist? Your state? Your region of the United States? The United States itself?"
2. "How much is racism present in corporate America? What forms does it take in corporate America? What are the ways in which it is seen? Not seen?"
3. "What effect does racism have on people of your acquaintance?"
4. "Is racism present in the public schools?"
5. "What effect does racism have on early schooling? Secondary schooling? College? Graduate education?"
6. "How do you know this? What information or observations do you have to support this conclusion?"

The next questions addressed awareness of racism in society, again drawing out content that fit with the contentions of the defense attorneys that the present allegations were part of an excessive sensitivity to race issues well beyond the reach of the present alleged discrimination.

7. "When did you first become aware of racism in society? In schools? In social relationships? In economic aspects and business relationships? What events happened to promote your awareness? What led to your present point of thinking?"

The next three questions regarded individual differences between African Americans and other Americans in their understandings and perceptions of racism. The purpose of these questions was to examine whether the plaintiffs would in some ways be open to describing themselves as oversensitive to what may or may not be racist actions.

8. "To the best of your knowledge, are there specific ways that African Americans versus whites view patterns and manifestations of racism?"
9. "Why is it that some African Americans see much racism and others see little racism?"
10. "How does one decide who is more correct and who is less correct when there are such differences?"

In this series of steps in preparing the defendants to be deposed and their attorneys to depose the plaintiffs, the consultant pursued two objectives. The first was to assist the defendants in handling what was an emotional issue, stemming from their life histories. The second objective was to inquire respectfully but thoroughly into how much racism the plaintiffs perceived in their business, their lives, and the lives of others. It should be noted that many scholars and observers believe that racism is present everywhere. However, the task for the case at hand was to address allegations of possible discrimination in a responsive, honest, and, at the same time, effective manner. The method used was modified from a procedure identified by Greenberg, Feldman, and Brodsky (1987), in which the plaintiffs' own expertise (in this case, on racism) was mobilized to be used against them.

CONCLUSION

The ways in which witnesses present themselves can have a powerful impact on how much they are believed. Both verbal self-presentation and the nonverbal behaviors in which it is seated can be influential in witness credibility. The early history of attorneys horse-shedding witnesses to produce sometimes falsified testimony has given way to attorneys and consultants seeking to modify the behaviors of witnesses to make them more effective. A parallel task to improving the credibility of witnesses is the effort of opposing counsel (and consultants) to ask questions that diminish the credibility of witnesses.

Trial consultants can bring practical and research knowledge to both the preparation of witnesses and the preparation of cross-examinations and depositions. The practical knowledge is seated in the behavioral science conceptualizations of problems in the witnesses' self-presentation, and then developed by taking steps in the form of behavior rehearsals and direct feedback to correct those problems. The research knowledge is drawn from studies that have identified significant witness variables such as confidence, powerful speech, posture, and narrative versus fragmented testimony. In contrast to direct preparation of witnesses, the consultants' work with cross-examinations and depositions usually assists attorneys in addressing both general and case-specific aspects of testimony of opposing expert and lay witnesses.

Chapter 5

PREPARATION AND EXAMINATION OF EXPERT WITNESSES

It was the first time the young physician had ever testified. I was at the attorney's office to help prepare him for his deposition. The deposition was part of a lawsuit against a corporation that owned a residential complex with many inexpensive rentals in which an unsanitary and perhaps toxic environment had been present for decades. The people living in the rental units had repeated infections and diseases, reminiscent in a number of ways of the true story portrayed in the 2000 film *Erin Brockovich*. The doctor was going to testify in a forthcoming deposition that there was a causal link between the presence of the toxicities and the residents' illnesses, but he was worried, as was the attorney for the plaintiffs. They were both concerned that his inexperience in the courtroom and in medical-forensic work would be a problem. The doctor was clearly anxious. The attorney sought to reassure him, but indicated to me privately that the doctor was fretting.

We set up a mock deposition. First, we went over the doctor's curriculum vitae. Playing the role of opposing counsel, I challenged his experience, his credentials, and his knowledge of MRSA (methicillin-resistant *Staphylococcus aureus*). We then went to the heart of his attorney's concerns, the fact that the physician had only looked at medical records and had never seen any of the complainant-residents personally. The doctor did not do badly, but he was diffident, sometimes reluctant to give much information, and hesitated a lot before answering. He was not convincing.

We worked on his testimony for hours, with some success. Still, something was missing. Finally, I asked about how he had become the person he now was, professionally and personally. A story of transformation unfolded. The doctor told how arrogant and self-centered he used to be in his work and in his life. Five years ago, he explained, he realized that he had been more interested in himself than others, and he had believed that he was superior to other people. With this insight, he decided it was a bad way to be, and that awareness changed his life. He committed himself to becoming humble, unassuming, and respectful of others. At first, it was difficult. He kept catching himself being insensitive and overbearing. The same drive that brought him near the top of his class in medical school was mobilized in this struggle. After months of effort, which included some time off from medical practice, he accomplished his goal. The attempted humility that had been a foreground and demanding priority finally emerged, became background in his thoughts, and eventually changed into an automatic way of being.

That opened up our consultation work in a good way, because a problem-solving process emerged. We focused on his deeply ingrained bending over backward to be humble and unassuming, a behavior that got in the way of being appropriately assertive and effective as an expert witness. Our objective became the resurrection of enough assertiveness and expressed self-confidence for him to be an effective witness. The principles that were used to help this doctor, and the attorney who retained him, were drawn in part from my books about expert testimony (see Brodsky, 1991, 1999, 2004) as well as from what I have found in my research. This chapter addresses the question of how to prepare expert witnesses for testimony, and we begin with the issue of why preparation is needed.

EXPERT WITNESSES ARE NOT NECESSARILY EXPERTS WHEN THEY ARE WITNESSES

It is a paradox that individuals who are often exceptionally skilled as professionals or scientists can be ineffective when they are on the witness stand. The reason is that expertise is situation-specific. The person who is wonderful at forensic medical analyses may be dreadful when called to present the findings of such analyses in a public forum. It is the same reason that many talented scholars in the academic community are not exceptional lecturers; engaging and teaching students calls for a different skill and role than conducting research successfully. To become an effective expert witness means to commit oneself to assuming that role. Some expert witnesses learn through experience, and others by reading about how to testify. Still others benefit from formal preparation in the form of workshops, short courses, and consultation. Some expert witnesses never truly become convincing or effective.

Let us note that expertise is defined specifically for witnesses. The Federal Rules of Evidence (FRE, 2007–2008), which are largely followed by the states, define an expert as a person qualified to offer an opinion on the basis of education, training, skills, knowledge, or experience. We delve more into the FRE criteria later in the chapter. What sets expert witnesses apart from lay witnesses is that they are permitted to offer opinions in their areas of expertise, with the customary limitation that they may not offer certain ultimate legal opinions, such as guilt or whether a defendant is legally insane. These legal decisions belong to the triers of fact: the jury or, sometimes, the judge.

Everyone who is a frequent observer at trials can see some experts hesitate, mumble, swallow their words, or become rattled. Even experts who are compulsively organized in their own work domains can become disorganized and hard to follow on the stand. In this chapter we speak to how experts should prepare, and should be prepared, for testifying in court. Then, following the same order as in the preceding chapter, we move to consultation with attorneys to conduct cross-examinations of experts.

ROUTINE VERSUS DEMANDING EXAMINATIONS

Many experiences of testifying in court are routine and unremarkable, in which few difficult questions are asked and in which the proceedings are contested at a low level of energy and challenge. Even in those circumstances, some witnesses have difficulty. They are visibly distraught and obviously uncomfortable. It is particularly true for inexperienced experts who may have worried excessively, who may not have slept well the night before, and whose discomfort may rise to a point at which the substance of their testimony is obscured or diminished by their manner. However, for experienced witnesses testifying in routine hearings, such as mental health experts testifying in involuntary commitment or recommitment hearings, not much happens that is challenging. Most expert witnesses manage to do well in routine testimony.

Of more interest is testimony when there are issues that are strongly contested and when the opposing attorneys are skilled in depositions and cross-examination. Under those circumstances, experts sometimes melt and their talking points become amorphous. When challenged in thoughtful and aggressive ways, their poise may dissipate and their professional demeanor may be replaced by defensive or weak answers. It is demanding testimony that is of most interest, because if expert witnesses can handle the questioning of skilled, prepared attorneys, they can manage almost any challenges to their testimony.

The common ways in which attorneys present major challenges can be categorized as bullying or substantively confrontational in cross-examinations (or depositions), as well as combinations of the two. Bullying attorneys often substitute an aggressive manner, a loud and accusatory tone of voice, and yelling for substance. That is, they often do not do the basic groundwork, and instead depend on intimidation as their style of examination.

Let us consider a case study of an attorney who combines substantive preparation with a bullying style: Thomas Moore, who is a plaintiffs' attorney in malpractice and wrongful death actions and who is a member of the Inner Group of Advocates.[1] In 1985, Libby Zion was admitted to the emergency room (ER) at New York Hospital and subsequently died (Robins, 1996). She had been given Demerol, which had been noted in the *Physicians Desk Reference* (a compilation of prescribing information and side effects of prescription drugs) as a substance that could have a fatal interaction with the particular antidepressant she had been taking. Part of the defense argument was that Ms. Zion had not told the hospital staff about the cocaine and other drugs she had taken. Her parents filed a wrongful death suit against four doctors and the hospital, and the case was eventually tried in 1995. The jury found for the most part for the plaintiffs, finding three of the four physician-defendants negligent and awarding damages of $375,000 to Ms. Zion's family. This award and decision influenced medical training to reexamine its long-standing overwork and exploitation of medical residents, with its accompanying sleep deprivation and potential interference with the development of good practices and values in residents (Green, 1995; Chandra, 2004; Zion versus New York Hospital, 1995). Videotaped excerpts from the trial are available from CourtTV and the transcript of the trial is widely available.

What are not obvious from the transcript of this trial, but are obvious from the CourtTV video, are the gestures, the body movements, and intensity and volume of Moore's voice as he asked the questions. He wheeled about, pointed at the witnesses, and challenged them loudly; he spoke just short of a shout. The physician-defendants were obviously distressed. Sometimes they answered incompletely. Sometimes they capitulated. They chewed at their lips. The crossed their arms in front of them protectively. They looked guilty.

The Thomas Moore example is meaningful for me because I worked on witness preparation in a case in which Moore was the plaintiff's lawyer.

---

[1]The Inner Group of Advocates describes itself as an organization of 100 of the best plaintiff lawyers in the United States. See *www.innercircle.org/history.php* for more information.

The person to be prepared was a physician who had been retained by the defense in a malpractice case to examine medical evidence and then to testify as an expert witness. The expert retained me, in turn, to help him be effective against Moore's cross-examination.[2] We did three things typical of preparation of expert witnesses:

1. *Past testimony.* We went over videotapes of prior testimony by this witness. As part of this consultation, I identified the aspects of his testimony that did and did not work. This doctor had been warm in manner, a good teacher, and compelling in testifying during direct examination. Once cross-examinations came up, he underwent a nasty metamorphosis. He became unfriendly. He pretended he did not understand the questions. He was defensive in response to all challenges. With difficulty, we reworked his style of responding to cross-examination, so that he was more able to be the same affable, friendly teacher in court that he was in his normal work situation at his office and the hospital.

2. *Anxiety.* Even though this physician had testified before in both depositions and trials, he had gut-wrenching anxiety about facing Thomas Moore. We worked at length on his anxiety. He mastered breathing exercises. He learned to present himself to others as relaxed, so that more comfortable emotions could follow his relaxed behaviors. We went through a series of desensitization exercises that reduced his anxiety somewhat.

3. *Role-playing.* Moore has a distinct style. As I role-played him, I whirled around suddenly and asked his kind of carefully phrased questions, trying to simulate his fierce manner. The expert learned to wait, and not answer at the same rushed pace as the mock Moore. He learned to take a deep breath before any answer. He acquired the ability to think through what was asked and precisely what his answer should be. Finally, he learned to sort out the substance of what Moore asked from the sweeping dramatics wrapped around it.

As in most civil litigation, this case never went to trial. With the considerable preparation and improved skills, the expert was both relieved and confident as the scheduled trial date approached. He often—but not always—handled our version of Moore's accusatory (but excellent) questions in a lucid and composed manner. He felt more in control of himself and reported that he was better equipped to deal with demanding and harshly critical cross-examinations in the future.

---

[2]I have changed just enough of this description to disguise the identity of this expert.

SUBSTANTIVE PREPARATION

As we discuss the preparation of expert witnesses, it is possible to conclude falsely that the medium is the message; that is, that the style of presentation is the essence of what one should master. In fact, the essence of the testimony is the professional or scientific foundation. It would be irresponsible for a trial consultant to prepare a person to be effective in court who did not know what he or she was talking about. Substantively prepared experts should know the current scholarly and professional research and practices related to their fields.

This assertion may seem obvious. However, many practitioners struggle to find time to squeeze in professional reading and the completion of continuing education requirements for licensure. Whether the practitioner-witness is competent in actually delivering mental health or medical services may be beyond our reach. However, checking out whether he or she is reasonably current in knowledge is part of the consultant's responsibility, because being current usually is necessary for effective testimony. When experts are not current—and this quickly becomes evident in role playing—then short-term actions for getting the witness somewhat current and long-term plans for regularly staying current become part of the consultation process.

Think of preparation in this way: When experts testify about what they know about the issue at hand, they are offering their conclusions and sometimes opinions. When experts testify about the basis for their testimony—which is how they know what they know—then the scholarly literature and related issues emerge, with the objective of showing the expert as being current and masterful about the literature. A well-prepared opposing attorney may ask what articles in refereed, scholarly journals support the ways in which the expert chose to investigate or assess the trial-related questions. The experts who simply answer that their practices reflect the way they were taught, or how they have always done it, or that what they have done is the standard of practice, should anticipate a series of further challenging questions about the literature and standards.

I often prepare forensic mental health professionals. If they are asked how many of the 5,000 plus published articles on forensic assessment they have read, and they are not ready to respond, they may appear ill read or insecure. A reasonable answer is that nobody actually counts the numbers of articles and books he or she has read.

The reason for such preparation should not be simply to be ready for tough cross-examinations. Instead, expert witnesses should be masters of their knowledge for intrinsic reasons, appreciating that good knowledge is what permits them both to practice and to testify as experts. Offering defensive, self-protective testimony is not an effective way of being masterful.

ANXIETY REDUCTION
FOR EXPERT WITNESSES

The two worst instances I know of expert witnesses having excessive anxiety were, first, a woman having tears streaming down her face during her entire cross-examination testimony, and second, a man having a panic attack and passing out. When I ask participants in my expert witness workshops what they most fear about testimony, the single most common response is that they fear being unable to remember anything. My goal is to aid them in controlling the effects of anxiety, a very different goal from eliminating anxiety.

Worry and anxiety about testimony in new experts often take the form of restless sleep and nightmares as the day of testimony approaches, a visible hand tremor, knees shaking, dry mouth, and various forms of abdominal and gastrointestinal distresses. Diarrhea, upset stomachs, and frequent urination are reported. Expert witnesses are sometimes easier to prepare than lay witnesses because experts have had many successful experiences of presenting themselves competently to others. They now need to learn to shift the presentation of a competent self to the new setting. Furthermore, many experts tend to be more psychologically oriented than do lay witnesses and thus more receptive to consultation help.

I have mentioned breath control already. With anxious experts, I have them briefly engage in the paradoxical process of breathing quickly and shallowly while mock testifying, and then shifting to deep, slow breathing until the latter is practiced and automatic. This behavioral approach promotes their potential for a calmer and self-controlled presentation style on the stand.

Next, I advise experts to use anxiety reduction techniques with which they are already at ease. They should not try new chemical aids like antianxiety medications or new-to-them psychological approaches, such as always trying to have the last word, unless they really have a grasp on them. Otherwise, they run the risk of being distracted by the new technique or having their mental acuity compromised by a new psychotropic medication.

Finally, I encourage them to habituate to the courtroom setting in which they will testify. For instance, they should look for an opportunity to sit in the chair on the witness stand when nobody else is in the room. I advise them to watch other experts testify. The first time on the witness stand can be uncomfortable. New witnesses are acutely and accurately aware that everyone is looking at and listening to them. When objections are made to some aspect of their testimony,[3] new witnesses may become distressed. They

---

[3]Hearsay objections are fairly common and are based on the witnesses' reporting that they depended in part on what others have said to them. Hearsay objections in this context are usually overruled.

can ask retaining counsel to ask the judge to waive the rule that excludes witnesses from watching other witnesses. If opposing counsel does not object—sometimes they do not—then the whole experience becomes more understandable and less scary, as experts see how ordinary are so many of the proceedings and how human and fallible are the participants.

MEETING WITH COUNSEL AND PREPARING FOR DIRECT EXAMINATION

Some lawyers are wonderful in seeking out their experts and meeting several times with them in advance of the deposition or trial. Other lawyers are overcommitted in time and, either because of personal style or heavy workloads, tend not to meet with their experts. When asked for meetings by the experts, they often reply, "You will be fine. Don't worry about it. I will meet with you in the corridor before you testify." Such a dismissal by an attorney serves the expert witness poorly. When faced with this situation, it is worthwhile to actively pursue a meeting in person, if possible, or alternatively, by telephone or using e-mail planning.

The prepared witness should know what to expect during direct examination. One cannot anticipate everything that will be asked during cross-examination, but expert witnesses should have a right to know every question to be asked during direct examination. If they are so prepared, there are no surprises. Witnesses should know every question and have had a chance to think through every answer.

This preparation concerning direct examination questions and answers offers security to the witnesses as well as to the attorneys. Moreover, attorneys should never be surprised by their experts' answers, and poorly phrased questions sometimes elicit surprising and unexpected answers. In the practice run-through with retaining counsel,[4] experienced experts often say, "If you phrase that question in this manner, I will have to give you this particular answer. If you rephrase it, I can answer in a way that gets more clearly and effectively at my findings."

What happens if the attorney is insufficiently experienced or knowledgeable to prepare the expert properly for direct examination? In that case, the expert may choose to lead the pretrial discussion of direct examination questions. While always being respectful of the attorney's role and responsibility for the trial, expert witnesses can suggest both individual questions and lines of questions. If experts are testifying repeatedly about the same

---

[4]Trial consultants usually sit in on these meetings and participate in them, so there is a chance to integrate what the experts and consultants have done in their preparation.

content areas, they can often become familiar with the questions that are best asked to elicit the nature of their credentials and experience, a rationale and description of the tasks undertaken, and then the results, conclusions, and opinions.

NARRATIVE TESTIMONY

Jurors who are exposed to lengthy professional and scientific testimony often have trouble finding ways for the testimony to be meaningful for the case and personally meaningful for themselves. The task for the expert witness is to testify in such a way that the information comes alive. At a minimum such engaging testimony calls for an animated style of speaking, explaining scientific or technical terms in a manner that unfolds ideas, maintaining a sense of personal contact with the jury, and using words, phrases, and language that promote understanding and interest. As is shown in Chapter 2 in the discussion of story and narrative in case conceptualization by trial consultants and attorneys, individual expert testimony can be improved if it takes the form of telling a story.

In his book *Linguistic Evidence: Language, Power and Strategy in the Courtroom*, William O'Barr (1982) distinguished between narrative and fragmented testimony. Fragmented testimony takes the form of brief answers, the kinds of yes–no replies that cross-examining attorneys seek to elicit. On the other hand, narrative testimony takes the form of answering in sentences and explanations, so the potential is there for the content to be personally meaningful and clearly tied into case issues. O'Barr presented the results of several studies that strongly conclude that narrative testimony is superior in persuasion. Cross-examining attorneys work at constructing questions that produce answers that are brief and counter to the expert witnesses' general opinions. Still, simple yes-or-no questions merit simple yes-or-no answers unless they unfairly simplify or mislead. Misleading questions are often introduced with a request or demand that the witness give only a yes-or-no answer. In the case of a misleading or complex question, the witness has the option of responding that there is no simple yes-or-no answer to that question and asking to explain.

PRIMACY AND RECENCY EFFECTS

When the retaining attorney announces, "The state now calls Dr. Smith to the stand," the attention of the courtroom is galvanized. Jurors, attorneys, observers, and the judge watch the expert witness come into the room and observe how he or she approaches the stand. Some witnesses approach confidently and with poise, with a measured, comfortable stride, and know where to walk to be sworn in. Other expert witnesses look uncertain from the beginning, hesitating, looking around to see where they should go, and approaching tentatively. First impressions are far from the whole package from which judges and jurors draw conclusions about witnesses, but they can make a difference. On one occasion, I entered a courtroom in a rural county walking with my typical effort to simulate good posture, simultaneously seeking to maintain a manner of respectful confidence. Then I tripped over an electric outlet with an elevated metal protective cover over it in the middle of the courtroom floor. I stumbled, started to fall, and regained my footing; then I carefully and slowly walked toward the witness stand. I did OK in my testimony, but I could have done better if the stumble had not stayed with me.

Parallel advice applies to leaving the stand. Witnesses should be told: No matter how the testimony has gone, whether splendidly or problematically, step down from the stand as if you have been wonderfully competent as a witness. The observers in the courtroom will, in part, take their cues from you on how well you did. If you communicate that you thought you did well, so may they. An expert I know tripped stepping down from the witness stand, papers scattering all over the floor; he felt certain that his testimony was diminished by his fall. A physician who could not quite figure out which way to go to leave the courtroom after his testimony, at the least, was embarrassed and at the most had his credibility a little impaired. The recency effects were detrimental.

Primacy effects—first impressions—and recency effects—last impressions—are, of course, less important than the content of testimony. However, peripheral cues like initial and last impressions may make a difference in how a witness is perceived overall.

Trial consultants should think of preparing experts this way. Instruct them to walk in and then present themselves on the stand with a visible presence of competence and mastery. Tell them to admit it nondefensively if they do not know the answer to a question. Instruct them to offer a modest nod or gracious smile, if they can do so without it feeling phony, to the judge or attorneys when the testimony is over. Further instruct them to leave with visible (but not immodest) satisfaction and an absence of hubris in manner.

The clothing of an expert may be considered part of the primacy effects. I am always astonished at how much worry and fuss there is about what clothing expert witnesses should wear to testify. At the far extremes of clothing options, it can be a problem. Think of Joe Pesci playing a defense attorney in the film *My Cousin Vinny*. In one scene Pesci appears in court wearing a burgundy tuxedo in period style with ruffles; this example is one extreme of problematic clothing. Alternately, think of the occasionally underdressed expert witness who comes to testify in jeans and a casual shirt or T-shirt. In this same category of clothing discrepant with the competent witness role was Roy Scheider playing the insurance company executive in the film *The Rainmaker;* he wore a blue polyester leisure suit that cried out "sleazy." For most experts who worry about their clothing for courts, the distinctions are much finer. Books on how to dress for success have titles like *Image Matters for Men: How to Dress for Success* (Henderson & Henshaw, 2007) and its sibling *New Women's Dress for Success* (Molloy, 1996). Such books and similar television shows have made many professionals overaware of clothing options that may help or harm impression management. Rehman, Neitert, Cope, and Kilpatrick (2005) have reported that medical patients are more disclosing and open with physicians who are dressed professionally. However, at my expert witness workshops, I am always asked much narrower questions about what participants should wear in court. "Do I need to avoid browns?" I am asked. "Are pinstripes essential?" I know of no research about clothing and courtroom effectiveness and credibility,[5] but I advise expert witnesses not to obsess about clothing. Instead, they should wear their normal dressier professional clothing. Women should not avoid pantsuits if that is what they wear in their professional work. Light or dark colors probably do not make a difference. If experts normally wear dark suits when they dress up, then dark suits make sense. An additional guideline is that expert witnesses should not wear clothing in which they feel uncomfortable. People who feel uncomfortable are at a disadvantage.

CONSULTING WITH ATTORNEYS ABOUT DIRECT AND CROSS-EXAMINATIONS AND DEPOSITIONS

A professional activity related to expert witness preparation is consultation to attorneys for preparing to examine their own as well as opposing witnesses. A good direct examination often ties into the story model discussed in Chapter 2. That is, the attorney, sometimes in collaboration with a trial consultant, has sufficiently thought through the narrative goals so that opening statements, closing arguments, and witness testimony all help develop the continuity of the theme.

Good direct examinations seek to have effective witnesses speak in their own voices, with their own language, and their own patterns of use of verbs and adjectives, repetitions, and naturally occurring dysfluencies. The majority of witnesses called to testify are not naturally effective. As

---

[5]An older study by Dacy and Brodsky (1992) indicated that dressier clothing in psychotherapists led to high initial ratings of competence.

I discuss in Chapter 6, there are some proven ways to prepare witnesses and improve the quality of their testimony, while respecting the integrity of their own experiences and perspectives. Some witnesses are good at making initial points in answering direct questions, but then subvert the power of their answers by adding tangential content. Preparation for these witnesses consists of clarifying for them the point at which a question has been answered and helping them to develop the focused self-awareness to tell when they are drifting away from a relevant answer. In other cases the style of answering or distracting mannerisms impede the clarity and effectiveness of the answers. However, style and mannerisms also lend themselves to being modified, while staying true to the content.

Trial consultation for cross-examinations seeks to bring out weaknesses and problems, rather than, as in direct examinations, minimizing them. In the forensic psychologist aspect of my professional life, I often serve as an expert witness and testify in court. Every now and then I became aware that a trial consultant has been working with opposing counsel.[6] The consultants who assisted the attorneys have prepared some of the best-developed and most thoughtful cross-examinations I have faced. When I have been called to testify on the stand, the consultants for opposing counsel were usually psychologists or persons with both psychology and law degrees. In some cases the consultants sat at the attorney's table, writing notes with suggested questions and passing them to the attorney. In other cases the consultants had prepared questions before the time of my testimony, and the attorney was well armed for the cross-examination. Witnesses do not always know whether opposing counsel has had assistance. In some instances, I discovered only much later that consultants had prepared questions when they mentioned it at a professional meeting. However, consultation for cross-examinations is not typical.

Why and when should attorneys turn to consultants for assistance in preparing cross-examination or deposition questions? Most attorneys do not, of course; most attorneys are content with the quality of their own questions. Sometimes a consultant is brought in to assist because of the specialized nature of the issues. Sometimes it is because of how much is at stake. At still other times, it is because attorneys have had good experiences

---

[6]As a psychologist who teaches experts how to manage difficult cross-examination and who conducts research on effectiveness of testimony, it may seem paradoxical that I also offer information for attorneys on how to prepare challenging questions for witnesses. When I mention this to participants in my workshops on testifying in court, the participants have been distressed that the attorneys they face may have had my help with questions to dissect their testimony. I also hear gently phrased hints that I am a traitor to the shared professional family obligations of expert witnesses. What I tell workshop participants is this: Good knowledge belongs to everyone and good questions promote the quality of justice.

working with consultants, having received their help in other trials or in the preparation of voir dire and deposition questions.

THE FRE CRITERIA

The content of cross-examination questions related to expert witnesses is often drawn from the fivefold criteria in the FRE for admission of experts (Thompson-West, 2007). In its entirety, FRE 702 reads:

> If scientific, technical, or other specialized knowledge will assist the trier of fact to understand the evidence or to determine a fact in issue, a witness qualified as an expert by *knowledge, skill, experience, training, or education*, may testify thereto in the form of an opinion or otherwise, if (1) the testimony is based upon sufficient facts or data, (2) the testimony is the product of reliable principles and methods, and (3) the witness has applied the principles and methods reliably to the facts of the case. (emphasis added)

The basis for admission of professionals, scientists, or other individuals as experts has been addressed in the Sales and Shuman (2005) book *Experts in Court*. In their review of admissibility of expert testimony these authors discussed the foundations of testimony from the Supreme Court decisions in the *Daubert, Kumho*, and *Joiner* cases[7] that led to points 1, 2, and 3, mentioned in the preceding excerpt, regarding sufficient data, reliable methods, and reliable applications to the case. The word *reliable* is used there in a legal context, referring to valid methods on which one can depend, rather than the customary psychometric definition of *reliability*, meaning "consistent." Sales and Shuman concluded that "this trilogy raises more questions than it answers" (p. 42), in part because of the lack of scientific training or acumen in judges, especially in resolving complex scientific issues. Furthermore, judges may choose to ignore the *Daubert, Kumho*, and *Joiner* criteria. Sales and Shuman asserted that the goals of the FREs to produce reliable testimony and experts "are not being consistently met, and often are thwarted" (p. 95).

CHALLENGES TO KNOWLEDGE

During cross-examinations and depositions, the five issues in the FREs are often addressed: knowledge, skill, experience, training, and education of the

---

[7]Of course, many states use the *Frye* criteria or a combination of *Daubert* and *Frye*.

expert. Cross-examination challenges to knowledge start with the under-standing that no expert knows everything about his or her field. Within every professional discipline, experts specialize, and even then they do not know everything within their specializations. One of my favorite *New Yorker* cartoons shows a patient in a doctor's examining room with the shoe and sock off his right foot. The doctor is apologetically saying, "I'm sorry—I'm a left-foot podiatrist." The skilled consultant helps the cross-examining attorney probe for specialized knowledge that the expert does not have—the equivalent of right-foot podiatry. Many experts who are in professional practice, as opposed to research scientists, do not have the time—or choose not to allocate the time—to stay fully current in the knowledge that makes up the scientific underpinnings of their practice. The prepared attorney can ask probing questions that bring out the limitations on current knowledge and challenge the witness on that basis. How should attorneys specifically proceed in challenging expert knowledge? Here are some lines of question-ing[8] with typical answers in parentheses.

"Doctor, is it important to stay current in your field?" (Yes.)

"Would you say it is essential to stay current in your field?" (Yes.)

"Why is that so?" (New developments and knowledge emerge.)

"How many journals have you fully read so far this month?" (Not certain.)

"In the last 2 months? Three months?" (I don't know.)

"How many professional books in the field of _____ have you read in the last 2 months?" (Sometimes specific books are named.)

"What were these books? And articles?" (Witnesses sometimes stumble.)

Shifting briefly to the perspective of opposing counsel in this scenario, we now consider the consultant preparing the expert witness to face cross-examination of this sort. The focus is on being nondefensive and honest. No experts have read everything in their fields, and a comfortable acknowl-edgement of that fact helps take the sting and effectiveness out of the cross-examination questions.

CHALLENGES TO SKILL

The issue of skill may seem on the surface to be related to knowledge. How-ever, *knowledge* refers to mastery of a body of specialized information. *Skill*

---

[8]Admission of these particular questions is dependent on the jurisdiction and the judge. They are presented as issues that are sometimes raised.

refers to the *application* of knowledge and methods integral to the professional tasks. It is reasonable to assume that some knowledgeable physicians may be poor practitioners, and some excellent practitioners may be limited in their academic knowledge base. Challenging experts about their skills can evolve into a perceived attack that is personal in nature. What consultants can bring is an understanding of the common gaps in skills and practices of the clinicians and how to expose and emphasize the gaps.

How should expert skill be specifically challenged? One way is through careful examination of an expert's report submitted to the court. In one instance, I read a report by an experienced and bright psychiatrist in which he inconsistently described various life events of the evaluee. Although not necessarily clinically significant, this inconsistency suggests a carelessness that should have been addressed by the psychiatrist in his review of the report and surely should be addressed during cross-examination. Later in the report, the defendant was described as claiming that he had no memory of the murder, even though there was no excessive use of alcohol or drugs at the time. A logical part of the challenge to the skills of the expert therefore would be the unaddressed question of whether the defendant was deceptive in replying or honest.

CHALLENGES TO EXPERIENCE

The third FRE area in which expertise is defined is experience. Attorneys are sometimes impressed by long curricula vitae (CVs) and many years of experience in practice and as an expert. Furthermore, the codification of experience as a legal criterion for admission of expert testimony can blind observers to the fact that highly experienced practitioners in psychology, medicine, and other fields are not necessarily adept. Experience is not the same as skill. Many practitioners are what one speaker[9] at a conference on the training of psychologists (Korman, 1976) quipped: "They are like the Bourbon kings: they learn nothing, forget nothing." There is a substantial body of knowledge to support the position that experience by itself is not indicative of expertise. In his review of 14 research studies on experience, Garb (1989) concluded that experienced clinicians were not more accurate than less experienced clinicians in personality assessment. Morris, Haroun, and Naimark (2004) compared the evaluations of experienced and inexperienced forensic clinicians of a vignette in which a clearly dis-

---

[9] I recall this quip with clarity. The remark was not included in the proceedings and I have been unable to retrieve the name of the speaker.

turbed defendant was reported to completely understand the nature of the criminal proceedings. Many more experienced clinicians were likely to incorrectly describe this individual as incompetent to stand trial than were less experienced clinicians. Garb and Grove (2005) point out that psychologists do not receive direct and immediate feedback on their diagnoses, which is why they do not learn from experience. Elsewhere Garb and Boyle (2003) similarly described reasons why experience is not the best teacher—and, indeed, is a poor teacher. Empirical data were gathered by Faust et al. (1988), who sent 1 of 10 different known professional case descriptions to 600 clinical neuropsychologists and requested that they come to diagnostic conclusions. A series of statistical analyses found experience and diagnostic accuracy to be unrelated. For some of the actual questions used to challenge experience, we turn to Ziskin (1995, p. 72) for these suggested queries:

Q: So your confidence stems largely from your experience in this kind of work?

A: Yes.

Q: Do you consider yourself fairly experienced?

A: Yes.

Q: Are you aware of the great number of studies which show that more experienced psychiatrists are no more accurate in their assessments than inexperienced ones, or even lay people?

This line of questioning continues by further contrasting experts' belief in their experience with the critical research literature. The eventual end point is reached when experts either concede that they do not know the literature or agree that their own belief about the positive worth of their experience is subjective and not scientific.

CHALLENGES TO TRAINING AND EDUCATION

The fourth area concerning expert qualifications in the FRE is training and the fifth area is education. The two topics are closely related and are discussed together here. *Training* refers to systematic instruction designed to make one more proficient in a profession. *Education* refers to instruction and schooling in a formal setting that is dedicated to the preparation of scholars, scientists, or professionals. In contrast to the findings on experience, there are considerable and compelling reasons to conclude that training and education improve performance of all sorts, and certainly of mental health and medical experts.

Nevertheless, the operating rule for assisting attorneys as they prepare to examine an expert about training and education is that there is always something that the expert is not. There is always a credential, a level of certification, or an achievement that the expert does not have. To find such gaps calls for knowledge of the expert's field, and, for that reason, it is worthwhile to bring in a consultant with background (dare I say experience?) in the same field.

In questioning experts about their training and education, two pathways are possible. The first option is cross-examination questions to cast genuine doubt on the foundations of their knowledge. As noted earlier, experts who testify about what they know should always be queried about *how* they know what they know—that is, the methodological and scientific underpinnings of their work. The scope of these particular questions may extend through all of the five criteria of knowledge, skills, experience, training, and education. For queries that raise doubt about education and training, experts should be asked about omissions of case-specific training and experience. If the case involves, say, a Native American plaintiff suffering from a bipolar disorder, the experts might be asked about what aspects of their training and experience specifically addressed cultural correlates of bipolar disorders in Native Americans raised on (or, if the case facts indicate otherwise, off) a reservation. This question may have a follow-up about the variations found between various tribes, contrasting, for example, Lakhota Sioux and Porch Creek tribes. Because virtually no professional training or education addresses details like these found in clients' histories, gaps can be shown in almost all training.

The second pathway utilizes gaps in training or education to shake the confidence of the expert. If experts are brought to the point of saying that they have not been sufficiently educated or do not have particular skills, then their sense of assuredness diminishes. There are good reasons to believe that lowered confidence of experts results in lowered credibility to the jury (see, for example, Cramer, Brodsky, & DeCoster, in press).

CONCLUSION

We have examined the substantive and personal ways of testifying that should be mastered by the expert witness and aided by the trial consultant. These methods are useful throughout testimony, but most consultations are particularly directed toward preparation for direct examination. What happens after the witness has been prepared? The expert learns what he or she can in terms of confidence, awareness of routine versus demanding testimony, specific knowledge of the literature, reduction of anxiety, meeting with counsel, and primacy and recency effects. We then discussed conducting and managing the most difficult questions and situations in a cross-examination, which can be challenging for expert witnesses. The FRE criteria for admissibility of experts offer both an outline for general cross-examination questions and a list of topics, which the prepared expert should routinely be able to address.

Chapter 6

———◆———

WITNESS PREPARATION

Findings from the Lab

The fourth floor of the psychology department building at the University of Alabama used to be dedicated to animal research. When I joined the faculty more than three decades ago, my colleagues were conditioning pigeons and running experiments with Norway hooded rats. One colleague studied the behaviors of quail that froze in place when exposed once or twice to the passing overhead of the silhouettes of red-tailed hawks (Martin & Melvin, 1964). Others taught the physiology of the brain by having graduate students perform surgery—sometimes satisfactorily—on the brains of anesthetized rats. As animal research became less important, the floor was renovated repeatedly, eventually resulting in two rows of faculty offices and research rooms. On the east side of the hallway, with ramps still in place that had been used to wheel up and down the racks of pigeon and rat cages, are mostly faculty offices, because these spaces have windows. On the west side of the hall are the less desirable rooms without windows, back against the eaves of the building. That is where my Witness Research Lab is located.

In this long room we constructed a witness stand on an elevated platform, with a large and comfortably padded witness chair, microphones, and an inside shelf attached to the stand. Behind it are paneling, a curtain, and an American flag. Facing the stand are a freestanding podium, a tripod with a high-resolution digital camcorder, 6-foot-high cool lights that heat neither the room nor witness, and a cart with a teleprompter monitor, a DVD recorder and player, and large-screen monitor. On each side of the cameras and witness stand are places for actors who play attorneys or judges.

The Witness Research Lab is the home for our studies of expert (and

74

sometimes lay) witness effectiveness, studying particularly which behaviors and responses work best when confronted with aggressive cross-examinations. The research plan for each of the studies is similar. We identify one specific aspect of expert testimony. We use a standard cross-examination scenario (Krauss & Sales, 2001) about which we have considerable data, or we develop scripts or locate transcripts that apply to the topic being studied. We vary experimental conditions studying the witness response under investigation, with equal time allocated to a control condition. We often recruit mental health professionals who have experience on the witness stand to play the roles of testifying experts. We use outcome measures of verdicts, of sentencing or damages, and of witness credibility, often drawing on our standardized rating scale of credibility (Griffin, Brodsky, Blackwood, Abboud, & Flanagan, 2005), which is described in more detail shortly. For the most part, undergraduate students in introductory psychology serve as research participants. We ask them to take seriously the task of pretending they are actual jurors.

Now our discussion moves to the research itself.

PERSUASION THROUGH WITNESS PREPARATION

The first study in the Witness Research Lab was based on a model for preparing witnesses. The model is called Persuasion through Witness Preparation (PTWP) and was developed by Marc Boccaccini as a dissertation at the University of Alabama (Boccaccini, 2004). Parts of it were published in two subsequent articles (Boccaccini, Gordon, & Brodsky, 2004, 2005). In discussions of witness preparation, the issue of ensuring the integrity and truthfulness of the testimony is consistently raised in the context of discussions of improving the quality of testimony. Thus, we suggested:

> The ultimate goal of witness preparation is to improve witnesses' credibility and persuasiveness without altering the substantive content of their testimony. Attorneys and consultants recommend using similar testimony delivery skills to achieve this goal, including making eye-contact with attorneys and jurors, maintaining good posture, speaking clearly, responding honestly, limiting answers to the questions that are asked, and being comfortable with answering "No" and "I don't know." (Boccaccini et al., 2005, p. 660)

The research on PTWP drew first on a cohort of mock defendants, in the form of 55 university undergraduates, and then a second cohort of 8 real defendants being represented at a public defender's office. The mock defendants were asked to describe minor crimes they had been accused of, but had not committed.

In the preparation of these student participants, the "crimes" for which they had been falsely accused led to the creation of an average of 18 direct and 13 cross-examination questions. The participants were randomly assigned to a preparation or control group. All participants had three study sessions. The preparation group had two witness preparation training sessions, led alternately by a white male graduate student in clinical psychology and a female African American graduate student in clinical psychology, both with experience in preparing actual criminal defendants to testify in court. Eight testimony skills were the predominant focus (the percentage of defendants taught these skills is indicated):

Improving posture (71%)
Reducing hand fidgeting (71%)
Improving clarity of responses (54%)
Reducing guesses (32%)
Improving phrasing (29%)
Reducing nervous smiling (29%)
Increasing use of gestures to facilitate communication (25%)
Reducing inappropriate facial expressions of anger and contempt (25%)

Six evaluators blind to the conditions of the participants served as raters. Significant differences were found on 11 of 13 skill measures. The behavioral targets of the witness preparation are shown in Table 6.1. The prepared defendants were rated as more credible. The mediating effect of the testimony skills training was both high (.71) and significant. Similar effects were found in preparation of actual defendants from the public defenders' office. The importance of this study is that witness training was systematically broken into components and studied, using a carefully matched control group.

At the same time, two unintended effects were found. The prepared participants were rated as being less expressive and less emotional than before they were trained, a change that was attributed to trying to avoid the appearance of deception. We concluded, "It is difficult to both suppress fidgeting and increase expressiveness," (p. 685) but were unclear about the trade-off: Less fidgeting is desirable, but it is associated with the negative quality of less expressiveness.

The PTWP addressed specific behavioral elements in the defendants' behaviors. Table 6.1 identifies the behaviors that were the target of the mock defendants' preparation. A similar but less comprehensive list was used for the actual defendants. These targeted problem behaviors and constructive behaviors are parallel to but separate from the substantive content of the

TABLE 6.1. Witness Behaviors

Poor posture

Posture tilt to side
Head tilt to side
Slouching (R)
Forward lean

Fidgeting (R)

Excessive shifting of posture
Hand to body or to face fidgeting and touching
Hand to hand fidgeting
Excessive foot movements
Excessive leg movements
Mouth movements when not speaking

Expressiveness

Gestures to facilitate communication
Head movements
Facial expressions of interest
Overall facial emotion
Overall vocal emotion
Vocal expressions of interest
Smiling

Gaze

Gaze while listening
Gaze while speaking

Voice quality

Softness of voice (R)
Voice clarity

Response quality

Narrative responses
Fragmented responses (R)
Strong negative assertions
Weak negative assertions (R)
Head movement up and down or sideways instead of words (R)
Uses grammatically correct speech
Testimony is understandable

Contempt (R)

Facial contempt
Vocal contempt

(continued)

Individual items
_____
Vocal hesitations (uh, um)
Polite speech
Makes guesses
Hedges (sort of, kind of)
Facial uncertainty
Legs apart

General credibility
_____
Intelligent
Believable
Convincing
Trustworthy
Respectful
Composed
Attentive
Cares about what is going on
Likeable
Friendly
Knowledgeable
Honest

Confidence
_____
Confident
Assertive
Shy (R)

Emotional
_____
Emotionality
Energetic
Nervous

Note. Drawn from a table of all targeted behaviors in Boccaccini et al. (2005, pp. 664–665) and rephrased in some cases for this chapter.

testimony. They describe how the testimony was delivered and provide an empirical starting point for preparation of defendants and witnesses. The letter "(R)" following a behavior identifies a clear problem needed to be addressed.

GENDER AND WITNESS TESTIMONY

Maureen O'Conner and Mindy Mechanic (2000) presented a paper reporting that no male expert witnesses they interviewed had ever been asked personal questions during cross-examination, whereas one-fourth of the women experts had been asked such questions. I was one of the men they later interviewed to double-check their findings. Had I ever been asked on the stand if I had been sexually or physically abused as a child? No. Ever been asked if I had been raped? No. How about ever filing a sexual harassment charge? No, again. "Ah, yes, right," I was later told. That preliminary report led us to the study of gender and expert testimony in our lab, much of which has been researched by Bridget Larson (Larson & Brodsky, in press) and by Tess M. S. Neal (Neal, 2007; Neal & Brodsky, 2008). The research was based on the O'Connor and Mechanic (2000) work, what I had heard from women participants in my expert witness workshops, and a study by Memon and Shuman (1998) that reported that women experts were rated lower than men, even though they were matched on levels of professional competence. Thus, our initial working hypothesis was that in gender-intrusive cross-examinations, women would be rated less favorably than would men.

When we decided to study gender issues in testimony, we constructed scripts drawn in part from real cases, in which both male and female expert witnesses were asked on cross-examination if they had ever been physically attracted to their clients or to litigants they had evaluated, if they had been physically or sexually abused, if they had ever been drunk, spanked their children, been married and divorced, and so forth. Men and women experts were videotaped testifying on the stand in the witness research lab. The O'Connor and Mechanic research had indicated that women were much more likely than men to be asked such personally intrusive questions. In the intrusive questions conditions, men and women playing expert witnesses alike answered assertively that this topic was inappropriate. Larson and Brodsky (in press) had 293 introductory psychology students serve as participants. They were exposed to a male and a female expert matched on perceived attractiveness, honesty, intelligence, and responsibility. A case scenario of a murder trial was taken from Ziskin and Faust (1988). Four experimental conditions were investigated: male expert, nonintrusive questions; male expert, gender-intrusive questions; female expert, nonintrusive questions; female expert, gender-intrusive questions.

The essential findings were that the male expert was rated more positively than the female expert on all four components of the credibility scale. An equally compelling finding was that both experts were rated more positively in the gender-intrusive condition than in the nonintrusive condition. In response to the intrusive questioning, such as being attracted to the defendant, the expert scripts called for assertive responses, stating clearly that this questioning was inappropriate and that professional conclusions rather than personal opinions were being offered. This unexpected finding, that both men and women were rated more credibly in their assertive replies to intrusive questions, has a major implication for preparing experts for court testimony.

Consultants working with expert witnesses, and probably with lay witnesses as well, may assume that most men probably do not need assistance in knowing how to answer sexually intrusive questions. Such questions are unlikely. However, with women experts and intrusive questions, the assertive responses that Larson studied were effective and increased credibility and should be included in the menu of trial consultation goals. The implications of the Larson research are that women witnesses should be neither passive nor defensive when they are asked such intrusive questions. Instead, the answers that work well are strong statements indicating that these questions are an intrusion of privacy and that questions of this kind have nothing to do with the examinations of defendants or plaintiffs. Would the same kinds of strong and assertive responses work for women who are testifying as lay witnesses or litigants? No data are available about those women, and research surely needs to be conducted with women lay witnesses; however, the best information we have is that extrapolated from the Larson research, which suggests that such assertive responses may be a desirable option.

In a related study, Neal (Neal, 2007; Neal & Brodsky, 2008) studied the effects of low, medium, and high eye contact on male and female expert credibility. She had hypothesized that women would be less credible than men in the high and medium eye contact (with the audience) conditions. Eye contact units of 5, 30, and 50 seconds per minute in a 5-minute video of testimony represented low, medium, and high eye contact. The eye contact consisted of the witness's looking directly into a camera. Of course, attractiveness has a strong influence on social judgments. In a pilot study two male and two female experts were not significantly different on credibility and attractiveness, and the male and female with the closest absolute scores on credibility and attractiveness were used in the main study itself.

The findings were that the woman in the high-eye-contact condition had significantly higher credibility ratings than the same actor in the medium- and low-eye-contact conditions. Gender played a role in all three eye contact conditions, with the woman rated as more credible than the man. The implications of this study support in part the Larson study. Experts who are women and who take the assertive nonverbal action of looking at listeners directly in the eye for long periods are seen as more believable. Although the same improvement in credibility with eye contact occurred with men as well, the women were decidedly more believable. Thus, women should not fear being seen as brash or uppity, but should assume the direct, perhaps challenging, "looking them right in the eye" posture, because it increases how likely they are to be credible. In earlier investigations by other researchers, negative judgments were made about women who looked others in the eye. The present study points to the role of expert witness, with all of its associated positive value, as a factor that allows women to be strong, challenging, and nonverbally confrontational.

CONFIDENCE ON THE WITNESS STAND

There are compelling reasons to support the notion that more confident individuals are more likely to be believed or persuasive than less confident persons. The Confidence Heuristic Model (Thomas & McFadyen, 1995; Price & Stone, 2004; Pulford & Colman, 2005) offers an explanatory framework. The heuristic itself states that decisions are made in part because of the expressed confidence of speakers. The model posits that when expressed opinions or conclusions are presented confidently, it signals the presence of higher-quality information. When a great deal of information is presented and the targets of this information have to make quick decisions and cannot process information themselves, confidence of the speaker is a key component of the statements' being seen as correct and believable. If the opinions expressed are in the form of highly confident judgments, as in the case of the vastly overvaluing of stocks by a simulated financial advisor, it is the people with right-wing authoritarianism and a high need for cognition who most accept these opinions (Price & Stone, 2004).

Cramer (Cramer, 2005; Cramer, Brodsky, & DeCoster, in press) studied confidence on the witness stand in our lab. Modifying the Krauss and Sales (2001) stimulus tapes of prediction of violence, he exposed 317 mock jurors (undergraduate students) to witnesses testifying with low, medium, and high levels of confidence. The findings showed significant differences between the conditions. Credibility was highest for the medium-confidence witness, followed by the high-confidence witness, and then, with a great drop-off in scores, by the low-confidence witness. The conclusions drawn from this research were that in the expert role, lack of visible confidence most diminishes believability, but also that being too certain may be seen as arrogant and be off-putting. A five-factor personality inventory was also given to the mock jurors who observed these witnesses. Juror extraversion emerged as the main factor associated with belief in confident testimony, a finding that has implications for choosing jurors when a strong, confident, assertive expert is a key witness.

EXPERT WITNESS CREDIBILITY

As of this writing we have conducted eight studies in our lab that either developed a measure of witness credibility or validated it in other studies. On the basis of our research, we have reason to believe that four components make up good expert testimony: knowledge, confidence, trustworthiness, and likeability.

In the first step of development, we drew on the Osgood, Suci, and Tannenbaum (1957) studies of the measurement of meaning, in which several hundred paired adjectives were developed and factor analyzed. Osgood et al. found factors of evaluation, potency, oriented activity, stability, tautness, receptivity, and aggressiveness, with the evaluation factor loaded highest. The evaluation factor included items like good–bad, positive–negative, and trustworthy–untrustworthy. Items were also examined from the Stone and Eswara (1969) likability[1] scale, which was developed as part of a study investigating how communicator likeability served to persuade an audience. Each choice for initial inclusion in the credibility scale came from sequential and independent group evaluations designed to identify characteristics that jurors use to determine an expert's credibility. We hypothesized that the credibility scale would include measures of professionalism, likeability, believability, trustworthiness, and intelligence, drawing from the literature on witness effectiveness (e.g., Boccaccini, 2002) and from the components identified by Brodsky (1991, 2004) in narrative descriptions of expert witness effectiveness. We used a 10-point Likert-type scale to maximize variance and specificity of the responses. Forty-one paired adjective items (e.g., trustworthy vs. untrustworthy) were chosen from the Osgood et al. and Stone and Eswara studies.

This first measure of 41 items was administered to 264 undergraduate participants, who were instructed to rate an expert witness after they watched a recording of simulated testimony. As in many of our other studies, the testimony was drawn from the Krauss and Sales (2001) study of clinical versus actuarial expert testimony in the sentencing phase of a capital murder trial. From the nine scenarios developed by Krauss and Sales, we used clinical testimony about likely future violence by the defendant, testimony that was subjected to a vigorous and knowledgeable cross-examination. This scenario was chosen because clinical testimony is common and because the cross-examination was well informed and critical. After viewing the video, participants rated the experts on the 41 items.

A factor analysis was conducted in which principal axis factoring converged after seven iterations. The original 41-item questionnaire yielded a 20-item credibility scale consisting of four subscales: Confidence, Likeability, Trustworthiness, and Knowledge, with all items loaded on their corresponding factor at the .50 level or above. We then chose five items for each subscale, with the rationale that the four components should be assumed for the

---

[1]The word *likeability* is spelled with an *e* throughout this book, except in the present case of a study that was published and a scale developed with the alternate spelling of *likability*. In these instances, I have accepted the authors' spelling option when referring to their work.

time being to equally represent expert witness credibility. Items that loaded equally on two or more factors were deleted to ensure distinct factors. The scale is reliable (alpha = .945). In addition, each subscale is individually reliable (Confidence, alpha = .89; Likeability, alpha = .86; Trustworthiness, alpha = .93; Knowledge, alpha = .86).

The research on the Witness Credibility Scale (WCS) produced a usable and systematically developed measure of believability of expert witnesses; as noted, it is made up of four factors: Confidence, Likeability, Trustworthiness, and Knowledge. Although these factors have elements in common with those of previous theories of source credibility, the WCS is a specific and quantified measure of the perceived credibility of an expert witness.

To this point we have considered paths to mastery on the witness stand. We now shift to the other side of the same issue, which is how specific manners of testifying reduce effectiveness. One of the ways in which witnesses may lose their credibility is for them to panic on the stand. Panic may be defined as a sudden and overwhelming sense of anxiety or fear. The anxiety feels uncontrollable and unmanageable. When somebody is testifying, panic may result from fear of the general situation, from concerns about the high stakes involved, or from an attorney's question that leaves the witness feeling guilty, inept, or trapped.

PANIC AND TESTIMONY

A woman came to work on her testimony in a forthcoming personal injury trial. She had had a panic attack at the deposition. In normal conversation, this woman was able to discuss in a thoughtful and moving way the issues and events at work when she had been sexually touched and personally harassed. When she was deposed, she could not talk very much about these events and felt as if she could not breathe. Her ex-employer had made serious accusations against her as a seducer and flirt, and she was not able to talk about the accusations. Instead, she stammered and gasped and could not speak clearly in presenting her own version of the events.

The experience of panic is not confined to our contemporary era, nor to being in court. A historical example emphasizes how panic may be related to the fall of nations. The fall of Constantinople in 1453 has been attributed to a widespread panic in the defenders (Herrin, 2003; Nicolle, Turnbull, & Haldon, 2007). Constantinople, the capitol of the Byzantine Empire, fell to Mehmed II, the Sultan of the Ottoman Empire, after a protracted siege. When one of the key defenders was wounded and asked to be treated within the inner walls of the city, the great door was opened for him. The Constantinople army had been fighting fiercely while locked out of the city. Its troops stopped fighting and rushed to get inside the opened door, and the

Ottoman attackers fell on them and slaughtered them. The defenders were outnumbered, but had been putting up a good resistance until panic set in. So it goes on the witness stand. Individuals who are doing well are sometimes overwhelmed at a key moment and lose their ability to stand up for what they believe.

We now return to our own time and to the woman who had panicked in her deposition. This plaintiff in the personal injury case engaged in repeated behavioral rehearsals, examination of videotaped mock depositions and trial testimony, and relaxation exercises and received directed feedback about the ways in which her self-presentation was problematic. With intensive instruction, she became more assured and more credible in the practice sessions, behaviors that carried over to her real testimony.

CONCLUSION

In this chapter we have looked at how lab and research studies have been conducted on the credibility and effectiveness of lay and expert witnesses. The Boccaccini model of witness preparation has been studied sufficiently to conclude that witness preparation efforts can have a substantial and important positive effect on testimony, albeit at the cost of a loss of perceived spontaneity and perhaps fidgeting being replaced by too great a sense of being fixed in place. The research we examined hardly covers all witness preparation and behaviors, and most of it needs practical investigations with real rather than simulated witnesses. Furthermore, there may well be case- and context-specific factors that make a difference in how witnesses are perceived. Nevertheless, in the witness preparation component of trial consultation, it is encouraging to see the beginnings of an empirical database on which direct consultation may be built.

Part III

❖

JURY SELECTION PRINCIPLES AND CASE STUDIES

It is tempting and appealing to use easily accessible data like appearance and occupation in drawing inferences about members of jury pools. Chapter 7 considers the heuristics that are associated with such decisions and why these foundations for striking jurors are so limited. It then concludes with a detailed report of research underlying a jury selection in a civil case.

The case-driven format continues in Chapter 8, in which the problems and constructs associated with jury selection in a criminal case are developed. We review the literature on Internet sex offenses and entrapment defenses, key issues in the case. The sequence of conceptualizations about the key issues is described along with the measures that were identified or designed to assess these concepts.

Chapter 9 discusses the process of deselection, which involves focusing on and identifying the jurors one may wish to strike. The deselection process is more targeted than a general information survey about all potential jurors, and the trial consultant's tasks in deselection are not always apparent. In this chapter we organize the tasks with special attention to what kinds of questions and what ways of asking them assist in deselection—without tipping one's hand to opposing counsel.

Chapter 10 is about reversals, or the times at which conventional wisdom and assumptions are not applicable and are set aside, in part, in favor of opposite assumptions. The chapter delves into this nonobvious aspect of jury selection, as it describes an application of a reversal in thinking to a jury selection in a criminal case. It outlines the principles associated with a reversal of assumptions about selection of jurors, so that the kinds of jurors one would normally never strike in a criminal case are assigned a high priority for striking.

Chapter 7

❧

JURY SELECTION

Basic Approaches

Some jury consultants approach their work with emotional displays of brag-gadocio and declarations of competence beyond the reach of anyone's abil-ity. No book on juries has a title that captures this excess better than the Demitrius and Mazzerella (1999) book *Reading People: How to Under-stand People and Predict Their Behavior—Anytime, Anyplace.* Or take, for another example, *Judge the Jury: Experience the Power of Reading People*, by Weiser and Hargrave (2001), or Lisnek and Cochran's (2003) *The Hid-den Jury: And Other Secret Tactics Lawyers Use to Win.*

Can anyone tell what a person is truly like by his or her appearance? A positive answer to this question is seated in common beliefs: Many people and most attorneys assert that they can tell a great deal about others by physical appearance. I have an acquaintance who observes other people and with blazing speed projects their intelligence, politics, behaviors in relation-ships, sexual orientation, levels of sexual desire, and social class. My initial inclination is to say, "Humbug!"

Fiction author Terry Goodkind (2005) put the process of reading peo-ple more positively in this way:

> Appearance, after all, was a reflection of what a person thought of [him-
> or herself] and therefore, by extension, of others. A person crippled by
> self-loathing or self-doubt reflected those feelings in [his or her] appear-
> ance. Such visual clues did not inspire confidence in others because, and
> while not always completely accurate, for the most part they did reflect
> the inner person—whether or not that person realized it.

No self-respecting bird in good health would allow its feathers to look ruffled. No confident cougar would let its fur long remain matted and dirty. A statute meant to represent the nobility of man did not convey that concept by portraying him disheveled and dirty. (p. 432)

Let us now consider attorneys, who commonly draw on appearance, first impressions, and ordinary common sense to select jurors. Attorneys typically express satisfaction about their reliance on the use of common sense about appearance in jury selection. The major sources of advice in the trial lawyers' literature draw heavily on ordinary commonsense assumptions about predispositions in potential jurors toward verdicts of guilt or innocence (Black, 1999; Miller, 2001). For example, defense attorneys in criminal cases often routinely rule out male engineers and accountants as acceptable jurors on the working assumption that men in both occupations will be tough-minded and impersonal. It is equally true that sometimes trial consultants make these assumptions. Yet some observers (e.g., Kressel & Kressel, 2002) have concluded that in big money civil cases, even attorneys who denounce trial consultants as practitioners of voodoo rarely forgo retaining them.

At the same time, a body of research literature has addressed the utility of "thin slices" as predictors of interactive skills. Thin slices refer to brief observations—less than 5 minutes—of fluid and dynamic information about behaviors, with nonverbal behaviors most likely to be useful. Ambady and colleagues have conducted a series of studies indicating that such thin slices yield distinct and sometimes useful impressions. Ratings of three 10-second silent video clips of university teachers were significantly correlated with end-of-term course evaluations. Similarly, findings also show students' and principals' ratings significantly correlated with later judgments of schoolteacher effectiveness (Ambady & Rosenthal, 1993). Thin slices of mock screening interviews have predicted the outcomes of employment interviews, and thin slices have predicted patients' satisfaction with their doctors. Particular success has been found in predicting the performance of salespersons whose effectiveness depends on interpersonal skills. The caution about depending on these thin slices—and in jury selection it is often only thin slices that are available—is that there are reasons, with supporting data, to be skeptical about using thin slices for predicting the outcomes of task-related and noninterpersonal skills, descriptors that more closely approximate roles of jurors (Ambady, Krabbenhoft, & Hogan, 2006).

This limitation appears to apply to attorneys and consultants who are heavily dependent on quick impressions and commonsense judgments. The components in their selection of jurors include direct observations, brief answers to oral questions, and responses to simple questions about occupation and family. These processes often produce recommendations and common sense judgments that are questionably useful.

There are three major problems in this dependence on ordinary common sense (OCS):

1. *Poor scholarly foundations.* Common sense conclusions are drawn from heuristics that have found little scientific support. The term *heuristic* comes from the Greek word *heuriskein*, meaning "to discover." Heuristics describe rule-of-thumb or seat-of-the-pants learning, a form of intelligent guesswork that does not follow a reliable formula. In their classic article in *Science*, Tversky and Hahneman (1984) addressed how heuristics are especially employed when uncertainty surrounds important judgments to be made. They observed the operation of an availability heuristic and a representativeness heuristic, among others. The availability heuristic comes about when a vivid example is brought to mind and the example is more available and thus more compelling than statistical probabilities. In the same sense, the representativeness heuristic neglects base rates when a common quality is assumed to be present between people (or objects) that have similar qualities. Michael Perlin (1994) has built on these principles in his writings about how heuristics distort understandings of both justice and the insanity defense. Perlin wrote that judges have been "shamefully poor" in applying social science research and data because of this dependence on fallible common sense. What he wrote about judges applies to attorneys during jury selection: He wrote that "judges often select certain proffered data that adhere to their pre-existing social and political attitudes, and use both heuristic reasoning and false OCS in rationalizing ... decisions" (p. 411). The use of such common sense rules in jury selection is as appealing as it is unreliable, which is a great deal.

2. *Lack of feedback.* The nature of jury selection does not permit systematic feedback about the efficacy of OCS decision outcomes. Because so much probative evidence is involved in trials, and because the process of striking a jury leaves many reticent or self-concealing persons on the jury, trial outcome is a poor measure of success of OCS assumptions in jury selection.

3. *Stereotypes.* Excessive dependence on social and demographic variables of occupation, class, race, age, religiosity, and gender often blurs the ability to make good hypotheses about potential jurors. It is also unethical and illegal when used explicitly to discriminate against minorities (Sommers & Norton, 2003). Advantages for either side in jury selection are achieved by going beyond stereotypes and simple demographics. That is, not all social workers are caring, not all accountants are detached, and not

all retired military officers are punitive. What is important is the eliciting of individual juror experiences and attitudes that are integral to case-related issues, thinking, and feelings.

Hans and Jehle (2003) addressed the issue of stereotypes as they asked whether trial attorneys should avoid bald men and people with green socks. Their conclusion was that the more limited the voir dire, the more attorneys relied on demographic stereotypes. They asserted that only an enlarged pool of information in the form of jury questionnaires and expanded voir dire would identify actual biases rather than empty and meaningless stereotypes.

INACCURATE IMPRESSIONS: AN ILLUSTRATIVE REPORT

The fallibility of common sense judgments and the limits of social and demographic variables are seen in the case of the following actual juror. The descriptive information about him was presented to me by his spouse, who had attended a conference at which I had lectured about jury selection, and is given in her own words:

> "This juror is a 55-year-old white man, an insurance adjuster who works as a volunteer youth minister in his fundamentalist church. He describes himself as a Christian conservative, as well as a registered Republican who believes in the death penalty, the rights of the unborn, and the right to bear arms. His preferred form of clothing is a dark suit, white shirt, and tie. His facial expression is a persistent frown. By conventional criteria, he would appear to be exactly the kind of person on a jury panel to be savored by the state and struck by the defense. However, such conclusions would be premature.
>
> "His permanent frown is the result of a life-long, severe sinus headache. He loves rock and roll and rhythm and blues music. He believes deeply in civil rights and human rights. His wife reports that he wears tiny black European-style underwear. He distrusts the police because they do not follow their own rules, and he absolutely believes in rules. He has told acquaintances that the police will do whatever it takes to get a conviction. He has been called three times to jury duty, has always been selected to serve on criminal cases, and all three times he voted for acquittal of the defendant, resulting twice in hung juries."

There is an old saying, people believe what they see; the trouble is they are better at believing than they are at seeing. So too it goes with jury selection. Personal and subjective beliefs of the attorneys or consultants are often the driving forces in striking a jury. This chapter, and the others in Part III of the book, describe ways of understanding and improving the foundations that underlie jury selection.

THE EMPIRICAL APPROACH

In contrast to the "Once I see them, I can figure them out" school of jury selection, I focus here on the empirical approach to selection. There are two very different groups of people who bring empirical and scholarly research to the process. The first are the academics, researchers at major universities who also spend part of their time consulting with attorneys and working in jury selection. Most of them are seated in departments of psychology or communications, but these two disciplines do not, by any means, own the empirical research in jury selection. Schools of law and social work, and often political science, theater, and sociology, have a piece of the action. Along with graduate students who are completing thesis and dissertation requirements for research, these academics design studies that seek to capture one piece of jury selection applied to a particular kind of case. Their research tends to be careful, accountable, and scientific—at least the research that makes its way into scholarly journals. For every article that appears in a scholarly journal, there are several more good jury selection studies that have never been submitted for publication or have been submitted and never accepted (Gleser & Olkin, 1996; Iyengar & Greenhouse, 1988). As a result of this significant-findings publication bias, much of the completed research never makes its way into the public domain. The research that does appear is often designed so that it will have generalizability for other researchers, first, and for trial consultants, second.

A second group of people who conduct scholarly research in jury selection is made up of the trial consultants themselves. Trial consultants are mostly engaged in professional practice. When they gather data for some aspect of jury selection, it is in the context of a case in which they have been retained. Their primary audience is not a broad group of scholars, but rather the attorneys and/or firms with which they are working. These data are sometimes informal, often analyzed just enough to answer the questions raised in the case, and are infrequently published. Indeed, the results are sometimes gathered under an explicit agreement that they will not be shared but instead will be part of attorney work-product. Are these data generalizable? Yes and no. Yes, they are potentially generalizable by the consultant-researchers to other cases in which the consultants are working. Trial consultants as a rule do not do a lot of publishing; indeed, there is not a particular journal in which the results of such case-specific research can be regularly reviewed and published. Consultants do not seek to pursue what is accurately seen as the more academic pathway, but instead try to help their clients and build on their own knowledge base and sometimes that of fellow trial consultants. At the annual meetings of the American Society of Trial Consultants, few empirical studies are presented. The content is more likely to be information on "how to do it," after reporting on individual cases or practices.

As one of the academics, I gather data and seek to publish it, working with the graduate students who assist me. With my other hat on, when I work as a consultant for jury selection, not much of the case data lends itself to publication. A few components of those data collected by practicing trial consultants are publishable. This chapter now moves to an example of how to approach jury selection in a disciplined, scholarly way that may lend itself to generalization and to publication. To begin, let us examine the background of jury selection.

SCIENTIFIC JURY SELECTION

When jury selection by social scientists moved into the public view in the political and controversial trials of the 1970s, the term *scientific jury selection* (SJS) was used to describe the prediction of jury predispositions and trial outcomes. SJS subsequently fell out of favor as a way of describing the process of using data to select juries, largely because SJS was not clearly systematic, replicable, or scientific. In his incisive review, Michael Saks (1976) argued that SJS as practiced in the early 1970s was essentially useless. However, the concept of SJS has made a comeback. In their 2007 book, *Scientific Jury Selection*, Lieberman and Sales (2007) have identified and described the multiple components of SJS. Elsewhere, in his analysis of the literature and of data he gathered in 27 telephone surveys, Selzer (2006) concluded that there is no simple yes-or-no answer to whether SJS works. He stated that it depends on the "unique characteristics of each case" (p. 2432) and that

> It would be too simplistic to suggest that we can estimate our ability to predict.... There are simply too many problems with our instruments and our ability to replicate the jury experience in a mock trial, particularly a telephone interview. However, it is clear that when R^2s are "respectable" (i.e., > .15), our use of SJS is likely to be of some help in choosing the jury, particularly when there is limited voir dire. (pp. 2432–2433)

Because telephone surveys are among the common methods of gathering SJS data, the Selzer report of 27 telephone surveys is informative. He described sample sizes from 153 to 1,000, with most in the range of 300–600 respondents, with one-third of the cases civil and two-thirds criminal.

Selzer followed the logical procedure of not using trial verdict as a criterion of success, because much more than jury attitudes are involved in trial outcomes. Instead, he studied how highly and significantly background variances predicted the attitudes he was trying to assess. The R^2s ranged from .04 to .50 with a median of .18. By far the best success was found in two cases of pornography charges and one of civil liberties violations, with R^2s of .50, .45, and .44, respectively. The poorest successes in predicting the key case variables were reported for two criminal cases of terrorism and in sentencing (R^2s of .04 and .06, respectively) and a civil case of slander of a corporation (R^2 of .09).

How well did finding the "usual suspects" work? By usual suspects, I mean the demographic variables that many of us have observed attorneys using routinely in their own jury selection. Selzer (2006) offers some preliminary answers. He folded together the data from his telephone surveys ($N = 27$) and focus groups ($N = 9$). He reported that the following factors were most important: Education successfully predicted juror initial voting in the jury room, as assessed by posttrial interviews, in 31% of the studies, followed by race (28%); church attendance (28%); age (25%); and gender (17%). Among the least important were marital status, type of car, owned versus rented home, number of children, and income (all at 3%). We continue with more of the substantive literature about jury selection in the following chapters, but now we move to a case study.

JURY SELECTION IN A MEDICAL MALPRACTICE CASE

The following is an illustration of an empirical approach to jury selection in a civil action alleging medical malpractice. The facts of the case were that the plaintiff, a 31-year-old woman, was admitted to a regional medical center at the time that her unremarkable pregnancy had gone to full term and labor had begun. The obstetrician who had been her regular physician during her pregnancy was not available, and two of the doctor's associates in the practice were on duty. Over a long and extended labor, the woman repeatedly stated that something was wrong. The physicians periodically looked in and assured her that the labor was normal. After more than a full day of labor and hours of indications that the baby was in a breech position and in distress, a C-section was performed. The baby was born paralyzed from the neck down. Subsequent evaluations indicated apparently normal intelligence to the extent that it could be assessed. After an extended period of upset, then depression, and finally anger, the mother and father filed a medical malpractice action against the attending physicians. Expert witnesses for both sides evaluated the facts of the case; some were prepared to testify that the physicians were negligent, and other experts that the physicians were not negligent. To establish a background perspective for my role in this case, we turn to the nature of medical malpractice: Understanding and conceptualizing its history and essential issues can help put the trial consultation tasks in perspective. We begin with the history of medical malpractice.

Medical Malpractice: Historical Notes

The earliest origins of malpractice in English law can be found in the Medical Act of 1511, which indicated that only medical graduates of Cambridge or Oxford could practice medicine, or persons licensed by the bishop (Martin, 1973). The Acts of Henry VIII in 1544 were more specific, identifying the standards to be met in order to be a qualified practitioner of medicine. The Acts noted that surgeons "do oftentimes impair and harm their patients, rather than do them good" (Harney, 1973, p. iii). Mohr (2000) traced the origins of medical malpractice litigation in the United States to about 1840, when the minimal control over quality of medical services led to lawsuits. Mohr identified six factors that subsequently promoted malpractice litigation, including widely accepted standards of medical practice, availability of malpractice insurance, and contingency fees for attorneys.

Starr (1982) conducted a parallel analysis of 19th-century U.S. medicine, reporting that one major group of legislators and political theorists opposed any regulation of medical practice, holding that market forces would ensure that good care was provided. The early 19th century was characterized by "mutual hostility among practitioners, intense competition, differences in economic interest, and sectarian antagonisms" (p. 80). Furthermore, physicians, and then afterward the American Medical Association, were at war with the patent medicine makers who distributed medicines for any and all diseases. Until the mid-19th century, most families cared for themselves without medical help and physicians were minimally paid. Only when standards were established and professionalism promoted was there a major financial incentive to practice medicine in America, and that status was followed by legal vulnerability.

In their review of legal medicine in America, Sanbar, Annas, Grodin, and Wecht (1998) identified Dr. James S. Stringham as being the father of medical jurisprudence with his seminal article in 1804. Dr. Benjamin Rush, the first surgeon general of the United States, delivered a published lecture on medical jurisprudence in 1811. A series of other volumes followed, including the Isaac Ray (1838) book, *A Treatise on Medical Jurisprudence of Insanity*. Sanbar et al. reported that from the end of the Civil War through the middle of the 20th century medical jurisprudence became dormant.

Things have changed. The *Physician's Survival Guide* (National Health

Lawyers Association and American Medical Association, 1991) observes that the threat of lawsuits engenders deep-seated anxiety in physicians, so much that "the role of malpractice looms so large in the physicians' psyche as to often obliterate effective response to legal mandates" (p. 2). The *Guide* goes on to point out that two out of three obstetricians will be sued before retirement (p. 13). Anderson (2005) notes physicians' feelings of helplessness and fear of consequences of medical errors and the coming medical apocalypse (p. ix).

Like all torts, malpractice in the form of medical negligence begins with, first, the existence of a duty to offer care that meets certain standards of care (Flamm, 1998). The second element is breach of duty—the necessary quality of care was not given, and some damage or injury is present. The third element is causation, which means a causal relationship between the negligent act and the injury. The outcome of malpractice is damages, which is the actual award in the form of compensatory or punitive damages, the latter resulting from egregious or malicious errors. With this background in place, we shift now to the case study.

Attitudes toward Malpractice and Physicians

This report draws on the approach and analyses that I did with three colleagues (Brodsky, Knowles, Cotter, & Herring, 1991) when we were retained by attorneys for the plaintiff as part of the medical malpractice suit mentioned earlier. A random digit-dialed survey was conducted of homes with landline telephones in a southeastern U.S. county with a population of about 135,000 people. The task was contracted to a regional professional polling firm, with the callers blind to the purposes of the survey. Two sets of qualification questions were asked: first, whether the respondents were working with physicians, were related to physicians, were in a close relationship with a physician, or had been called to jury duty. The second qualifying questions, to ensure that they were eligible for jury duty, asked if they were registered voters and U.S. citizens. Forty-three respondents who answered yes to the first questions or no to the second set were thanked for their time, and the calls were terminated. A final sample was composed of 301 persons who were interviewed. The results are presented in Table 7.1.

A factor analysis was conducted to identify the common underlying factors from the survey data, in the 20-item Attitudes toward Physicians and Malpractice Scale, as well as an additional 30 items about the respondents' experiences with physicians and obstetricians, and then 15 items eliciting demographic information. We found two major factors and four minor ones, presented here with the highest loadings from the analyses.

TABLE 7.1. Results of the Attitudes toward Physicians and Malpractice Scale

Items	Strongly agree	Agree	Disagree	Strongly disagree
1. Doctors rarely make mistakes in treating their patients.	4.3%	49.3%	41.8%	4.6%
2. Doctors tend to have more patients than they can adequately care for.	10.3%	67.3%	21.0%	1.4%
3. Most doctors (in this area) really know what they are doing.	5.4%	77.6%	15.9%	1.1%
4. Doctors have a duty to make sure that their patients know what the responsibilities of patients are.	15.8%	75.0%	9.2%	0.0%
5. Doctors do not spend enough time helping people understand their illness.	11.5%	59.4%	28.8%	0.3%
6. Doctors should be held accountable for the mistakes they make.	15.2%	73.1%	11.7%	0.0%
7. It is a doctor's responsibility to see that [his or her] patients in hospitals are receiving the right treatment.	23.2%	75.2%	0.7%	0.3%
8. A person should be able to trust [his or her] doctor to give them the right care.	25.2%	74.2%	1.3%	0.3%
9. It is wrong to punish an otherwise good doctor for making one mistake, no matter the consequences of this mistake.	2.9%	51.1%	41.2%	4.8%
10. Doctors in this area are as good as those found elsewhere.	7.7%	68.2%	21.2%	2.9%
11. If I needed a doctor, I would not hesitate to go to one in this area.	7.5%	83.2%	7.9%	1.4%
12. Doctors associated with big medical schools are better doctors than those found in this area.	5.9%	40.0%	51.8%	2.4%
13. Doctors in this area are more concerned about money than they are with the welfare of their patients.	5.4%	28.0%	64.8%	1.9%
14. Jury awards against doctors for malpractice almost always are paid by insurance companies.	4.0%	81.7%	13.9%	0.4%
15. Patient greed is the major reason why the number of malpractice suits has increased.	5.3%	56.4%	36.7%	1.6%

TABLE 7.1. (*continued*)

16. The cost of malpractice insurance is a major reason why the cost of health care is so high.	7.2%	70.5%	20.9%	1.4%
17. In most malpractice suits, the doctor is actually negligent or in the wrong.	1.2%	44.0%	54.1%	0.8%
18. Most financial awards against doctors in malpractice suits are too high.	6.0%	69.0%	24.3%	0.7%
19. When patients sue their doctors, they tend to get greedy about how much money they ask for.	6.2%	71.6%	21.1%	1.1%
20. No amount of money adequately compensates a person who is permanently paralyzed as a result of a doctor's mistake.	18.8%	67.9%	13.0%	0.4%

- *Major factor 1: Knowledge versus Ignorance.* This factor had loadings of .87–.90 on four items about cesarean sections and childbirth. The following items or variables were also loaded heavily on this factor: being urban (.58), white (.43), more educated (.61), and living in the area less than 5 years (.54). In addition, this factor had negative loadings of .55 on "all children should be born naturally and without surgery."

- *Major factor 2: Attitudes toward Health Care.* Evaluative responses were loaded most heavily on this factor, especially evaluations of hospitals (.72), physicians (.66), and obstetricians (.57).

- *(Minor) Factor 3: OB and GYN Exposure.* One item was very heavily loaded on this factor—whether respondents had contact with obstetric or gynecological services (.89)—and the next highest item was whether anyone with whom they have had close contact has had a cesarean section (.52).

- *(Minor) Factor 4: Amount of Award.* The single item most highly loaded on this factor was, as the label suggests, the respondents' judgment for amount of appropriate award for a case like this (.78). No demographic category unilaterally predicted this factor, a finding of interest, given the common assumptions about how gender, age, education, and occupation would predict proneness to awarding high or low damages.

- *(Minor) Factor 5: Doctors' and Patients' Responsibilities.* Items 5, 6, 7, 8, and 9 on the Attitudes toward Physicians and Malpractice Scale were part of a complex variable in which respondents assigned responsibility either to doctors or patients (.60), but not to both. This judgment is what juries may eventually have to make in malpractice trials. The issue was of much importance and therefore called for further exploration with a carefully constructed set of voir dire items during jury selection.

• *(Minor) Factor 6: Unequivocal Support of Physicians.* Many of the respondents viewed physicians as meriting absolute support, no matter what, versus being suspicious and distrustful of physicians. The item loaded most heavily (.61) was "patient greed is the major reason why the number of malpractice suits has increased." Rural residents were somewhat more inclined to have such absolute belief in physicians (.31). This factor is linked logically to a key issue in malpractice litigation. Plaintiffs' attorneys should attempt to identify those with unequivocal support of doctors in order to strike such individuals whereas defense attorneys should seek to identify and strike people who have major doubts about and distrust of doctors. The first four items in the Attitudes toward Physicians and Malpractice Scale tap into this dimension of perceived fallibility or infallibility of doctors.

Implications of the Study

The survey data were designed to address underlying assumptions about litigation and physicians that are likely to influence how evidence about possible malpractice is processed. Despite the strong conclusions offered earlier in this chapter, there are vigorous disagreements about whether to rely on demographic data in jury selections. As noted, Selzer (2006) presents summarized case results that support the use of demographics, whereas Hans and Vidmar (1982), among many others, argue for contextual and evidentiary variables that tie into a case. The data presented fit with the Hans and Vidmar perspective.

Certain obvious questions follow. Are these data generalizable? Although they are produced by an accepted methodology and offer coherent findings, there is no reason to believe that a particular sample is sufficiently representative to be offered *ex cathedra* for use elsewhere. Checking these results with those in other jurisdictions in which malpractice actions are taken is the next step to generalizability. There is no shortage of malpractice actions.

Are attitudes toward physicians by themselves primary factors in the outcomes of malpractice trials? This question brings us back to the assertion made in the opening chapter of this book. The most compelling and cogent factors and data in jury selection make a difference only when the evidence is equivocal and the trial could go either way. When the evidence is very strong for either the plaintiff or the defense, it is not likely that jury selection will make a marked difference. In civil suits jurors always implicitly or explicitly sort out the responsibility of plaintiffs and defendants. In medical malpractice actions, trial attorneys should attend to preexisting attributions of responsibility to patients and physicians and to unequivocal perceptions of physicians' infallibility or fallibility.

CONCLUSION

The primary theme of this chapter is that selecting jurors may be nonobvious and often may lend itself to an empirical approach. Although attorneys often select and deselect jurors on the basis of their intuition, ordinary common sense, and other methods familiar to them, this intuitive and common sense approach may be problematic. The dependence on stereotypes to select and deselect jurors is often built on poor scientific foundations. However, because so many case-dependent variables are present in any given trial, feedback about the effectiveness of methods based on intuition is difficult to obtain. The outcomes of cases are not solely or even primarily dependent on the attributes of the jurors, a limitation that may mask the difficulties of intuitive jury selection as well as of more careful and empirical selection methods.

Research on scientific jury selection has shown that there is no simple answer to whether empirical jury selection methods work, but the research has also shown that some of the methods lawyers and consultants use are better than others. Thus, attorneys and trial consultants can incorporate what the research on scientific jury selection has found (e.g., that a juror's education has been observed to predict outcome 28% better than a juror's income). The goal in empirical research is to help attorneys and trial consultants appreciate what approaches work better than others. Still, just as lawyerly intuition will not hold up in every case, neither will empirical findings be applicable in every case. The task is to select those research investigations and empirical findings that apply most closely to a particular case and use them to identify individual juror attitudes and experiences likely to influence the way the jurors may think and feel during the course of the case. Hans and Vidmar (1982) argue for using contextual and evidentiary variables that tie into the case on an individual case-by-case basis, in addition to selecting the empirical findings that apply to the case at hand, and using them skillfully in voir dire may be the best any attorney or trial consultant can do for his or her client.

Chapter 8

JURY SELECTION
*Internet Sex Offenders
and Juror Sexual Values*

The focus for the trial consultant is not necessarily the same as for the trial attorney. Differences arise according to what each understands and values as important and, in turn, what each thinks about the particular trial and the knowledge and skills of each participant. As noted in Chapter 2, the trial consultant can be of particular help when trial attorneys require assistance in developing a conceptual frame of reference for case presentation. So it was with the trial of Professor Karol Lubic (a pseudonym). His defense attorney's focal point was entrapment. Mine was harsh critical judgments by potential jurors about sexual activities. For both of us, it was a long shot, because the charge was sexual seduction of a minor over the Internet and such charges almost always lead to conviction (Walsh & Wolak, 2005).

When I took a fiction writing class, I was taught *in res media,* or to begin in the middle of the plot. The middle of this case revolved around the sexually charged e-mails to be entered as evidence. The e-mails that Professor Lubic had written, and around which the prosecution's case was built, were not simplistically sexual. To the contrary, his e-mails contained detailed and explicit fantasies, flamboyant descriptions of proposed sexual activities and of great volumes of sexual fluids and sizes of organs, elaborate descriptions of planned uses of dildos and vibrators, and writings about varied sexual positions and behaviors. Drawing on his broad background in literature and his vivid vocabulary, Lubic painted a portrait of anticipated sexual activities that perhaps were the equal of well-known published literary descriptions of carnal desires and sexual adventuring. They were all addressed to the 15-year-old girl with whom he had been corresponding.

Professor Lubic was an associate professor of physics,[1] as well as a brilliant clarinet player,[2] and his scientific and musical accomplishments were widely known and admired. At the age of 33, he had accepted a new academic post and was getting ready to move. For a year he had been e-mailing the 15-year-old girl, Gail.[3]

Gail had been a typical teenager until her father was convicted of a major crime and imprisoned with a life sentence. Then everything changed. She started going out with older men and was sexually active with them. She also became a habitual devotee of Internet chat rooms where she "met" Professor Lubic. For 6 months she corresponded with him by e-mail about her schoolwork, her friends, her mother, and her daily frustrations. Professor Lubic wrote back about his studies and laboratory, about his musical performances and his physics students, and about each newly purchased used automobile that would quickly break down. They seemed to have little in common, but they wrote short, chatty, and superficial e-mails about their daily lives Their e-mails were all without sexual content, except when Gail described a negative physical encounter with a boy she had dated.

One day, Gail's mother read some of the e-mails and found out that her daughter's e-mail and chat room correspondent was a 33-year-old professor. Concerned already about Gail's being out of control, the mother called the police. Gail's e-mail privileges were suspended. An experienced 40-year-old male police investigator took over the e-mail correspondence, using Gail's name. In his first few e-mails, the investigator, pretending he was Gail, expressed sexual interest in Professor Lubic and made statements about her (Gail's) supposed sexual fantasies. Then the fireworks went off.

Until that time Lubic had been a subdued and proper e-mail buddy. Once the investigator wrote of sexual fantasies, Lubic's e-mails changed from two or three sentences every day or so to two pages of florid sexual content and proposals for sexual activity. After 5 months had passed, the police investigator arranged for Lubic to meet with the now imaginary Gail. No Gail was at the designated place, of course, and Lubic was arrested and charged with, among other things, crossing state lines for immoral purposes with a minor.

---

[1] Not really his field.

[2] Not really his instrument.

[3] A pseudonym, of course.

INTERNET SEXUAL OFFENDING

As with the medical malpractice case in the preceding chapter, we begin the case discussion with the social science and legal literature related to the case issue. This brief review of the literature is drawn from two perspectives: the law enforcement perspective and the defense attorney's perspective. The discussion starts with the law enforcement and victimization studies.

In their book chapter on Internet sexuality among adolescents and children, Longo, Brown, and Orcutt (2002) observed how easy it is for adolescents to have inadvertent access to sexual content and sites on the Net. Teens who are psychologically healthy and who have a positive sense of self are described as being relatively inoculated against harmful sexual content. It is not so for teens who are not psychologically healthy. Survey data indicate that as many as one in five youths received unwanted sexual solicitations over the Internet during a 1-year period (p. 97). One in 33 received aggressive sexual solicitations. Sullivan and Beech (2004) have described the process of targeting and sexually manipulating children on the Internet as "grooming." Grooming goes through the stages of asking about school, developing a rapport, discussing mutual interests, and, finally, introducing a sexual agenda (p. 75).

In a review of Internet sex crimes, Walsh and Wolak (2005) asked why adolescents are vulnerable to such nonforcible sex crimes. The answers they give are that adolescents are exploring their sexuality, some are troubled or seeking father substitutes, some are interested in sexual risk taking, and still others are susceptible to flattery and attention. In a thoughtful review of the outcomes, Walsh and Wolak concluded that for individuals charged with Internet-related sex offenses the outcome is likely to be conviction. Walsh and Wolak (2005) used information from the National Juvenile Online Victimization Survey, which examined the court dispositions of nonforcible Internet-related sex offenses with adolescents.

Their methodology was to survey 2,574 law enforcement agencies and conduct follow-up interviews with 612 case investigators of Internet sex offenses. They also interviewed 207 prosecutors. Looking at only completed interviews with 77 prosecutors from state, county, and local jurisdictions, Walsh and Wolak reported a number of observations about cases in which defendants had been arrested for Internet-related sexual crimes. They reported that, contrary to common public perceptions about its being difficult to convict these persons, 77% of defendants entered guilty pleas and 14% more who went to trial were convicted. Three percent of the defendants were acquitted, and 3% more had charges dropped.[4] Convictions were typi-

---

[4]These percentages add up to less than 100%; the remaining cases still had outcomes pending.

cal even when the victim was a willing participant in the relationship and an unwilling participant in the criminal proceedings. In the few cases in which the defendant was acquitted, the victim had been untruthful or similar prosecution problems had arisen. These investigators concluded that most defendants were incarcerated and then required to register as sex offenders.

Mitchell, Wolak, and Finkelhor (2005) reviewed the rationale for police posing as juveniles online. They reported the following observations:

- One in five youths receives sexual solicitations online, many from other youths and including fairly benign solicitations. This finding was consistent with the numbers reported by Longo et al. (2002).
- The anonymity of the Internet advances adult sexual approaches to minors and facilitates investigators posing as minors online.
- In proactive investigations no minors are actually involved. The investigators posing as minors are considered to be engaging in a form of undercover work.
- In 59% of the arrests the investigator communicated with the targets for a month or less.

Also drawing on the National Juvenile Online Victimization Survey, Mitchell et al. (2005) examined two samples of 124 and 129 arrests in proactive investigations. The practice, as in the present case, of an investigator posing as a juvenile to find and arrest potential predators accounted for 25% of these arrests for Internet sex crimes against minors. Mitchell et al. also reported that the individuals arrested had fewer arrest histories and less likelihood of deviant adult behaviors than other online offenders. However, they were comparable in their possession of child pornography.

Internet sex behaviors that have been viewed as problems are hardly unique to the United States. Countries as diverse as China, Great Britain, Sweden, and Egypt have reported a variety of problems, In Egypt, Internet entrapment has been a common practice to locate gay men who would otherwise be unknown to the authorities. Azimi (2005) has reviewed the history of Egyptian government antagonism toward homosexuals and has observed that surveillance and entrapment of homosexual men are pursued avidly through the Internet, typically followed by persecution and torture in the context of the nation's criminalization of homosexual behaviors.

Remarkably little is known about the psychology of Internet offenders. In his review, Hammond (2004) concluded that little information has been gathered and what is present is not revealing nor does it constitute a coherent body of knowledge. He observed that "the furtive and relatively solitary nature of the behaviour coupled with its recency have conspired to keep Internet offenders 'off the map' for researchers in sexual offending" (p. 86). He also reported that there is a lack of data available to compare individuals whose full sexual activities are on the Internet versus those whom he categorizes as contact offenders.

ENTRAPMENT

Entrapment is the subject of the second perspective in this discussion, one that arises from legal and defense views. The seminal U.S. Supreme Court case on entrapment is *Sorrells v. United States* (1932). In the state of North Carolina during Prohibition, Sorrells was introduced to a man who said he was a furniture dealer. The stranger indicated that he had served in the same division as Sorrells during World War I. With the apparent development of a friendship and as time went by, the stranger asked Sorrells seven times for a half gallon of liquor for a friend back home. Sorrells kept apologizing, explaining he did not have any alcoholic beverages. Finally, Sorrells left for 20 minutes and returned with a half gallon of liquor. The man paid Sorrells five dollars, and then arrested Sorrells for the illegal sale of liquor. The basis for the U.S. Supreme Court's overturning Sorrells's conviction was that the illegal sale of the liquor would not have taken place if the agent had not repeatedly and persistently solicited the sale. A subsequent Court decision (*Jacobson v. United States*, 1992) overturned the conviction of a man on possession of child pornography when his purchase of it followed 2 years of a federal agent's soliciting the sale. The essential element that emerged in later Supreme Court decisions was the strength of the defendant's predisposition to break the law, as compared with the strength of the inducements by the law enforcement agent.

In his article "Entrapment in the Net?" Sinott-Armstrong (1999) observed that "predisposition and inducement usually vary inversely in that more inducement is needed when there is little predisposition" (p. 98). He defined entrapment as existing when there is a weak predisposition and strong inducement and added, "Subjective predispositions can be especially hard to determine on the Internet, partly because feelings of anonymity on the Internet lead many users to pose as personae or write out fantasies that they would never really act on" (p. 100). He suggested that one element of inducement and thus entrapment on the Net is how long or eagerly a police officer pursues a target. Sinott-Armstrong also observed that Internet stings are less costly, less dangerous, and less intrusive than live sting operations. The issue of inducement on the Internet has been discussed in a broader context by Scottberg, Yurcik, and Doss (2002). They describe a bait-and-capture method used against Internet intruders whom they label as "Internet honeypots." In their discussion, Scottberg et al. conclude that only a fine line, drawn with minimal precedent from the courts, separates protection from entrapment on the Net.

THE CASE AND THE FOCAL POINTS

For the defense attorney in the case described at the beginning of the chapter, the focal point was entrapment. Nobody had been harmed, she prepared to argue during the trial. Gail herself had never had sexual correspondence with Lubic. The defense attorney held that the investigator had created the crime. We have noted that in the key Supreme Court rulings on entrapment, legitimate charges can be filed and convictions follow if the defendant had a substantial predisposition to commit whatever act was involved. The focal point of the defense was that without the sexual enticement by the investigator, there would have been no sexualized e-mails and no attempted seduction by Lubic. Was it a good practice for a 33-year-old physicist to correspond sexually with a person he thought was a 15-year-old girl? Definitely not! Was it a criminal act? The defense argued that it was not.

For me, acting as a trial consultant for the defense, the case focus was the flamboyant sexual language and suggestions. The trial was held in a federal district court in an area in which most counties were rural, sparsely populated, and religiously conservative. It was reasonable to assume that many of the people subpoenaed for jury duty would not have been comfortable with Lubic's graphic images and explicit sexual language. My working hypothesis was that sexual images and language would, by themselves, galvanize indignation and condemnation in many jury panel members. As a consequence, such jurors might rush to conclusions of the defendant's guilt well before hearing all of the evidence, arguments, and instructions from the court. My case conceptualization and that of the attorney did not necessarily compete. I sought to identify people for striking who would not be able or willing to listen to the legal argument of entrapment, her focal point.

I prepared a supplemental juror questionnaire, and the items reflected how the overall jury selection was approached. The rationale for the questions was based on four working hypotheses, each presented here with the actual items used to assess the hypothesis. The items were drawn or modified from items in existing research scales, a process discussed in Chapter 3 as part of the trial consultant's toolbox. Here are the stated hypotheses in the form of operational goals, followed by the items prepared to assess these dimensions. As with all such tasks, the intention was to identify only jurors who would be oriented toward opposing counsel's position, a technique discussed in the next chapter as part of the deselection process. The jurors were asked to check items with which they agreed. The items were phrased in such a way that agreement meant that the individual members of the venire would favor the prosecution.

- *Goal 1. Rule out people easily offended by the kind of explicit sexual language used by the defendant.*

FIVE ITEMS[5]

Instruction: Check if you agree.

____ I cannot stand being around anyone who uses four-letter words.

____ The common words used to describe the sexual act are offensive to me.

____ It is morally bad to use slang terms to describe men's and women's sexual organs.

____ I prefer not to be on a jury if a lot of very sexual language is presented.

____ I avoid books, films, and TV shows with clear sexual content.

• *Goal 2. Rule out people with noncosmopolitan outlooks because they may favor the prosecution.*

FIVE ITEMS[6]

Instruction: Check if you agree.

____ Individuals should not have sexual relations prior to marriage.

____ Society should keep a tight rein on what people do in their personal daily lives.

____ Drinking of alcoholic beverages is always problematic or wrong.

____ Society should not allow persons to take their own lives.

____ People should not be permitted to keep pornography for their personal use.

• *Goal 3. Rule out people with low need for cognition.*

FOUR ITEMS[7]

Instruction: Check if you agree.

____ I prefer to think about small, daily projects as opposed to long-term ones.

____ Thinking is not my idea of fun.

____ It's enough for me that something gets the job done; I don't care how or why it works.

____ I would rather do something that requires little thought than something that is sure to challenge my thinking abilities.

---

[5]High scores mean easily offended.

[6]High scores mean noncosmopolitan.

[7]High scores mean low need for cognition.

• *Goal 4. Rule out persons who overvalue police fairness and entrapment actions by police officers.*

SIX ITEMS[8]

Instruction: Check if you agree.

____ Police treat rich people the same as poor people.

____ Average people do not realize how much their lives and property are protected by police officers.

____ Undercover police should encourage possible offenders to violate laws, to be sure they get arrested.

____ Police understand human behavior as well as psychiatrists and sociologists because they get so much experience in real life.

____ In order to prevent crime, federal law enforcement officers should set skillful traps that lead people to a situation in which they might break the law.

____ I approve of police pretending they are customers so they can arrest prostitutes.

When the voir dire questioning was ready to begin, the jury venire was seated in the courtroom in order by juror number. The judge asked some of the voir dire questions, which he chose from a list submitted by the prosecution, as well as a longer list that I had prepared with the defense attorney. The jurors were asked to stand if the question applied to them and occasionally were asked to explain their answers.

The questions submitted for the voir dire were designed to overlap in part with the jury questionnaire items, but also to tap into domains not covered in the questionnaire. The overlap permitted the trial team, consisting of two defense attorneys, two of my assistants, and me, to observe the members of the venire as they spoke aloud their responses and to note the nature of the accompanying emotions. The following voir dire questions were submitted to the judge, who modified them as he asked them.

Internet Familiarity Questions

The issue addressed here was awareness of what goes on, innocuous and otherwise, in Internet chat rooms as well as in Internet use in general. Despite what may appear to be universal knowledge among those of us for whom Internet use is a daily event, many people have a passing or suspicious outlook toward Internet use and computers. One estimate is that 27% of the

---

[8]High scores reflect high valuing of police and entrapment.

U.S. population has no access to the Internet and 30% more have only dial-up access (*New York Times*, February 4, 2007). We wanted to identify individuals for whom the Net was an alien world and was an alienating process, full of uncertainties, dangers, or threat. The jurors were told:

> "You may be called to serve on a jury in which computer e-mails that directly relate to the issues in the case will be presented. Some of the following questions are about your own computer knowledge.
>
>> "Please raise your hand if you personally own or use a computer. [For *yes* responders]
>> "Do you personally own one at home? Use one at work?
>> "How many hours in a typical week do you use a computer?
>> "How many hours in a typical week are you connected on the computer for social reasons?
>> "Raise your hand if you have been or are currently part of any chat room. Explain.
>> "Indicate if you have ever done Internet dating."

These questions were designed to provide a segue into the issues of the case. The working assumption was that jurors who found computers and Internet usage alien or alienating would not be in a position to listen to and think through the defense's arguments about what had happened. Six jurors were so isolated from computers that they were listed as possible strikes. One man said he had owned a computer and got rid of it in disgust. I noted the visible emotionality in his use of the word "disgust."

Sexual Language

The judge read aloud the following statements that had been prepared in a slightly different form than the jury questionnaire.

> "This trial may have some written statements introduced into evidence in which explicit sexual descriptions or sexual words are used. These next questions are intended to check with you about your comfort with such language.
>
>> "Please raise your hand if you find it difficult being around anyone who uses four-letter words. [Explain.]"

Two other sexual-content items were also read aloud.

>> "There may be evidence in this trial about sexual discussions between unmarried people. Please indicate if you believe that

individuals should not have sexual relations prior to marriage."

"Because of strong sexual descriptions that may be introduced,
indicate by raising your hand if you believe that people should
not be permitted to keep pornography for their personal use."

About two-thirds of the jurors answered at least one of these questions
affirmatively. One-third answered yes to all of the questions, with several
people standing to explain how they felt it was morally wrong to use sexual
terms, to have premarital intercourse, or to possess pornography. I noted,
"possibly strike" next to their names.

The judge then asked the questions we prepared about entrapment-
related issues. He read:

"It is possible that one argument made during the trial will be that police
have set up the defendant, pretending that they were somebody they
were not. These next two questions ask about that kind of action."

"Do you agree, that in order to prevent crime, law enforcement
officers should set skillful traps that lead people to a situation
in which they might break the law? [Explain.]"

"Indicate if you approve of police pretending they are customers
so they can arrest prostitutes. [Explain.]"

These two questions went to the heart of the entrapment defense, with
the prostitute question designed to get at the issue in another context. As
he read the questions, the judge explained that entrapment is a legitimate
tool in law enforcement. Nobody stood or raised a hand in response to the
entrapment questions, an inaction that we interpreted as passivity rather
than agreement with the premises of the two questions.

By the time the jury was struck, the defense team had a clear sense of
having eliminated many people who were ready to convict on the nature
of the case and not on the evidence and the law. No trial verdict is presented here. For the purposes of trial consultation, the essential issue was
that jurors who survived the selection process would be able to listen to the
defense.

CONCLUSION

The defense attorney believed that the jury selection and voir dire questions
were essential in approaching the case. As a trial consultant, I am always
cautious in coming to such conclusions. However, this case study leads to

three conclusions: first, identify key case conceptualizations. In reporting the nature of this consultation, it may seem obvious to pursue conceptual content and working hypotheses, but at the time of the initial entry into the case, it was not at all obvious. The second conclusion is that evaluation of jurors on the case conceptualizations needs to be fine-tuned. Simple inquiries yield simplistic answers. Differentiated inquiries yield the kind of multifaceted products that allow one to go past generalities and stereotypes. Finally, the case study reflects how trial consultation can be especially apt in cases in which much personal opinion and emotionality may be present in the jurors. It is not easy to ensure that jurors are open to listening to the arguments; a minimal necessary step is to find and strike those who enter with the likelihood of a closed mind. In trials with issues of sexuality, jury selection needs to focus on the ways in which the sexual attitudes and experiences of potential jurors can influence the cognitive processing of trial evidence and arguments. Similar case conceptualizations need to be addressed in every case in which much emotion will be generated.

Chapter 9

⊰⊱

NO QUESTIONS BUT DESELECTION QUESTIONS

Route 43 and Tierce Patton Road come together just north of Tuscaloosa, Alabama, creating a chronically dangerous intersection. Drivers on Tierce Patton Road look for a chance to slip into the flow of heavy traffic moving south toward the city, and they dart through a line of cars into the south-bound opposite lane of the highway. In the early hours of the day when many drivers were heading to work or school, a woman accelerated her late model Buick toward the space between two cars, and the side of the Buick was struck by the trailing car. The driver's mother was in the passenger seat. The air bags failed to inflate. The mother was killed. General Motors was sued.

Fast-forward now to the trial. I was on jury duty. The attorneys for the plaintiffs and for General Motors (GM) each were given up to an hour for the group voir dire. The questions that were asked were not prepared or assisted by consultants. They were often rambling and poorly formulated. Examining some of these questions can serve to begin this discussion of deselection questions only.

The attorneys for the plaintiffs asked few questions, among them:

> "Does anybody here work for any General Motors company, dealer, or
> supplier, or have you worked for GM in the past, or has any mem-
> ber of your family worked for General Motors?"

Seven of the 60 people in our venire raised their hands. The people who worked for GM were later challenged for cause or struck by the plaintiffs.

What was wrong with that? Anybody who has family or friends in the auto business knows how variable the work experience is. Some salespeople and mechanics are exceptionally loyal and protective of GM. On the other hand, some workers at dealerships, as well as assembly line employees, are bitter about the ways in which they have been mistreated. In order to make a meaningful peremptory strike, the plaintiffs should have asked the necessary follow-up question about whether anybody felt he or she had a personal investment in or positive inclination in any way toward the welfare, success, or image of GM. Instead they ended up eliminating both friends and foes.

One more unanticipated consequence of these questions could have occurred. The opposing defense attorneys for General Motors could have picked up on some of the cues and identified the people who worked for only a very short time for GM or a GM supplier, or in whom there was a reason to suspect a negative attitude. In other words, the question served both sides. Could questions have been asked that would avoid helping the opposing counsel? Perhaps. That topic is what this chapter addresses, finding the questions that help you make strikes—deselecting jurors—without assisting the other side. At some point the plaintiff's counsel could have asked our venire the bottom-line question: Do any of you feel a particular occupational, patriotic, car brand, or personal loyalty to GM? Affirmative answers could then have been followed up.

In contrast to the plaintiff's attorneys, the defense attorneys asked many questions, most of which addressed ownership—or lack of ownership—of GM and other American cars. Two women in the venire stood and indicated that they currently owned Hondas and had never owned American cars. Most of the venire had owned American cars, and many of these people had owned GM cars. That included me. Because I did not raise my hand in response to the question about not owning GM cars, I was asked no further questions.[1]

The defense attorneys missed a lot. I have owned two used Oldsmobiles. The first one was an Oldsmobile Super 88 I bought as a junior in college. It lasted 6 months before the engine seized up and the car had to be junked. The second was a compact Oldsmobile Achieva I bought for my stepson to use when he was in high school. We kept it for a year. The transmission had to be rebuilt at considerable expense shortly after I got it. The Olds was not the disaster that my college car had been, but it had many problems. The

---

[1]Whether I personally was asked any questions at all was moot. As a psychology professor, forensic psychologist, and trial consultant, I correctly knew that I would not be selected to be on this jury or any other jury.

ownership question asked of the panel by the defense attorneys had insufficient depth. They could have asked if any of us had had bad experiences owning GM cars. My hand would have shot up.

One man on the panel told me afterward that he had worked as a mechanic in a local GM multibrand dealership. His supervisor was nasty and critical without reason. He repaired a lot of cars brought in with major problems that should have been prevented during assembly or fixed at the factory. If the defense attorneys had done their job well, he would have been challenged for cause. As for me, I had a very different reason to be biased against GM. For 20 years, GM had led the successful lobbying effort against the proposed requirement that airbags be installed in all new cars. Over that time, at least 50,000 people who had died in auto accidents might have survived. The number of people who would have had less serious or no injuries at all, had airbags been installed, was surely in the millions. I personally, perhaps irrationally, considered GM responsible. I don't know how completely fair I would have been on that jury, but I would have gone in with a decidedly unsympathetic attitude toward GM.

Even if the ownership questions had brought out more information, they equally served the plaintiffs' attorneys as well as the defense attorneys. Because of the defense attorneys' questions, the plaintiffs' attorneys now had the identities of the people who owned GM autos and other American brand cars.

What should have been the basic objective in the questions of the GM defense attorneys? They should have sought to find out who would be biased against GM without revealing who was biased in favor of GM. They did not succeed on either count because of how poorly their questions were developed and phrased. Once again, let us suppose they had asked the essential question directly: Do any of you have any reason from your own experiences or opinions, or for any other reason, to have a negative attitude toward General Motors?

This jury selection story brings us to the fundamental principles of this chapter:

1. Good voir dire questions and jury questionnaires address the core factors to be considered in deselection decisions, and not in positive selection judgments about whom one wants on the jury. Attorneys should attend to individuals they do not want.
2. Successful and skilled voir dire questions and jury questionnaires do not do any of the spadework for opposing counsel.
3. Even when drawing in part on excellent standardized scales, reducing the numbers of items to allow for practical courtroom use and for deselection purposes always diminishes the reliability of a scale.

DESELECTION QUESTIONS
ABOUT PUNISHMENT

Assume you are conducting a research study about attitudes toward the punishment of offenders. You would go through the usual process of developing a large pool of possible items, conduct preliminary studies in which items that do not contribute much to the attitudes scale are discarded, check on reliability and factor structure validity, and eventually end up with a scale that yields a wide range of scores so that diverse attitudes are assessed. For example, in the development of the Melvin, Gramling, and Gardner (1985) Attitudes toward Prisoners Scale, among many others, this developmental procedure was followed and the logical outcome was a completed scale appropriate for research studies. This particular scale has good reliability and can be used in Spanish-speaking countries and populations (Ortet-Fabregat, Perez, & Lewis, 1993).

The use of scales to select jurors in terms of how punitive they are, as approached during voir dire and identified with SQJs, is different from their use in research. Suppose we look at jury selection in a criminal case in which a key issue is sentencing. We would be concerned with how punishment-oriented the potential jurors are, and our objective in such a case would be narrower and more focused than it would be in the course of a research study. In research we typically want to investigate the full range of responders, no matter where they fall in the distribution. In jury selection, if a scale like the Melvin et al. scale is administered, it helps both the prosecution and defense equally.[2] In research, typically, with the use of a scale measuring attitudes toward the punishment of prisoners, the following item might be presented:

Prisoners should be under strict, harsh discipline.

    1.   Disagree strongly
    2.   Disagree
    3.   Undecided
    4.   Agree
    5.   Agree strongly

When the respondents choose one of the five response choices, they present reasonably differentiated information on the single item. Prosecution attorneys might consider striking individuals who responded 1, 2, or 3. Defense attorneys might strike people who write or say a 4 or 5—*Agree* or *Agree strongly*. In contrast to this conventional use, see what happens when

---

[2]Equal assistance to both sides assumes that both sides have access to knowledgeable interpretation of the results. This assumption is not necessarily accurate.

the same question is posed in a clearly deselection-focused manner by the defense in voir dire questioning or in a supplemental juror questionnaire:

Check (or raise your hand) if you agree with the statement.

1. ____ Prisoners should be under strict, harsh discipline.

What this altered format does is identify only the most punitive jurors, without identifying the relative positions of the jurors who do not respond. In other words, the defense does not ask a question that does the prosecution's work. Here are other questions about punishment that seek to identify only punitive extremes and those jurors whose punitive attitudes may generalize toward the sentencing of a defendant. Items 2–8 were developed in my own work. Items 9–16 were also defense-deselection scored and drawn from the Smith and Capps (Capps, 2002) 15-item Punitiveness Orientation Scale.

Check if you agree with the statement.

2. ____ Juries and judges are too soft.
3. ____ Police are handcuffed in their work by court decisions.
4. ____ Prisons don't really punish.
5. ____ Prison inmates should not get an education at state expense.
6. ____ Prison inmates should not be allowed to watch television.
7. ____ Prison inmates should serve tougher time.
8. ____ Prison inmates should not be allowed to have hot water in their showers.
9. ____ In most cases probation is simply an unjustified way of putting criminals back on the street.
10. ____ Three-time losers deserve to be sentenced to life without the possibility of parole.
11. ____ Spanking is often the most effective way to teach children not to hit others.
12. ____ Physically punishing misbehaving children may hurt them in the short run, but it will help them in the long run.
13. ____ I think private citizens should take matters into their own hands if the courts are unwilling to punish criminals properly.
14. ____ If children refuse to eat what their parents serve them, they should be required to stay at the table until they change their minds.
15. ____ If your teenagers use drugs, you should turn them in to the police.
16. ____ If I were a juror I wouldn't hesitate to cast the decisive vote to send a murderer to death row.[3]

---

[3]Some judges may not permit this item to be asked.

Among this pool of items, a further sorting of punitive attitudes may be constructed. Items 5, 6, and 8 mention specific privileges of education, television, and hot showers, which are available in almost all American prisons; thus, endorsement of these items reflects a markedly punitive view. Items 11, 12, 14, and 15 all endorse punitive actions over leniency in raising children. The remaining items signal more global inclinations toward punitiveness, a tendency that Capps (2002) presents as a persistent personality trait. If the potential jurors endorse many punitiveness items, they would be rated more likely for peremptory challenges by the defense. If they do not respond to many items, there is still much unknown about their attitudes toward the punishment of offenders and the prosecution still has much of its own work cut out for it.

DESELECTION QUESTIONS
ABOUT AUTHORITARIANISM

Between the 16 authoritarianism scales described by Christie in Robinson et al. (1991) and others by Corcoran and Fischer (2000), many instruments are available to measure this construct. Authoritarianism itself is discussed in Chapters 3, 10, and elsewhere, but let us note briefly that researchers started by measuring fascist attitudes, and the construct has evolved to include measures of right-wing authoritarianism and personal rigidity and other related constructs. Authoritarianism is also inversely related to class. Christie has offered considerable reason to favor the Ring-Wing Authoritarianism Scale (see Christie, 1991, p. 552–555, and Altemeyer, 1981, 1988) that has received unusually positive reviews; thus, the first 3 items of this 24-item scale are examined for content:

1. Laws have to be strictly enforced if we are going to preserve our way of life.
2. People should pay less attention to the Bible and the other old traditional forms of religious guidance, and instead develop their own personal standards of what is moral and immoral. (Reverse scored)
3. Women should always remember the promise they made in the marriage ceremony to obey their husbands.

The other items are also sometimes lengthy and often have multiple elements. The third item in the list might be difficult to interpret in a time in which the "obey" part of the vow is often replaced by the word "cherish," and the phrase "always remember" is ambiguous. Even if one wished to assess potential jurors with the full 24-item Right-Wing Authoritarianism Scale, it may not be practical to administer. This difficulty arises, in part, because many of the items would be seen by the court as intruding excessively on the personal privacy of jurors, and, in part, because they would assist both sides equally. The lesson is worth repeating here: Opposing counsel should do its own work in gathering information.

Examining the options for measuring the trait of authoritarianism, I have combined items from the scale by Heaven (1985) with items from the closely related construct of dogmatism, the last two items in the following list. This format can be accepted as part of a supplemental juror questionnaire and it may not appear unduly intrusive. Agreement with an item is scored as suggesting the presence of authoritarianism–dogmatism. The items are introduced under the heading "What you think."

1. Does the idea of being a leader attract you? Yes ____ No ____
2. Do you like to have the last word in an argument or discussion?
   Yes ____ No ____
3. ____ Check here if you believe people should observe moral laws more strictly than they do.
4. ____ Check here if you believe that under almost all circumstances a police investigator's report of what happened at a crime scene will be accurate.
5. Once you make up your mind, do you really stick with it?
   Yes____ No ____

The advantage of these items is that the attitudes are commonly held. The disadvantage is that the product of five items is a markedly diluted measure of authoritarianism, with lower reliability than when the entire scale is used.

AVERSION AND DISGUST

In most trials involving allegations of violence, photographs or videos of wounds or injuries are presented as evidence. Individual jurors have a wide range of reactions to such visual content, and photos of bloody and disfigured corpses have the potential for causing such a strong emotional reaction that it may be difficult for jurors to evaluate other evidence and attorney arguments dispassionately. Instead of engaging in central processing of the key evidence of guilt or innocence, the jurors may be absorbed and biased by the visual drama of the exhibits. In a case in which a defendant was charged with capital murder of an infant, the following questions were asked of the venire, starting with an introduction to the rationale for the questions. The first three items go to the heart of the evidence to be offered by the prosecution. The last eight items are drawn from the more tangential 32-item Disgust Sensitivity Scale (Haidt, McCauley, & Rozin, 1994), a measure that has been used to study revulsion about spiders, cockroaches, vomit, and other arguably disgusting objects and actions.

Instructions: It is possible that this trial will have photographs of a severely injured and dead infant introduced into evidence and shown to the jury. Please check the following statements about photographs and other topics if they apply to you.

1.____ I would not be able to look at photographs of a dead infant.
2.____ I would find it difficult to examine photographs of a severely injured infant.
3.____ If I looked at photographs of a badly injured infant, I might become so emotional that I could not be an objective juror.
4.____ It would bother me tremendously to touch a dead body.
5.____ It would disturb me to see someone accidentally stick a fishing hook through his finger.
6.____ If a friend's pet cat dies, I could not pick up the dead body with my bare hands.
7.____ It bothers me to see someone in a restaurant eating messy food with his fingers.
8.____ Seeing a cockroach in someone else's house upsets me very much.
9.____ If I see someone vomit, it makes me sick to my stomach.
10.____ It would bother me to see someone put ketchup on vanilla ice cream and eat it.
11.____ I would be disgusted if I took a sip of a soft drink and then realized that I drank from the can or glass that an acquaintance of mine had been drinking from.

The scoring of these items was divided into two categories. The first was made up of the first three items, specific to the trial evidence. The second category was made up of the last eight items drawn from the Disgust Sensitivity Scale, which is a step farther removed from the evidence to be introduced.

ATTITUDES TOWARD THE DEATH PENALTY AND CAPITAL PUNISHMENT

In many capital murder trials the evidence overwhelmingly points to guilt. In such a capital murder trial, the combination of a properly Miranda-ized confession, compelling forensic evidence, and eyewitnesses make it unlikely that that a verdict of not guilty would emerge. In these cases, the jury selection addresses attitudes toward capital punishment. Among death-qualified jurors,[4] that is, persons not absolutely opposed to the death penalty, the question arises about which questions would better serve the goals of the prosecution or the goals of the defense. In standard and supplemental juror questionnaires, a variety of items are commonly included. For the present purposes, I discuss one of the many available scales for assessing attitudes toward the death penalty: the 15-item scale developed by O'Neil, Patry, and Penrod (2004). In their article, these authors presented a cogent case for use of the scales in jury selection, concluding that there is a direct correlation between attitudes toward the death penalty and sentencing verdicts. They wrote, "The primary effect of attitudes is direct—supporters of the death penalty, those who believe it is a deterrent, and those who believe that defendants sentenced to LWOP [life without parole] nonetheless get out on parole were more likely to sentence the defendant to death, irrespective of their findings of aggravating and mitigating factors" (p. 463).

Starting with a pool of 59 items, O'Neil et al. (2004) went through successive iterations and factor analyses, reducing their scale to 34 items, then to 19 items, and then to the final 15-item form, reflecting four separate factors.[5] The 15 items are listed below. Asterisks indicate reverse-scored items.

1. I think the death penalty is necessary.
2. It is immoral for society to take a life regardless of the crime the individual has committed.*
3. No matter what crime a person has committed, executing them is a cruel punishment.*
4. The death penalty should be used more often than it is.
5. The desire for revenge is a legitimate reason for favoring the death penalty.
6. Society has a right to get revenge when murder has been committed.
7. There are some murderers whose death would give me a sense of personal satisfaction.
8. The death penalty is just one way to compensate the victim's family for some murders.
9. The death penalty does not deter other murderers.*

---

[4]More recently, assessment of life-qualified jurors is undertaken, in which jurors absolutely personally committed to the death penalty are identified for possible challenges for cause or peremptory challenges.

[5]I have not presented the factor structure and loadings here, but the four factors, in order from beginning to end of the scale, are General Support, Retribution and Revenge, Death Penalty Is a Deterrent, and LWOP Allows Parole.

10. The death penalty makes criminals think twice before committing murder.
11. Executing a person for premeditated murder discourages others from committing that crime in the future.
12. It is more cost-efficient to sentence a murderer to death rather than to life imprisonment.
13. Executing a murderer is less expensive than keeping him in jail for the rest of his life.
14. Even when a murderer gets a sentence of life without parole, he usually gets out on parole.
15. There is no such thing as a sentence that truly means "life without parole."

Now, we again take the intentional risk of response bias in the form of yea-saying, or the tendency to agree with inquiries and to respond "True" to true–false questions. We then go through the scale in order to delete items that help the prosecution, working on the assumption that we have been retained by attorneys for the defense. All of the reverse-scored items are deleted—thus, items numbered 2, 3, and 9 are dropped, leaving 12 items. Item 8 is somewhat vague and had the lowest factor loading based on the research that has been done with the items, so we delete that item. Items 12 and 13 are repetitive, so item 12 is deleted. In the same sense, items 14 and 15 are repetitive, so item 15 is deleted, leaving a smaller and more focused deselection scale of 9 items for defense purposes. Because judges may be severely restrictive and the time limited, it is typically required that an abbreviated scale be used. The 9 final items are as follows:

1. I think the death penalty is necessary.
2. The death penalty should be used more often than it is.
3. The desire for revenge is a legitimate reason for favoring the death penalty.
4. Society has a right to get revenge when murder has been committed.
5. There are some murderers whose death would give me a sense of personal satisfaction.
6. The death penalty makes criminals think twice before committing murder.
7. Executing a person for premeditated murder discourages others from committing that crime in the future.
8. Executing a murderer is less expensive than keeping him in jail for the rest of his life.
9. Even when a murderer gets a sentence of life without parole, he usually gets out on parole.

DESELECTION PERSPECTIVES
ON POLICE INTERROGATIONS

The Miranda warnings were designed to give suspects information about their rights before they consent to speak in interrogations. Few suspects choose with thoughtful clarity to remain silent, to have a lawyer present, or to decline otherwise to participate in an interrogation. As a result, the nature of admissibility of interrogations and the interpretation of confessions are frequent issues raised by the defense. As part of the deselection of members of the jury pool, participants are often asked questions about how they see interrogations and confessions. In this content area, the problematic questions that are asked by defense attorneys tend to be open-ended, with the jurors often replying in narrative statements. In the context of our present purpose, of posing only deselection questions, six questions are presented here. Observe how the questions are designed only to elicit agreement with the perspective of the police interrogator and of the prosecution.

Check the statements with which you agree.

1. ____ Suspects are always treated fairly during police interrogations.
2. ____ Police who interrogate suspects have only one interest, which is in learning the truth even if they do not find the offender.
3. ____ It is only on television or movies that police officers force or trick people into confessing.
4. ____ Police do not use scare tactics to make innocent people confess.
5. ____ Police use scare tactics only to make guilty people confess.
6. ____ A defendant's confession is always reliable proof of guilt.

GENERAL PRESUMPTIONS
ABOUT INNOCENCE AND BURDEN OF PROOF

When I first started constructing questionnaires and voir dire questions about the presumption of innocence, I was surprised to find that a large number of people presume guilt. The last time I asked these questions, 40% of more than 100 people agreed that the defendant should have to prove his or her innocence. Using the request "*Tell us your opinions about the law,*" the following questions are sometimes posed. Respondents are asked to make a checkmark if they agree with the following presumption of innocence or guilt questions, which I have used in a number of cases.

1. ____ A defendant is innocent until proven guilty beyond a reasonable doubt.
2. ____ If the prosecution goes to the trouble of bringing someone to trial, the person is probably guilty.
3. ____ There are two kinds of people in this world: those who are basically decent and those who are not.
4. ____ Regardless of what the law says, a person who is accused of a crime should be required to prove his or her innocence.
5. ____ People who have a lot of money are sometimes treated better than other people by the legal system.

Items 2 and 4 are the key queries. What happens in the actual voir dire is that persons who respond *agree* to these two queries are next asked by the prosecutor or judge, often as a group, if they can follow the instructions of the court and assume that the defendant is innocent until all of the evidence has been presented, the closing arguments completed, and the judge's instruction given. They all agree. It would be difficult to disagree. They are not successfully challenged for cause. However, they do become more likely candidates for peremptory challenges.

OPEN-ENDED QUESTIONS

There may be occasions when an open-ended question can, at least in part, serve the purposes of deselection. The overriding principle remains that questions that can be answered unpredictably may benefit both sides. An example of a sometimes useful open-ended question is one that follows a closed-ended question. Consider this query that can be used in either a supplemental juror questionnaire or during voir dire questioning:

Indicate whether you believe that you would be a good juror for this case, based on what you know so far.
   Yes, I would ____ No, I would not ____

Please explain your answer. _____

Jurors who answer the question *no* in court often will have an opportunity to explain to the judge individually. The *no* answer may represent a personal explanation of biases related to the nature of the allegations. The explanation sometimes leads to a successful challenge for cause.

A *yes* answer by a juror may call for further questioning, because some jurors see their personal roles as being to redress perceived injustices in the legal system. Where they perceive that prior juries or judges have failed, they may seek to ensure that a compensatory balance is introduced. Individuals with this kind of agenda may be prone to attend as much to their internal mandate as to the facts of the case. At the same time, some people do answer *yes* out of a reasonable and accurate assessment of their own impartiality, in which case little harm is done by this self-identification. An additional factor in weighing types of jurors desired and not desired is the strength of the evidence on each side. When the strong weight of evidence is against their side, attorneys often should be encouraged to seek jurors who will react nonobjectively and emotionally. In contrast, when the clear strength of evidence is with them, identifying the unpredictable and more subjective jurors for striking can be helpful.

The same question about being a good juror can also be stated the opposite way, in terms of self-identification as an unfair juror. This issue may be pursued through a question like:

"Would the nature of the charge of [murder/assault on a police officer/ illegal drug sales/or other specific allegation] affect your ability to be a fair and impartial juror?"

Judges often seek to "rehabilitate" many of the jurors who answer affirmatively because many judges are conservative about allowing challenges for cause. However, persons who are so forthcoming about bias are always possible targets for challenges for cause and may be moved up in the hierarchy of likely peremptory challenges.

THE DESELECTION PROCESS APPLIED TO THE JUROR BIAS SCALE

The Juror Bias Scale (JBS) is examined in Chapter 3. However, its wide usage makes it a good case study scale for the final aspect of the phrasing of questions that are a central part of deselection. Here are the steps that make the scale useful for one side, for the moment the defense. The full scale is presented first:

Instructions: This is a questionnaire to determine people's attitudes and beliefs on a variety of general legal issues. Please answer each statement by giving as true a picture of your position as possible. Asterisks indicate reverse-scored items.

RESPONSES

1 Strongly agree
2 Mildly agree

3   Agree and disagree equally
4   Mildly disagree
5   Strongly disagree

1. *Appointed judges are more competent than elected judges.*
2. A suspect who runs from the police most probably committed the crime.
3. A defendant should be found guilty if only 11 out of 12 jurors vote guilty.
4. *Most politicians are really as honest as humanly possible.*
5. Too often jurors hesitate to convict someone who is guilty out of pure sympathy.
6. In most cases where the accused presents a strong defense, it is only because of a good lawyer.
7. *In general, children should be excused for their misbehavior.*
8. The death penalty is cruel and inhumane.*
9. Out of every 100 people brought to trial, at least 75 are guilty of the crime with which they are charged.
10. For serious crimes like murder, a defendant should be found guilty if there is a 90% chance that he or she committed the murder.
11. Defense lawyers don't really care about guilt or innocence, they are just in business to make money.
12. Generally, the police make an arrest only when they are sure about who committed the crime.
13. Circumstantial evidence is too weak to use in court.*
14. Many accident claims filed against insurance companies are phony.
15. The defendant is often a victim of his or her own bad reputation.*
16. If the grand jury recommends that a person be brought to trial, then he or she probably committed the crime.
17. Extenuating circumstances should not be considered—if a person commits a crime, then that person should be punished.
18. *Hypocrisy is on the increase in society.*
19. Too many innocent people are wrongly imprisoned.*
20. If the majority of the evidence—but not all of it—suggests that the defendant committed the crime, the jury should vote *not guilty.**
21. If the defendant committed a victimless crime, like gambling or possession of marijuana, he should never be convicted.*
22. *Some laws are made to be broken.*

Note that out of the 22 items, 5 were filler items and are *italicized* above. They are items 1, 4, 7, 18, and 22. These are deleted. Next, let us assume that the jury selection assistance is for the defense. In this instance, the 6 reverse-scored items, 8, 13, 15, 19, 20, and 21, are deleted.[6] Each of these 6 items, if answered affirmatively, indicates skepticism about the prosecution's perspective. Defense attorneys do not want this skepticism made public, as it would help the prosecuting attorneys decide whom they did not want as well. For example, item 21 as presented below helps only the prosecution.

If the defendant committed a victimless crime, like gambling or possession of marijuana, he or she should never be convicted.

With the 11 filler and reverse-scored items removed, 11 items remain. Two of them concern the role of lawyers and are deleted because they are likely to reveal negative and subjectively influential attitudes toward attorneys. One item asked if many claims against insurance companies were phony. This item could be kept, because it has a less obvious connection to a criminal case, but we delete it for the reason of nonobvious connection. One remaining item uses the word *extenuating*, a word not in common usage among some jurors. For that reason, it is deleted, leaving 7 items, as follows. Note that items 2 and 5 below might not be allowed as part of a supplemental juror questionnaire or voir dire, because the judge or opposing counsel may object to asking questions that are in opposition to rules of law.

1. A suspect who runs from the police most probably committed the crime.
2. A defendant should be found guilty if only 11 out of 12 jurors vote guilty.
3. Too often jurors hesitate to convict someone who is guilty out of pure sympathy.
4. Out of every 100 people brought to trial, at least 75 are guilty of the crime with which they are charged.
5. For serious crimes like murder, a defendant should be found guilty if there is a 90% chance that he or she committed the murder.
6. Generally, the police make an arrest only when they are sure about who committed the crime.
7. If the grand jury recommends that a person be brought to trial, then he or she probably committed the crime.

CONCLUSION

These deselection procedures are only as good as the conceptual frame of reference from which they are derived. If a consultant or attorney has been

---

[6]If deselecting for the prosecution, these items would be retained. The other items would be either discarded or rephrased to identify defense-leaning jurors.

able to think through the core and nuanced issues in the case, then deselection has promise of making a worthwhile contribution. If the conceptualization is simplistic and limited, so will be the results of the deselection methods.

As mentioned, the greater the departure from the original and standardized scales, the more there will be a shrinking down of the original scientific utility and knowledge. At the same time, the shrunken and downsized scale items still have merit in having been systematically developed. If one starts with a robust scale with high reliability, high item–total correlations, and strong single factor structure, it will be more likely to survive the pruning fairly well.

We should be aware that the deselection methods constitute a transparent strategy. Opposing counsel who take the time to examine with care the nature and phrasing of the items may well legitimately object to their inclusion in supplemental juror questionnaires or voir dire questions. They may alternatively propose items that serve to balance the degree of leaning one way by members of the venire. As legitimate as this effort may be, it is not frequent. Most attorneys choose not to construct items, but prefer to use what they have tried before.

The thoughtful trial consultant looks for opportunities to check out the reliability, validity, and factor structure of the scale actually put to use. Many trial consultants use the same items in different trials. With the knowledge of likely future applications, a separate study of the psychometric qualities of truncated deselection scales can provide a sound basis for their use.

In this chapter a way of thinking has been presented for the process of preparing items for juror questionnaires and voir dire questioning. Like so much in the field of trial consultation, good item preparation and careful jury selection does not override the strong weight of evidence. As with other aspects of trial consultation, deselection procedures may also have positive indirect effects in terms of the mental set of the attorneys being more optimistic and confident, and, as a consequence, their being better able to represent the client and negotiate a favorable plea or settlement.

The deselection procedures are steps in an uncertain process. They assist in moving toward identifying and perhaps striking certain jurors, but they are by no means the only method nor do they necessarily always yield the most undesirable jurors, which an attorney may wish to strike. I know of no empirical research that can fully validate the deselection method itself, but it is reasonable to conclude that the results of this soliciting of one-sided biases can make a difference. The good face validity of this method—it *looks* as if it makes a difference—is far from what we should expect in making it a regular part of jury selection. The concluding verdict: promising and interesting, but not proven.

Chapter 10

JURY SELECTION

Reversals

Reversals in trial consultation refers to selecting the opposite, or reverse, of what one would normally do or think, because of the specifics of a case. I have described reversals as a strategic approach to court testimony, in which the well-prepared and fully honest witness gives the opposite response to what the cross-examining attorney has expected (Brodsky, 2004). Reversals in jury selection work in similar ways. The opposite, or reverse, of common criteria are chosen. Reversals have the potential advantage of being nonobvious to opposing counsel and introducing an element in which commonsense assumptions are discarded. Hutson (2007) has described cases in which juror reversals are seen, writing: "When psychologist Robert Bothwell asked 10 mock juries to look at the Kobe Bryant case, he found that people with a healthy respect for authority, who might be expected to punish the defendant, actually blamed the victim" (p. 93).

Indeed, the historical cases that helped found trial consultation as a profession were based in part on reversals. The trial of the Harrisburg Seven protesters against the Vietnam War used just such nonobvious findings. College graduates and others with more education would conventionally be assumed to be more defense-oriented in criminal trials. In the Harrisburg, Pennsylvania, area, the more educated people were found by jury consultants to be prosecution-oriented. More educated people were struck by the defense without the prosecution understanding why, and other counterintuitive criteria were also used to strike other jurors. The jury was made up of individuals sympathetic to the protesters and neutral about the case. The jury deliberations lasted almost 60 hours. Charges were dropped for

all seven defendants following a hung jury, and the verdict was widely cel-
ebrated as a victory for the right to protest, a victory in the struggle against
conspiracy charges against war protesters, and a victory for applying social
science knowledge to jury selection (Lieberman & Sales, 2007).

Jury selection is case-specific. A body of practical and research knowledge has been generated to apply to jury selection and strikes and to related
issues of interest to prosecution, plaintiff, and defense attorneys. However,
these practical and research findings always need to be considered afresh
in light of the specific allegations and nature of the evidence. This chapter
addresses the process of going further than reconsidering assumptions in
jury selection and, instead, turning the assumptions on their heads because
of the demands of the case.

The general rules that are brought into jury selection have already been
discussed, including the following:

- Ask only those questions that elicit information to identify people
  whom you may wish to strike.
- Avoid the commonly asked open-ended questions in jury questionnaires and in voir dire questioning that help both sides. After all,
  trial consultants and attorneys do not and should not want to be fair,
  in the sense of both sides equally benefiting from questions. That
  information equity is what often happens when excellent open-ended
  questions are posed.

This chapter focuses on the reversal, and major modification, of typical
strike assumptions. Part of the rationale is that trial consultation and theories of jury selection should follow the contours of the case, rather than use
the same template in most cases. The case presented in this chapter concerns
a police officer on trial for assault and misconduct while on duty.

THE FACTS OF THE CASE

The facts of the case coming to trial were not in dispute. In a poor, predomi-
nantly African American, and crime-ridden city, the police had organized
an intensive surveillance effort to combat illegal drug sales. The mayor had
insistently pushed through city council an ordinance of uncertain constitu-
tionality whereby persons flagging down cars, waving their hands, or wan-
dering aimlessly in a known drug area could be arrested and charged with
loitering.

While assigned to a town square known to be the nexus of drug dealers
and that had been designated as a Federal High-Intensity Drug Traffick-
ing Area, nine police officers were stationed in threes, sitting in unmarked

cars or SUVs. All of the officers and the suspect described here were African American. The police officers' instructions were firm. They were to be aggressive, to stop suspicious people, to search them, and to arrest people possessing or selling illegal drugs.

The police officer who later became the defendant was Ulysses Fish.[1] He was 31 years old, 5'5" tall, weighed 165 pounds, and was exceptionally fit and athletic. He had been on the force for 36 months. With two other officers, Fish had been assigned to duty in this area using an unmarked automobile.

On the evening in question, Fish was sitting inside a car. The automobile itself had been parked in a position allowing him to watch and to be available to serve as a backup for a parked SUV with an Officer Brown and two other officers. A solitary man, Abram Ashton, was observed moving and behaving in a manner that arose the suspicions of the police. Ashton was ordered to stop by Officer Brown. Ashton at first refused, then argued and complained, and as Brown attempted to pat him down and search him, Ashton kept slapping away Brown's hands, all the time attempting to get away. Brown threw Ashton to the ground, handcuffed him, searched him, and found no drugs. Ashton swore during this process, calling all of the officers "a bunch of weak bitches" and asserting that he did not give a f*** about the town or the police. Ashton was then informed by the supervising officer that if he would calm down and stay quiet, he would be released and allowed to move on. Ashton did become quiet and the handcuffs were removed. Ashton was ordered to move away.

In an act of explicit defiance, Ashton stood where he was. While making eye contact with Officer Fish in the backup vehicle, he started directing insulting remarks to all of the police officers, but especially to Fish. He said, "None of you officers ain't shit and if you took your badges off, I would beat your bitch asses." Ashton called the police "pussies," "not really men," "cowards hiding behind their guns and uniforms," and much more, in a display of vivid street profanity. He continued to direct his remarks especially to Officer Fish, now standing outside the car, commenting on how small Fish was, how he was not a man, and how Ashton would thoroughly beat Fish to a pulp if Fish did not have a badge and a gun.

Because the remarks were directed particularly at him, Fish was offended. The officer in charge ordered Fish to arrest Ashton for disorderly conduct and loitering. Ashton started walking away as Fish ordered him to stop, instructing him that he was under arrest. Ashton declared, "You ain't taking me to jail tonight."

As Fish moved toward Ashton, Ashton tried to grab Officer Fish around

---

[1]All names are pseudonyms.

the waist. The much smaller Fish put his own arms around Ashton and wrestled him to the ground. Ashton's head hit the pavement. He was briefly unconscious, and blood flowed from both of his ears. All of the other eight officers on the stakeout watched the takedown. Two officers later reported to investigators that Fish had banged Ashton's head on the pavement after Ashton was down. The other six officers stated that the only blow Ashton suffered occurred as part of the takedown.

If there had been no adverse outcome for Ashton, the incident would not have had any further consequences. However, Ashton suffered headaches and memory problems and lost his job. Furthermore, he filed a personal injury suit against the city and against Ulysses Fish. The attorneys representing the city reached a settlement of $100,000 with the attorneys representing Ashton. At the same time Ashton's lawsuit became public knowledge, Fish was dismissed from the police department. Three charges were subsequently filed against him in federal court, the most important of which was assault. Two minor charges were filed alleging that Fish had falsified his report of the incident on the departmental incident report form.

EXCESSIVE FORCE BY POLICE

One can conceptualize excessive force by police as being organizational, contextual, or individual in nature. Organizational influences on excessive force consist of implicit, or occasionally explicit, policies and encouragement for officers to act violently. Contextual influences are those that arise from the particular situations in which officers find themselves. Thus, taunting by individuals who are perceived as being high risk to fellow officers and the accelerated unfolding of confrontations may lead to acts that can be labeled by observers as police brutality. The individual perspective holds that particular officers are bad apples, in the sense of having a low tolerance for frustration or ambiguity and a tendency to respond to demanding situations with an early and strong reliance on physical control. Of course, the causes of police violence do not necessarily relate to any single theory, but can be a combination of these influences coming together at a point in time.

In a societal-level analysis of how racially identified charges like those leveled at the four officers in the Rodney King beating (and in a number of other cases), Lynn Chancer (2005) has observed that legal issues sometimes become social causes. As a result, the guilt or innocence of a defendant is transformed into either an affirmation or rejection of broader social causes. The resultant legal decisions are rarely satisfying to groups that experience a sense of social ownership in the outcome. In contrast, attention to the individual defendant leads to an arguably simpler and potentially more satisfying outcome.

An example of the individual perspective has been developed by Toch (1996), with his construct of the violence-prone police officer. Drawing on a 4-year database of allegations of excessive force in the Los Angeles Police Department (LAPD), Toch described the results for officers reported to have used force. Allegations of excessive force or improper tactics occurred at the rate of 0.6 allegations per officer, when all officers were studied. In contrast, a subset of 44 officers with 6 or more allegations had an average of 7.6 allegations each. Toch suggested that these officers had a personal propensity to use violence and could be considered chronic deviants. He described these officers as having "an across-the-board aggressive, proactive, and peremptory approach to encounters with citizens that leads to escalations of conflict" (p. 100).

Nevertheless, Toch placed police violence in a broader context as well. He pointed out that police recruits are socialized toward violence when their instructors regale them with war stories involving force. Toch observed that conflict-aversive officers may be held in lower esteem by fellow officers and that an initial willingness to be physical is a mark of achievement. There was organizational approval for active physical activity on "hot calls." Danger and fear by themselves contribute to violent acts.

Data have been gathered on contextual influences. The Police Services Study (PSS) in three metropolitan areas arranged for trained observers to join police officers on patrols, and they recorded what occurred in 5,688 police encounters with citizens (Worden, 1996). Some of the contexts in which excessive police force was shown included violent offenses, the presence of at least four bystanders and more than one officer, African American male offenders, and hostile or antagonistic behaviors by the individual citizen. Hunt (2006) added that symbolic or real assaults on the authority, property, or person of an officer are often perceived by police officers as situation-specific justifications for excessive force.

In the case described earlier, the alleged victim, Mr. Ashton, chose to pursue the paths of both taking civil action in a personal injury suit and serving as an active participant in a criminal prosecution for excessive force by Officer Fish. Although civil lawsuits are common, criminal prosecutions of officers are infrequent. Klockars (1996) has examined why civil rather than criminal litigation is pursued in excessive force allegations against police. He observed that in civil suits discovery rights are more generous, that the threshold for proof is only preponderance of evidence (instead of beyond a reasonable doubt, as in criminal cases), and that there are major financial incentives for attorneys to initiate such suits and for officers and departments to settle such suits.

Klockars (2006) has also raised the moral question of whether the means justify the ends in the use of excessive police force. Calling this issue "The Dirty Harry Problem" (p. 403), Klockars described excessive force as a dirty means, even if it serves the purpose of movement toward a morally justified end. Indeed, in the present case, the question arises as to whether Officer Fish had indeed employed dirty means in the form of his perhaps unnecessarily aggressive takedown of Mr. Ashton.

VOIR DIRE QUESTIONS

In this case, which was typical of felony assault charges, no supplemental jury questionnaire was allowed. A standard two-page questionnaire, routinely administered to citizens called to jury duty in this particular federal court, was used. Although that questionnaire yields some general information from which tentative inferences may be drawn, the primary resource in this case was the voir dire questioning. In this section, the voir dire questions are described, along with the accompanying rationale.

An initial and uncharacteristically open-ended question was prepared to initiate the voir dire process. This question read:

"The brief questionnaire you filled out before you came today asked about family or personal employment with law enforcement or attorneys. Please raise your hand if there are other ways in which you or your family have had contacts, interactions, or working relationships with law enforcement, district attorneys or other attorneys."

The central part of the voir dire questioning then proceeded. Five components of the screening were identified:

- The police stand-up-for-self factor
- The macho factor
- Juror experience with police mistreatment
- Presumption of innocence and setting up theory of case
- Antiauthoritarianism

The Police Stand–Up–for–Self Factor

• *Working hypotheses:* Prosecution-oriented jurors will believe that police officers should quietly accept whatever verbal abuse is directed their way. Defense-oriented jurors will believe that there is only so much in personal insults an officer should take before he is entitled to act "like a man."

Because Fish was accused of going beyond the normal boundaries of aggressive intervention, the defense wanted to strike jurors who would have preferred a patient, waiting, hands-off attitude. The stand-up-for-self jurors would presumably endorse more assertive acts.

• *Voir dire questions:* Three questions were prepared for inquiries about the stand-up factor; they tapped into personal, obscene, and insulting verbal abuse. In most conventional criminal cases, a voir dire for the defense would seek to identify possible police-affiliative jurors to strike; that is, the defense would consider peremptory challenges for jurors who believed that officers should aggressively and assertively respond to citizen abuse. In our reversals case, it is just the opposite. The jurors the defense would seek to strike would be those who presumably would identify with the prosecution and perceive an extremely high threshold for officers reacting to abusive language. They would want police to be able to passively and nonreactively accept abusive language as part of the job. The Fish defense team then went about constructing voir dire questions to tap into this issue. As always, the following three questions were phrased so only prosecution-oriented jurors in the Fish case would be identified:

"Raise your hand if you think police officers should just take verbal abuse from citizens, no matter how personal the verbal abuse is."
"Raise your hand if you think police officers should just take verbal abuse from citizens, no matter how obscene the verbal abuse is."
"Raise your hand if you think police officers should just take verbal abuse from citizens, no matter how insulting the verbal abuse is."

Follow-up question:
"Will jurors who have raised their hands please explain?"

The Macho Factor

• *Working hypothesis:* Mr. Fish acted in a hypermasculine, highly macho way, showing a behavior consistent with what has been called hegemonic masculinity (Kilmartin, 2006). Prosecution-oriented jurors will disapprove of macho masculinity, whereas defense-oriented jurors will be able to identify with the officer. This topic is of special interest to me because I regularly teach courses on the psychology of men and masculinity and I am a member of the American Psychological Association (APA) Division 51, the Society for the Psychological Study of Men and Masculinity.

• *Voir dire questions:* The voir dire questions addressed what it means to be male, masculine, and a police officer. The working assumption was that pro-prosecution jurors would have a value system holding that officers should submerge male role identity in favor of the constraints of police roles. Thus, the questions instructed the venire as follows:

> "Raise your hand if you believe that good male police officers show willpower and submerge the desire to stand up for themselves as men."
>
> "Raise your hand if you believe that good male police officers always are officers first and men second."
>
> "Raise your hand if you believe that forceful male police officers should be identified, reprimanded, and then punished much more than they are now for what they do on the job."

Juror Experience with Police Mistreatment

• *Working hypothesis:* Jurors who have had police officers act unfairly, rudely, or violently toward them or their families will generalize from these experiences and, as a consequence, would be likely to be biased against Mr. Fish.

• *Voir dire questions:* The voir dire questions broke down the concept of police maltreatment into three domains of self, family, and friends. The questions used the descriptors *hold, hit,* and *hurt* as the units of physical maltreatment and unfair treatment, and as an indication of specific negative experiences. The jury pool was instructed:

> "This case will deal in part with an allegation of mistreatment by a police officer. Please raise your hand if you personally have had a police officer physically hold, hit, or hurt you."
>
> "This case will deal in part with an allegation of mistreatment by a police officer. Please raise your hand if a member of your family has had a police officer physically hold, hit, or hurt him or her."
>
> "This case will deal in part with an allegation of mistreatment by a police officer. Please raise your hand if a friend or someone you know has had a police officer physically hold, hit, or hurt him or her."

Follow-up questions were prepared that addressed nonphysical abuse or harm, using the next issues:

> "We now move to asking about other kinds of contacts with police.
>
> "Please raise your hand if you personally have been treated unfairly or unjustly in any way by a police officer."
>
> "Please raise your hand if a member of your family has been treated unfairly or unjustly in any way by a police officer."

"Please raise your hand if somebody else you know has been treated
unfairly or unjustly in any way by a police officer."

Further follow-up question:

"Will jurors who have raised their hands please briefly explain?"

Presumption of Innocence and Setting Up Theory of Case

• *Working hypothesis:* Some jurors will be inclined to accept the
account of events as unnecessarily aggressive and excessively forceful from
Mr. Ashton and the two officer observers instead of the more moderate versions from Mr. Fish and the six other officers on that assignment.

   • *Possible voir dire question:*
   "There may be presented in testimony some different accounts of events
      that occurred on the reported date. From your own understandings
      and what you have seen yourself, are you inclined to accept stories
      about officers intentionally harming a citizen?"

This closed-ended question gets at the essential heart of the case.

   • *Related question:*
   "At the beginning of testimony, some officers may say that say the
      defendant harmed a man. Would that be enough to make you think
      Mr. Fish is guilty?"

Antiauthoritarianism

• *Working hypothesis:* Jurors who appreciate that police sometimes
have to act unilaterally and be completely in command would be defense-
oriented. These jurors would be inclined to accept authority and perhaps
to be authoritarian themselves. However, jurors who are more likely to follow social demands, more likely to accept societal rules, and comfortable
in submitting to others in their own lives would be skeptical about what
the defendant officer is alleged to have done. They could be prosecution-
oriented jurors who should be identified and possibly struck. Two measures were selected from a book of scales discussed in Chapter 3: *Measures
for Clinical Practice: A Sourcebook, 4th Edition* by Fischer and Corcoran
(2007). Items were drawn from the Patrick Heaven Authoritarianism Scale
(AS) (Heaven, 1985) and the Rigby (1987) Authority Behavior Inventory
(ABI), which assesses submission to authority. The 20-item AS has a Cronbach alpha of .79 and the ABI has a Cronbach alpha of .90, both sufficient
to use as part of an inventory.

• *Voir dire questions:* As with the use of almost all psychological instruments in courtroom applications, only a few items can be drawn for use in voir dire questions. The fundamental approach is to examine the pool of items, to find those that fit most closely with the concepts of interest, and to use only items that help to identify jurors that favor opposing counsel. Toward that goal, the following four items about passivity and nonauthoritarianism were selected from the AS (Heaven, 1985).

• Raise your hand if this applies to you.

____ If you dislike having to tell others what to do.
____ If you would rather take orders than give them.
____ If it would upset you a lot to see a child or animal suffer.
____ If even when your anger is aroused, you don't use strong language.

The Rigby ABI (1987) has 24 items, 12 of which are reverse scored. Three items were selected that identify people who do not accept or submit to authority and who, presumably, may be more likely to put themselves in the position of identifying with Mr. Ashton:

____ Do you encourage young people to do what they want to do, even when it is against the wishes of their parents?
____ Do you question what you hear in the news?
____ Do you speak up against your boss or person in charge when he or she acts unfairly?

These seven items from the AS and ABI made up the measure of antiauthoritarianism. Members of the jury pool who agreed with these items were hypothesized to be likely candidates for us to strike.

Other Case Issues

Not all constructs that emerge from the process of trial conceptualization lend themselves to focal points or assessment during the voir dire. For purposes of illustrating the vetting of constructs, five additional constructs or options are presented that were considered and not used.

• *Intentionality:* Was Mr. Ashton's hitting of his head on the ground an accidental consequence of the fall with Mr. Fish, or was it caused by intentional pounding by Mr. Fish?

• *Credibility of the two complaining officers.*

• *Standards of practice in law enforcement* with respect to disorderly conduct by citizen and associated use of physical force by police.

• How do social class, education, age, and race of jurors relate to empathy with Mr. Ashton versus empathy with Officer Fish?

• *Preparation for testimony:* Does Mr. Fish need preparation to be an effective witness on his own behalf?

CONCLUSION

The judge in charge of the jury selection screened out some of the questions. The defense's part of the voir dire process was much longer than that of the government, lasting about 3 hours for the 60 members of the jury pool. By the end of the voir dire questions, a clear sense emerged of persons who might be bad for the defense. It was a strange feeling to be striking the liberal, empathic, intelligent jurors and to be keeping the authoritarian, punishment-oriented, and law-and-order jurors. Still, that is the nature of reversals: to have compelling reasons to deselect exactly the jurors one would want to keep in conventional trials.

Parenthetically, I would like to add my observations about the defendant during the voir dire. He kept cracking his knuckles. I instructed him to stop. He kept touching his face, holding his hands against his forehead and cheeks. I told him that research indicates that self-touching like that is a sign of anxiety and that it would not serve him well. He tried to stop. He kept shifting in his seat and, every now and then, reached his arms above his head. It made him look ill at ease. Not a good idea, he was told.

In many cases, trial consultants are present throughout the trial, offering observations, advice, and perspectives. In this case the consultation stopped when the jury was selected. The agreed-upon tasks had been completed. At the least, the attorneys for Mr. Fish had much more information on which to base their decisions and representation in court.

Part IV

—◆—

CHANGES OF VENUE

This part addresses pretrial bias and changes of venue. In Chapter 11, we look at the legal foundations and social science issues surrounding likely bias in communities and jury pools. Then we consider the issue of local variations in attitudes, drawing in part on the example of the change of venue in the criminal trial that followed the 1995 bombing of the federal building in Oklahoma City.

Sometimes the considerable information collected about pretrial bias does not lead to the trial being moved to another location, even for a case in which the nature of the alleged offenses are heinous or bizarre. In the continuing spirit of our case-driven approach, Chapter 12 describes the methodology of assessing pretrial knowledge and attitudes in a highly publicized capital murder case. The method included a repeated survey of prospective jurors to determine to what extent attitudes had changed.

Chapter 11

CHANGE OF VENUE CONSULTATIONS

As compared with the available data in many other areas of legal scholarship, information about changes of venue is meager. When I searched my university's law library for books exclusively about change of venue, I found none. When I looked under the history of change of venue in English common law, my search was also relatively unproductive.

The notion of venue itself has a long and respected place in common law and refers to the place in which actions should be brought and tried. Bosek, Knickerbocker, and Muskus (2000) observed that the original use of the term *venue* was in the context of the "fact-venue." In this original common-law usage in the 14th century, the jurors were the actual witnesses of the facts in dispute. Individuals served as jurors because they had personal knowledge of the parties involved as well as the facts of the case. As for location, it was typically at the place of the offense, although the trial officially was held wherever the king of England's court chose. Bosek et al. (2000) reported, "An important consequence of the original doctrine of venue was that it restricted jury trials to merely local issues. All actions were local [and] ... the venue of every action being the place where the fact arose" (p. 242). The law eventually changed to allow the action to be tried anywhere in the "action-venue," or where the authorities chose.

In current Western usage, common-law definitions have given way to a definition in which the legal proceedings are held where the act took place, where a court has jurisdiction, or sometimes where the defendant resides (in civil cases). The two requirements are that the location must be both fair and convenient. The issue of fairness brings us directly to questions of pretrial prejudice in the pool of possible jurors.

PRETRIAL BIAS AND THE VENUE

Pretrial publicity is the most common source of presumed bias. The most sensational trial in the early decades of the United States had pretrial bias as a core issue. The case was the trial of Aaron Burr for treason in 1807 (Curtner & Kassier, 2005; Melton, 2001). The allegation was that Burr, the former vice president and attorney general of the United States, planned an insurrection in which he and his followers would take New Orleans, invade Mexico, and form a new empire stretching from the southwestern United States through to Mexico City. Presiding over the trial was John Marshall, the chief justice of the Supreme Court, who sought to combat the extensive pretrial bias by conducting a detailed and fierce voir dire.

President Thomas Jefferson had ordered up to 20,000 militiamen to New Orleans to thwart Burr, and the entire U.S. Navy, weak and fragmented as it was at the time, to go there as well. In early 1807 President Jefferson proclaimed of Burr that his "guilt is placed beyond question" (Melton, 2001, p. 151). Finding an objective jury was difficult, for this was the single most sensational, politicized, and publicized trial of the new nation. In the first day of the voir dire questioning by Justice Marshall, only 4 men were selected out of 48 in the pool. The other 44 men admitted that their opinions had been deeply influenced by the reports in newspapers. Eventually, the trial began, with Marshall ruling that the potential jurors who had been only "lightly impressed" by the newspaper reports could maintain an open mind. The government argued that Burr was the mastermind of a complex and treasonous plot. In turn, the defense argued that no physical acts of levying a war of insurrection had taken place and, therefore, no treason had occurred. Justice Marshall gave a narrow definition of "levying war" that was to be followed by the jurors. The jury then acquitted Burr, a remarkable outcome, given the widespread pretrial knowledge of the case and the marked extent to which Burr was detested by Washington, Adams, Jefferson, and many other influential founding fathers of the nation. The Burr trial outcome indicates that, at least with a careful, conscientious, bright[1] judge presiding, prejudicial impressions can sometimes be overcome.

In jury selection the process of searching for dimensions on which to deselect jurors can be sophisticated, not at all obvious, and sometimes

---

[1]The term *brilliant* is more accurate than *bright* in describing Justice Marshall.

labyrinthine. In contrast to such multifaceted conceptualizations and tasks in jury selection, the search for case conceptualization in change of venue evaluations and consultations is often straightforward. Furthermore, the apparent simplicity of the presenting issues and of the compelling prejudicial factors do not necessarily add unexpected or even useful information beyond what almost everyone active in the case already knows. It is a situation that seems to cry out for a Yogi Berra (1999) aphorism,[2] one of those quips that Petsko (2003) describes, only partly tongue in cheek, as being the thoughts of a quintessential sage. Few of us left-brain types are good at creating paradoxes in the manner of Yogi Berra aphorisms, but I propose this one for change of venue assessments: " When everyone involved already knows that almost every possible juror is biased against the defendant, it is time to go to find out if it is so."

The "everyone involved," in actuality, may initially describe the judge, defendant or plaintiff, many of the attorneys, and other trial team members working in both criminal and civil litigation. In this chapter, we consider the legal and scholarly foundations in change of venue assessments. We look at cases in which attorneys were indeed convinced that almost every person in the area from which the jury pool would be drawn first, was, close-minded about the case and, second, had concluded that the defendant was guilty (or, more rarely, innocent) and should be punished (or acquitted). Finally, we move to the specific issues of seeking data and understanding the implications of trial consultation as consultants address and study the presumed biases. First, we look at why attorneys pursue changes of venue.

WHEN ATTORNEYS ARE UNEQUIVOCALLY CERTAIN OF PRETRIAL BIAS

Two out-of-county attorneys had agreed to represent a defendant in his capital murder trial and had traveled 200 miles to the county in which the accused murderer was jailed and in which the trial presumably would take place. They had spent much time going over the television and newspaper reports of the killings, the repeated stories in the media of the particular violent acts alleged, and the media reports of the eventual arrest and indictment of their client.

The two attorneys were visiting the distant county to file motions and

---

[2]The famous sayings attributed to Berra include "It ain't over 'til it's over," "The future ain't what it used to be," and "It's déjà vu all over again." Petsko (2003) observed wryly that these statements are really about the future of genomics. I think they are really about trials.

were having breakfast in the restaurant of the hotel in which they were staying. The waitress asked what brought them to town. They said they were there for legal work. She then piped up with, "I hope you are not here defending Mr. W, who did those horrible killings. He should be executed!" The attorneys instantly became firmly convinced that the venue was irreparably tainted.

When I met with these two attorneys, they described their fierce indignation at how the entire county had already decided against their client. Even though the killings themselves had taken place 3 years earlier, they sought to convince me that the circumstances and publicity were such that the whole venue was prejudiced. With passion they explained that essentially every adult citizen and every potential juror was biased. When I raised doubts in the form of the time that had passed since the killings and the substantial transient population in the county, they dismissed them. They had a simple request; they wanted empirical data followed by court testimony to support their observations. With their input, I constructed a survey that addressed the case-specific issues. The survey itself was conducted by a professional polling firm that employed telephone interviewers who were blind to the research questions.

The results came back in a direction opposite of what the attorneys had anticipated. About 65% of the 300 respondents had heard something about the crime. Most were uncertain about the guilt of the defendant. A majority of respondents indicated that they were open-minded about the case. Cases like this illustrate the reasons that consultants seek to gather survey data. Personal and subjective impressions are to be distrusted.

SURVEY DATA IN CHANGE
OF VENUE MOTIONS

As far back as the middle of the 20th century, social scientists made attempts (and then sometimes reported them in the literature) to bring survey data into court decisions for changes of venue. Woodward (1952) described the use of a survey conducted by his national polling firm, the Roper Poll, in a case brought by the National Association for the Advancement of Colored People. In July 1949 four African American men had been accused of raping a white woman in Lake County, Florida. One man was shot and killed, one was sentenced to life imprisonment, and, after a Supreme Court decision stating that the jury selection procedures were racially biased, the cases of the two remaining defendants, who had been sentenced to death, were sent back for retrial in a different county. Both men were subsequently shot "attempting to escape" the sheriff (quotes were in the original report), and the one imprisoned survivor, Walter Irvin, was retried in an adjoining county, Marion County. In a remarkable effort, 1,500 face-to-face interviews were conducted by Roper interviewers despite repeated threats from some county officials. Of the whites interviewed in Marion County, 43% were sure Mr. Irvin was guilty, and 20% more thought he was guilty. In contrast, only 1% of the 151 African Americans interviewed were either sure he was guilty or thought he was. The trial judge ruled that the interview data could not be admitted because they were drawn from hearsay evidence and because "no respondent had been put on the stand to testify that his opinions were as actually set forth in his questionnaire blank and to submit to cross-examination" (p. 452). The judge did admit testimony by leading citizens of the county called by the state, all of whom testified that a fair trial could be held in the county. The trial was held there and Mr. Irvin was convicted. In a related but more encouraging early journal article, Geiser and Newman (1961) reported that public opinion polls have a useful place in assessing pretrial prejudice, observing that polling "provides the courts an opportunity to base a necessary assessment of public sentiment on a scientific, rather than a speculative foundation" (p. 656).

In their chapter on surveys and change of venue, Nietzel and Dillehay (1986) addressed how public opinion surveys are used in trial consultation and what role they have in motions for changes of venue. Nietzel and Dillehay observed:

> Venue surveys are especially potent tools for the trial consultant for two reasons. First, they provide data that permit informed jury selection and litigation strategies sufficiently in advance of trial. Second, although it is not frequently granted, a change of venue is the most effective technique available for improving the chances of selecting a favorable jury in a case with excessive publicity. (p. 63)

In the case of the two attorneys influenced by the waitress's comments, the attorneys did not have survey support for a change of venue motion; indeed, they did not file their motion. However, they did have information about the demographic characteristics of citizens who had already made up their minds about the guilt of the defendant. That is, they could look at the age, gender, race, education, and income of the citizens who, before the trial began, were open-minded, closed-minded, and uncertain about guilt.

Pretrial publicity also has the potential for working toward predispositions of innocence as well as guilt. In a small-sample study, Green and Loftus (1984) looked at the effects of reading an article in *Reader's Digest* about a well-publicized case of a man who had been accused of a series of horrendous crimes in which there was clear eyewitness testimony identifying him. The article reported that the real offender was identified later and confessed. The study participants were individuals waiting at the Seattle-Tacoma airport who agreed to read a transcript of a different case. Of the *Reader's Digest* regular readers who remembered the article, 15.4% gave a guilty verdict to the different case, whereas 39.1% of those who did not recall the article rendered a guilty verdict, a significant difference.

LEGAL FOUNDATIONS

The Supreme Court has addressed the question of venues that would be so biased that the bias cannot be remedied. Consider the case of Leslie Irvin, who had been charged with and convicted of murders and sentenced to death in Vanderburgh County, Indiana. The trial followed considerable publicity about six murders committed in December 1954 and March 1955 in the same area and the media coverage of Irvin's confession to the murder for which he was tried, as well as his confession to many other crimes. The defense motion for a change of venue was granted, but the trial was moved only to Gibson County, adjacent to Vanderburgh County, and Gibson County had been exposed to the same pretrial publicity. The Supreme Court held:

> Here the build-up of prejudice is clear and convincing. An examination of the then current community pattern of thought as indicated by the popular news media is singularly revealing. For example, petitioner's first motion for a change of venue from Gibson County alleged that the awaited trial of petitioner had become the cause célèbre of this small community—so much so that curbstone opinions, not only as to petitioner's guilt but even as to what punishment he should receive, were solicited and recorded on the public streets by a roving reporter, and later were broadcast over the local stations.... A barrage of newspaper headlines, articles, cartoons and pictures was unleashed against him during the six or seven months preceding his trial. (*Irvin v. Dowd*, 1961, p. 366)

Trial courts typically ask whether potential jurors can set aside their knowledge, biases, and opinions and decide on the basis of the instructions given to them by the trial judge. It is contrary to most understandings of cognitive processes to believe that jurors can set aside strongly formed and held opinions of guilt (Frame, 2001). However, there are empirical reasons to believe that judges' instructions about disregarding content and biases can somewhat shift opinions of venirepersons in nonbiased directions (Crocker & Kovera, 2008; Platania, Small, Fusco, Miller, & Perrault,

2008). It is a different story with powerful pretrial publicity. Consider the facts and opinion[3] written by Justice Thurgood Marshall in *Swindler v. Lockhart* (1990) as the Court denied certiorari.

> During voir dire, a majority of the 120 venirepersons indicated that they were aware that petitioner had previously been found guilty of the crime and that he was wanted in another State for allegedly murdering two teenagers. More importantly, an overwhelming majority of the venire—98 out of 120—either tentatively or firmly believed that petitioner was guilty. The strong local feelings regarding petitioner's guilt are reflected in the comments of venireperson Thomas Bricksey:
>
> Q. Have you discussed this case with anybody?
>
> A. Oh, yes, sir.
>
> Q. All right, and have these people expressed an opinion to you about this case?
>
> A. Yes, sir.
>
> Q. Could you tell me what those opinions were? Did they think the defendant was guilty?
>
> A. I am afraid it was almost unanimous.
>
> Q. Did you ever hear anybody state that they thought he was not guilty?
>
> A. No sir.

> Similar prejudicial attitudes surfaced in the voir dire of three other jurors whom petitioner challenged for cause but who, unlike Bricksey, ultimately served on the petitioner's jury. Each indicated that he believed petitioner was guilty as a result of exposure to pretrial publicity regarding petitioner's first trial.... Milton Staggs, another juror challenged by petitioner, when asked whether he had an opinion about the first verdict, stated, "Well, sure, based on what came out, I don't know how it could be otherwise, you know." ... The trial court, finding that each of the three challenged jurors was capable of setting aside his opinion regarding petitioner's guilt, denied petitioner's request that they be struck for cause. (p. 495)

So when should a change of venue be ordered? The standards derived from Supreme Court decisions and the American Bar Association (ABA) standards are similar. Both require that a reasonable likelihood of prejudice be present, sufficiently that a question is raised about the substantial possibility of an unfair trial. ABA Criminal Justice Standard 15-1.4b reads (in full):

---

[3]This was a dissenting opinion, but the case content is illustrative of strong pretrial attitudes.

A motion for change of venue or continuance should be granted whenever there is a substantial likelihood that, in the absence of such relief, a fair trial by an impartial jury cannot be had. A showing of actual prejudice should not be required. (ABA *Criminal Justice Section Standards*, 2007)

CONDUCTING A SURVEY ABOUT BIAS AND CHANGE OF VENUE

Nietzel and Dillehay (1986) organized a systematic and thoughtful guide for conducting surveys for change of venues. They proposed the following steps (pp. 70–79); I have modified the description of their procedures to fit with the developments and resources available since their guide was published more than 20 years ago, as well to reflect my own perspectives. More detail about the specific questions posed in change of venue surveys themselves is presented in the next chapter.

1. *Set aside a good deal of lead time before beginning the telephone survey.* Nietzel and Dillehay suggest that 2 months should be a minimum lead time. However, no particular time period is mandatory. The principle is to ensure that the key issues for the surveys can be identified, that planning can take place, and that one does not have to rush into what should be a considered, deliberate process.

2. *Identify key phrases used by the media as part of the preliminary analysis.* These phrases are usually repeated (e.g., "the hatchet killings," "the bathtub drownings") in the media descriptions of the charges or the crime, or of the defendant or the plaintiff. The media labels of case-specific issues by themselves may be prejudicial, especially when complex evidence is boiled down to a simple label or phrase.

3. *Work on the theory of the case with the attorneys who have retained you.* At least one extended conference is needed to make the theory of the case clear, explicit, and operational. More meetings are better. It can be useful to state aloud or write on a board the interim conceptualizations as the consultants and attorneys work together toward refining the theory of the case.

4. *Arrange for a survey.* Nietzel and Dillehay (1986) suggest recruiting and training the personnel to do the interviews. In contrast, I routinely use a professional polling firm with access to trained and experienced interviewers who are not informed about the purpose of the research questions.

5. *Design the instrument.* The survey always starts with a foot-in-the door introduction that engages the respondent. The question I use is "What do you think is the most pressing problem facing (identified) County?"

6. *Use standard questions about jurors' eligibility and attitudes toward law enforcement, crime, and punishment.* The eligibility questions simply inquire about age, citizenship, and other local criteria for serving on juries. If a person is not jury-eligible, he or she is thanked and the call is terminated. For example, Nietzel and Dillehay (1986, p. 71) approach attitudes by asking questions like this one: "How successful in fighting crime do you think each of the following actually is? Having harsh (long) sentences for convicted criminals. Would you say this is: Not at all successful? Somewhat successful? Very successful?"

7. *Develop special questions tailored to the case at hand.* Such questions ask in particular about whether members of the community have read, heard, or know anything about the facts and allegations of the case, as well as the name and character of the defendant and of the victim.

8. *Ask about knowledge of and attitudes about the defendant.* Nietzel and Dillehay (1986) give this example: "In your own mind at this time, do you think that Rowdy Dan Lawless, a man arrested in the Convenient Mart case, is probably guilty or not guilty of murdering Frank Burns?" (p. 72).

9. *Finally, ask questions about the pretrial publicity.* Such inquiries ask respondents about how much and what they have read, heard, discussed, or thought about the offense or charges. This step applies the content derived from step 7.

SETTING ASIDE BIASES
AND THE SET-ASIDE QUESTION

With predictable regularity, judges ask a cluster of questions of potential jurors who have reported pretrial knowledge, attitudes, or well-formulated opinions about a case. Friedman (1992) discusses what obligations judges have to question during the voir dire, drawing in part on the *Mu'Min v. Virginia* (1991) decision, in which the Supreme Court ruled that it was not required that "voir dire establish that jurors be totally ignorant of the facts and issues involved in a case, but only that the jurors be without fixed opinions of guilt or innocence that would preclude them from judging the facts impartially" (p. 920). In his law review article titled "Ma, Ma, Where's My Pa? On Your Jury, Ha, Ha, Ha!: A Constitutional Analysis of Implied Bias Challenges for Cause," Barnette (2007) not only argued that family members should be excluded from serving on juries when their relatives are part of a class filing the legal action, but more germane to our discussion, he addressed the truly broad discretion judges have in conducting and controlling the voir dire and ruling on challenges for cause. A judge inquires of the jurors as to whether they will be able to be objective, to set any personal opinions aside (the set-aside question), and to decide the case following the instructions given to them in court and based on the evidence they will hear. It is difficult for any juror to say no to this inquiry, first, because of the social undesirability of admitting bias to any significant extent and, second, because of the inability to decline a task requested by a major authority figure like a judge (Babcock, 1975; Spears, 1975). However, in cases in which there is an alleged offense that has a high base rate of victimization in the population, some jurors say they cannot set aside their biases. With child abuse or molestation, for example, there is a high incidence, perhaps in every community. Jurors sometimes come forth and offer an explanation that they cannot be objective and presume innocence. When the same question is asked of the jurors in a large group, whether by attorneys or judges, individuals who are aware of this bias are less likely to raise their hands, stand up and stand out, than when they have the opportunity to present their concerns in private and individual conferences with the judge and the attorneys. Babcock (1975) has addressed the ways in which jurors actively avoid admitting any socially unacceptable attitude because of personal discomfort or embarrassment.

The conformity reaction to the set-aside question is often what judges expect and, indeed, may depend on. Nietzel and Dillehay (1986) assert that "the demand characteristics for an affirmative answer to this question, particularly when asked by a judge in open court, are so strong that its utility as a screener of bias is dubious" (p. 73). However, once one or two potential jurors do stand or speak up and report their difficulty in setting aside biases, others often follow.

BOGUS QUESTIONS

A persistent question is, How valid are these surveys? For example, can change of venue surveys be invalidated by people falsely responding that they have been exposed to media items to which they have not? A study by Moran and Cutler (1997) sought to answer this question with data from two change of venue surveys with bogus items included. These bogus items were stories or facts that never appeared in the media. Thus, in a highly publicized case involving the shooting death of a young Miami police officer after a high-speed chase, Moran and Cutler included this bogus item in their telephone survey of 100 jury-eligible persons: "Do you remember seeing, hearing, or reading about police officers suspended from their jobs, without pay, for failing to respond to domestic dispute calls?" (p. 343). This item never appeared in the media, yet 23% of the sample reported that they had seen or heard of it.

The concept was that if bogus items are included in the survey and people correctly say "no" to having seen the false items and "yes" to having seen the actual items, the strength of the motion for change of venue is increased; respondents have accurately remembered what the media reported. However, if many people respond "yes" to both the actual items *and* bogus items, it should bring into question whether the people were exposed to the actual media items. Moran and Cutler (1997) studied whether the correlation between awareness of pretrial publicity and prejudgment of guilt would be different between people who indicated having read about the bogus items and those who did not. It was not. When people who reported seeing a bogus item were deleted from the samples, the relation between exposure to pretrial publicity and presumption of guilt remained unchanged. The implication is that an indiscriminating tendency to report awareness of fictional media events does not threaten the validity of change of venue surveys.

CASE CONCEPTUALIZATION

The conceptualizations for change of venue assessments in criminal cases can be almost self-evident, even if the methodology is not. Consider a typical criminal scenario: A citizen has been killed and the nature of the killing and the identity of the accused have been extensively publicized. The information and descriptions of the killing, the victim, and the accused have been present in the media repeatedly. The case results in enough notoriety prior to trial that citizens have repeatedly talked about the event and about what it means for the victim's family and for the community. When 32 faculty members and students at Virginia Tech were shot and killed by a student, it dominated coverage in the newspapers, at television stations, and on news websites. People throughout the country spent much energy talking about the horror of the incident and interpreting what it meant. In the Virginia counties of Blacksburg and Montgomery one can reasonably assume that the impact was much greater. If the man who did the shooting had survived, change of venue questions surely would have been raised concerning whether somebody in a situation like this should be tried in another jurisdiction.

The charging and subsequent trial of Timothy McVeigh for the bombing of the federal courthouse in Oklahoma City presents a parallel case, in the sense of the offense being of national significance and the subject of widespread publicity. Studebaker, Robbennolt, Pathak-Sharma, and Penrod (2000) described their analysis of pretrial publicity in the Oklahoma City bombing, as it came to be known. Starting from the empirically supported assumption that the impact of pretrial publicity is directly related to the amount of pretrial publicity, Studebaker et al. quantified the extent of the publicity of the Oklahoma City bombing case. The number of articles, total number of paragraphs, and amount of text and space, as well as length of the headlines and sizes of the fonts, were coded for the *Daily Oklahoman*, the *Lawton Constitution*, the *Tulsa World*, and a non-Oklahoma newspaper, the *Denver Post*. Between April 20, 1995, and January 8, 1996, the *Daily Oklahoman* (the Oklahoma City newspaper) published 939 articles about the bombing or the case, the *Lawton Constitution* published 251 articles, the *Tulsa World* 235 articles, and the *Denver Post* 174 articles (p. 327). Significant differences were found between the newspapers on most measures. Large and significant differences were reported in the negative characterizations of the defendants and the amount of emotional publicity. The researchers reported:

> The *Daily Oklahoman* contained more statements concerning emotional suffering, more statements describing the goriness of the bombing scene, more statements about the economic impact of the bombing on the Oklahoma community, more statements conveying themes of helping and togetherness in Oklahoma City, and more statements concerning connections between the bombing and the local community served by the newspaper. (p. 329)

Also presented in the change of venue hearing for this case were the results of public opinion surveys by political scientist Kent Tedin (as cited in Studebaker et al., 2000). He surveyed 400 citizens in four cities. Describing the results for three of the cities, Tedin reported that 54% of the Lawton respondents were absolutely confident of McVeigh's guilt, 47% in Tulsa were absolutely confident of his guilt, and 18% in Denver were absolutely confident of his guilt. In Steven Penrod's testimony in the change of venue hearing, he drew on other experimental studies and testified to the close link between publicity and attitudes toward McVeigh. The judge changed the venue for the trials of McVeigh and Terry Nichols to Denver, holding that a fair trial could not be held in Oklahoma.

Let us shift our attention to the general issue and assume a pending criminal trial of any defendant charged with much publicized heinous crimes. If a motion is made for a change of venue, there are perhaps four questions that the defense should be prepared to answer:

1. *Knowledge.* How much about the crime does the jury-eligible community know?
2. *Decisions.* To what extent have the citizens likely to be called for

jury duty already made up their minds about the guilt of the defendant?

3. *Certainty*. What degree of confidence do they have about their conclusions?

4. *Commitment*. How open or nonreceptive are they to additional information, instructions, or evidence possibly changing their minds?

CIVIL ACTIONS WITH MULTIPLE ISSUES

Sometimes considerable work is needed to sort out competing aspects or sources of possible pretrial bias. Consider a class action suit filed by former employees against a large factory that employed a substantial percentage of the adult workforce of a rural county. The suit alleged that toxic fumes, a byproduct of the operations in the factory, had harmed the health of many employees, some of whom had been unable to continue to work. The harm to their health took the form of common cancers and lung diseases, which are also found in lower percentages in the public at large. The attorney for the defense was worried that the friends and acquaintances of the ailing and deceased workers, as well as other people who knew of the allegations, would want to punish the owners of the factory severely, regardless of the evidence presented in the case. This county where the factory was located had fewer than 15,000 residents, and the illnesses and charges against the factory owners were a regular topic of discussion. As a result, the attorneys for the defense were considering a change of venue motion so that the word-of-mouth reports and beliefs about the poisonous effects of the factory would not bias the jury.

At the same time, this county had suffered losses of its long-time major industries, which included textile factories and lumber mills. The county had only one major employer, the defendant. The attorneys for the plaintiffs were concerned that jurors drawn from the county rolls would be motivated by a desire to please and keep this one last major industry, on which the economic well-being of the county was partially dependent. As a result, the plaintiffs' attorneys also considered filing a motion for a change of venue to get a jury less financially invested in the stability of the large company. This case illustrates how both sides in a civil case may have different but possibly valid concerns about a biased venire.

One more example may indicate how local issues may idiosyncratically affect the presumption of an unbiased venire. In this instance a civil suit was filed by a number of homeowners against a landfill that smelled foul. When the wind blew from the landfill toward the nice homes of the plaintiffs, the homeowners complained that the quality of their lives was compromised.[4] Their clothes and hair stank, they asserted. They were often nauseous. They could not comfortably sit outside, nor could their children play outside during the times when the wind shifted so that they were downwind from the landfill. The attorneys for the landfill owners sought consultation about possible pretrial bias.

Two possible reasons for widespread bias came out. First, the landfill was located adjacent to one of the main roads that traversed the county. Even though the homeowner-plaintiffs were few in number, a large but unknown proportion of county residents regularly drove past the landfill site. When the road was downwind from the landfill, not in the direction of the prevailing wind, drivers received a brief but pungent nose-full.

The second complicating factor was that one of the homeowner-plaintiffs was an active, visible member of the community and county; he was admired for his civic contributions and leadership roles. He was beloved. The possible pretrial bias was not media related, but instead due to widespread awareness and familiarity in a small community. The attorneys for the landfill owners feared that citizens would ally themselves with this person and with his position in the lawsuit. At the same time, the defense attorneys were not certain how many county drivers were personally offended by the landfill smells. Those of us who have lived in cities with nearby paper mills are aware of the diversity of sensitivity or insensitivity to the sulphur dioxide emissions that smell like rotten eggs. Furthermore, the attorney was not positive that the community leader who was central to the case was actually known to the new people in the county, inasmuch as there had been some transients in the population and some immigration. This example illustrates that there may be uniquely local factors in a community that arise from many close interactions, as well as the extent to which many people in a potential venire may have stakes or investment in a particular trial outcome.

CONCLUSION

Change of venue motions are common, but court orders for changes of venue are much less frequent. The scholarly literature on assessing charges of pretrial prejudice has grown, in the form of better methodologies of community surveys as well as structured analyses of reports in the media. Good

---

[4]I did ask why the landfill could not be quickly and fully cleaned up. The attorneys described a complex problem because of the technical difficulties involved and the differing views of multiple and absent owners.

community surveys require lead time and a careful and systematic approach. Analyses of media reports need to specify just what elements make up the different types of pretrial publicity. The identification of certain apparently straightforward causes of pretrial prejudice can be easy, and sometimes accurate. At the same time, many complex local and idiosyncratic factors also affect the ways in which community members and potential jurors may be influenced.

Chapter 12

SURVEYS OF
PRETRIAL BIAS

A Case Report

In the preceding chapter we examined the principles and methods that apply to the assessment of pretrial bias used in change of venue evaluations and in preparing to select jurors. We now put together principles and methods with a detailed case application. This chapter describes what happened when attorneys and a trial consultant were confronted with broad and continuing media coverage of a killing and the associated possibility of extensive pretrial prejudice in the jurisdiction. The background is presented, followed by how the issues were understood, and then the nature and results of community surveys. In earlier chapters, I have not reported the legal outcomes of trial consultations in which I have been retained. Because it serves the purpose of exploring how change of venue surveys are received, this chapter does report an outcome, with a discussion of how a judge decided the issue. With this introduction now in place, we move to the case report.

In early January 2004, two police officers in Athens, Alabama, responded to a call from 36-year-old Farron Barksdale, who asked first for an FBI agent and then for a police officer to come to his house. When two police officers arrived in their patrol car in response to the call, Barksdale was inside his house. While they were in the patrol car, Barksdale shot the first officer seven times and shot the second officer twice, killing them both. Then Barksdale lay down in the middle of the street, waiting to be run over by traffic. Two witnesses to the shooting held him until other police arrived.

Barksdale had a history of serious psychological disorders. He had

156

been involuntarily committed to psychiatric hospitals five times, and at each admission he had been diagnosed with paranoid schizophrenia. Among other symptoms, he thought that the government, police, and gangsters were directing microwaves at his brain. He had torn the television cable line out of his mother's home because of his belief that the television was being used to tap into his brain. He reported hearing voices directing him to harm others and himself. His disorganized and paranoid personal writings were included as part of an earlier petition filed by his mother to have him committed. Barksdale wrote, "The metal connected to the nervs [*sic*] in my teeth that makes people shoot rays in my brain … like a childs [*sic*] toy or a bunch of doctors secret pot-o-gold" (Fleischauer, 2004).

The two police officers who were killed were exemplary and well-known citizens in Limestone County, in which approximately 70,000 people reside. The funeral for the slain officers was attended by thousands of citizens and police, including police officers from four states. Newspaper and other media coverage was extensive and continued for some time. The attorneys for Mr. Barksdale questioned whether he could get a fair trial in this county because of the extensive publicity, the intense emotional reactions to the killings, and how beloved the victims were by so many people. Armed with many newspaper clippings, they sought out an independent evaluation of the pretrial bias toward Mr. Barksdale.

THE RATIONALE

In one of the earliest articles about the use of opinion polls as evidence in change of venue hearings, Geiser and Newman (1961) observed that the courts were generally reluctant to accept survey results as evidence. However, they also noted that, even at that time, one court had used survey outcomes in a change of venue hearing and that one other source reported court acceptance of a survey for change of venue. They further made the case for scholarly objectivity and careful, unbiased sampling. As an example of a biased sampling in civil litigation, Geiser and Newman described a silverware trademark case in which the issue at dispute was possible confusion between silverware patterns. A survey had been commissioned by the Oneida Company, the plaintiff, using participants in a large city near the location where the plaintiff's silverware was manufactured and where the plaintiff's silverware had high sales. In contrast, the defendant (National Silver Company) commissioned a similar survey questionnaire in a different state where other silverware brands were more established. The judge decided that neither survey had sufficient evidentiary value. It is encouraging to see that the Geiser and Newman (1961) recommendations for psychologists doing polling have been largely addressed: "They should be aware of the special considerations involved when a survey is prepared for use in litigation. Utmost attention must be given not only to the scientific planning and execution of the survey, but also to its legal relevance" (p. 690). Although the Geiser and Newman article concerned specific instances of surveys in civil actions, the same methodological considerations are present when surveys are prepared and conducted for pending criminal trials. The content of the survey needs to be designed to attend to the essential legal issues, the methodology should be designed with care and objectivity, and the implementation and reporting should be studiously even-handed.

Now we move to the survey about pretrial trial knowledge and possible bias in the Farron Barksdale case.

DESIGN OF THE SURVEY

This chapter describes the working conceptualization, the method, and the results of two telephone surveys of jury-eligible citizens of Limestone County for a change of venue in the Farron Barksdale case. The first survey was conducted in April 2004, and the second survey in August 2005. In each survey 300 residents were contacted via the method of random digit dialing, in which random numbers are used to call telephone numbers, using the prefixes found in the county. Only landlines were called because of legal restrictions against calling parties on cell phones when such a person might have to pay a fee for receiving a survey telephone call.

After examining newspaper clippings and meeting with the defense attorneys, we identified the key issues involved in possible pretrial bias and then designed a survey to address (1) the concepts and issues related to pretrial knowledge, (2) pretrial bias, (3) knowledge and opinions about the offense for which Mr. Barksdale was charged, and (4) reactions to the anticipated *not guilty by reason of insanity* defense. The design of the survey followed a model commonly used in assessing pretrial prejudice in other civil and criminal trials. We contracted with a professional polling firm to conduct the telephone interviews. The actual interviewers were blind with respect to who had developed the questionnaire and to the identity and objectives of the attorneys who had retained us.

The "last birthday" method was used to determine which adult in the called household would be interviewed. Households often have a designated "answerer" of phone calls. This method requests that the adult who had the last (most recent) birthday come to the phone, so ensuring a more random sample than possible by simply interviewing the designated answerer. The survey sought to identify individuals who were jury-eligible. Thus, persons were excluded if they were not currently registered to vote in the county and did not have an in-state driver's license.

In order to engage the respondent, we began with a foot-in-the-door question[1]: "Now, what do you think is the most important issue facing Limestone County at the present time?"

This question allowed the person to answer about a topic of common concern and sought to start the individual off on a pattern of replying.

RESPONSE RATES

As with all such telephone surveys, a large number of calls resulted in no answers, voice mail or answering machines, calls not completed, screened calls, or busy signals. The percentages of calls that were answered and in which the individuals agreed to answer the survey questions were approximately 20% and 24%, respectively. The completion rates in terms of persons who agreed initially to participate in the two surveys, along with other data, are listed here.

	April, 2004	August, 2005
1. Completed surveys	300	300
2. Break-offs during interview	54	55
3. Break-offs as percent of total	15.3% (54/354)	15.5% (55/355)
4. Completions as percent of total	84.7%	84.5%
5. Up-front refusals	1,182	877
6. Up-front refusals and break-offs	1,236	932
7. Completed surveys (row 1) as percent of total (rows 1 and 4)	19.5% (300/1,536)	24.4% (300/1,232)

The up-front refusal rate reflects the large numbers of people who do not respond to any surveys, who personally screen answered calls in the first few seconds after answering, and who interpret calls from unknown persons as telemarketing efforts or other unwelcome intrusions.[2] Indeed, research has shown that the number of unsolicited telephone calls people receive is

---

[1]The foot-in-the-door technique is a gradual-persuasion technique in which a modest initial request is followed by a more substantive request (Dillard, Hunter, & Burgoon, 1984; Rodafinos, Vucevic, & Sideridis, 2005). In this context, the foot-in-the-door technique refers to the tendency of people who answer a first question to continue to answer questions.

[2]I can offer my own personal experiences as the designated answerer of telephone calls in our home. I receive at least one survey call a week on our landline. I turn down most requests. Openly disclosing callers who inquire about topics of interest to me sometimes get my participation.

on the rise, and that people are turning to increasingly sophisticated technology to screen their calls (Keeter, Kennedy, Dimock, Best, & Craighill, 2006). The more revealing percentage of individuals in the preceding list is the approximately 15% who started to respond and then declined to continue, when they decided *after* starting the survey that they no longer wanted to continue answering the questions.

The fundamental issue is whether such survey results are representative of the public and provide accurate data. In the face of call screening, caller ID, and call blocking, the ability of survey data to accurately represent the populace's attitudes becomes more important. Even official government agencies with the perceived and actual powers to impose various and severe penalties on nonresponders have difficulty getting a high response rate.

Consider a letter mailed by the Alabama Department of Revenue to a randomly selected sample of 5% of the state's licensed automobile drivers, asking for verification of whether they had the mandatory auto insurance coverage. Between October 2006 and August 2007, more than 140,000 questionnaires were mailed and more than 74,000 drivers (or 52%) did not respond or had no insurance (Associated Press, 2007). The penalty for nonresponse was suspension of their vehicles' registrations. The study did not distinguish between uninsured motorists and nonresponders, but the base rate of uninsured motorists in the state had been about 25% for many years. The inference is that more than one-fourth of recipients of the mailed survey were insured but, by not responding, had their registrations suspended. Given the severity of the consequences, this rate of nonresponding points to the substantial number of people who will not participate in surveys, no matter what the incentive or penalty.

A question that should be addressed is how to interpret survey data when there are many nonresponders, when, indeed, it is always true that there are many nonresponders. Useful data on the issue of how representative responses are were reported in an April 2004 study by the Pew Research Center for the People and the Press and associates (Keeter, Best, Dimock, & Craighill, 2004; see also Keeter et al., 2006). The Pew Center compared people who were reached easily, who had response rates well below 30%, with respondents from a more rigorous (difficult to reach) sample, and with "hardest to reach" individuals. The hardest to reach participants had refused the interview at least twice before complying and required 21 or more calls to complete the survey; they yielded an overall response rate of 51%. There were few differences between the groups. The Pew Center report put it this way:

> Participants in the standard and rigorous samples were similar in their attitudes and values. There were virtually no differences in opinion toward

government, the poor, business, homosexuality and other issues. More-over, respondents in the standard and rigorous samples, and the hardest to reach people, differed very little in attitudes about evangelical Christians, about immigrants, about the root causes of poverty among blacks, or about the role of Islam in encouraging violence.

The implication of the Pew Center report, along with similar studies, is that somewhat low response rates can yield interpretable measures of attitudes. Individuals who are not readily available for polling do not seem to differ markedly from standard respondents. In other words, it was not unreasonable to extrapolate the present survey results to a broader group of jury-eligible citizens of Limestone County. The reliability of the data was also supported by the similar findings from two separate surveys conducted 16 months apart.

SAMPLE CHARACTERISTICS

The Limestone County respondents were mostly white (88%) and more than 60% were women. The median number of years the respondents had lived in the county was 25 years and 34 years, respectively, in the April 2004 and August 2005 groups. The median age was 46 and 51 years old in the two samples. The racial characteristics were generally similar to those in the results of the 2000 census reports, in which 84% of the county was white. The census median age in the county was 36, but our survey, as expected, tapped into an older group, because we excluded individuals younger than 19 years old. No census data were available for length of time of residence in the county.

FINDINGS

Knowledge

The first three survey questions asked about knowledge of the offense to examine how widespread and how lasting were the pretrial knowledge and publicity. The results indicated that almost everybody in both survey samples knew about the offense. These rates of more than 98% with knowledge are unusually high. Here are the response percentages:

"Do you remember reading or hearing anything about the killing of two police officers in Athens in [early][3] January of [this] last year?"

---

[3]Brackets indicate differences in phrasing of the items in the two surveys.

	April 2004	August 2005
Yes	100%	99%
No	0	1
Don't know, NA	0	0

"The two police officers were killed when they went to a house to arrest a man. The man inside the house has been charged with their murders. Do you remember reading or hearing anything about this incident?"

	April 2004	August 2005
Yes	99%	98%
No	1	2
Don't know/NA	0	0

"The two police officers were [named]. Do you remember reading or hearing anything about these officers being shot and killed?"

	April 2004	August 2005
Yes	98%	98%
No	2	2
Don't know/NA	0	0

Comment

Affirmative response rates for these three items were close to unanimous. It is rare to have any crime or charges be known by all but 1 or 2% of any sample, given that there is some normal immigration into a venue and that some people neither read newspapers nor follow the news on television or the Internet. These results represented an extraordinarily high level of knowledge of the offense and the victims. At this point, one may infer that the shooting and publicity were salient in the minds of almost all jury-eligible citizens.

Name of Defendant

As part of the inquiry into pretrial publicity, the respondents were asked if they knew the name of the defendant. More than one-third of respondents indicated that they did. When a follow-up question was asked, many did not immediately recall his name. The results to the following two questions indicate these response percentages.

"Do you know the name of the man who has been charged with the murder?"

	April 2004	August 2005
Yes	45%	36%
No	51	55
Don't know/NA/Not familiar with case	4	8

(If they said they knew the name of the accused, they were asked), "What is his name?"

Farron Barksdale	38%	32%
Other	2	2
Don't know name	55	64
Don't know/NA/Not familiar with case	5	2

Guilt versus Presumption of Innocence

The next two questions inquired about the respondents' beliefs about whether the defendant was guilty. In response to the first inquiry, presented in the next table, 72% and 70% reported that they thought Mr. Barksdale was definitely guilty, and 10% and 12% indicated that he was probably guilty.

The participants were also given an opportunity to indicate whether they thought he was not guilty. There were three points along the scale of indicators of Mr. Barksdale's being not guilty: (1) possibly not guilty, (2) probably not guilty, and (3) definitely not guilty. Added together, the three indicators yielded total responses rates of 2% and 1% not guilty in the two samples. Another 12% and 13% did not give an answer. In a follow-up question, respondents were asked how much evidence there was that Mr. Barksdale was guilty of murder; 83% (survey 1) and 79% (survey 2) replied "a great deal" of evidence. Here are the specific questions asked.

"The name of the person charged with killing officers [named] is Farron Barksdale. Based upon what you know about the Athens police killing case, do you think that Farron Barksdale is definitely guilty, probably guilty, possibly guilty, possibly not guilty, probably not guilty, or definitely not guilty?"

	April 2004	August 2005
Definitely guilty	72%	70%
Probably guilty	10	12
Possibly guilty	3	3

Possibly not guilty	1	0
Probably not guilty	1	1
Definitely not guilty	0	0
Don't know/NA/Not familiar with case	12	13

"Based upon what you know about the Athens police killing case, how much evidence do you think there is that Farron Barksdale is guilty of murder—a great deal, some, not much, or none at all?"

	April 2004	August 2005
Great deal	83%	79%
Some	8	6
Not much	1	0
None at all	0	1
Don't know/NA/Not familiar with case	8	14

Exposure to Media

The next three questions inquired about exposure to media reports of the incident. When asked how many newspaper articles they had read about the killings, 8% of the respondents in both surveys indicated that they had read no articles. Even fewer people had not seen television stories about the killings. Newspaper and television and radio stories were reported to be approximately equally influential.

"About how many newspaper articles would you estimate you have read about the killing of the police officers in Athens?"

	April 2004	August 2005
None	8%	8%
One	11	8
Two	11	6
Three	10	10
Four	8	6
Five	6	7
Six	5	4
Seven	2	2
Eight	4	1

(continued)

Nine–ten	9	8
Eleven or more	15	19
Don't know/NA/Not familiar with case	11	21

"About how many television news stories would you estimate you have seen about the killing of the police officers in Athens?"

	April 2004	August 2005
None	6%	5%
One	3	3
Two	10	7
Three	9	8
Four	10	6
Five	9	8
Six	6	6
Seven	2	1
Eight	2	2
Nine–ten	12	14
Eleven–fifteen	10	11
Sixteen or more	9	11
Don't know/NA/Not familiar with case	10	17

"Which of the following has had the greatest influence on your opinions about the Athens police officers killing case—what you have read in the newspaper, what you have seen or heard on TV or radio, the conversation you have had with others, or your own personal decision?"

	April 2004	August 2005
Newspaper	23%	24%
TV or radio	28	29
Conversation with others	14	13
Personal decision	31	28
Don't know/NA/Not familiar with case	4	6

Mental Illness of the Defendant

The final three questions inquired about memory of reports of the defendant's mental illness and judgments about guilt relating to the mental illness of the defendant. A high rate of affirmative responses was received for respondents who had read or heard about Mr. Barksdale's having a mental illness. The rates were 95% and 90% in the two surveys.

"Do you remember reading or hearing anything about Farron Barksdale having a mental illness?"

	April 2004	August 2005
Yes	95%	90%
No	5	8
Don't know/NA/Not familiar with case	0	2

"Suppose Farron Barksdale is shown to have a major mental problem. As a result, do you think he should definitely be found not guilty by reason of insanity, probably found not guilty by reason of insanity, probably found guilty, or definitely found guilty?

	April 2004	August 2005
Definitely not guilty by reason of insanity	6%	6%
Probably not guilty by reason of insanity	9	9
Probably guilty	22	15
Definitely guilty	49	49
Don't know/NA/Not familiar with case	14	21

"No matter what else you might hear about his mental illness at the time of the shootings, do you think Farron Barksdale should be criminally punished by the judge and jury?"

	April 2004	August 2005
Yes	82%	76%
No	7	8
Don't know/NA/Not familiar with case	11	17

When a motion for a change of venue was heard before the judge, the district attorney argued against it in these terms:

Limestone County District Attorney [named] opposes the change of venue, and has tried a capital murder case outside the county before. "It's very

difficult when you have to try to move your office," she said. "It's difficult on the witnesses; it's difficult on the jail. More importantly the crime
occurred here. The trial should be here. (in Stancil, 2005)

The judge denied the motion for a change of venue.

CONCLUSION

Some elements in the hearing in the Farron Barksdale case are noteworthy.
First, I did not testify in court. Because of scheduling problems around the
fixed date of the hearing, I was not free to testify. Instead, my report was
submitted to the court as part of the motion for the change of venue. Would
it have made a difference if I had testified? It is difficult to know the answer
to that question. Judges have great leeway in making a change of venue
decision. As a general rule, evidence offered in testimony rather than in
affidavits has the potential for greater impact, but it is unknown whether it
would have made a difference here.

Second, the knowledge of the citizens and their judgments about the
case were unusually clear. People in the venue had strong opinions that Farron Barksdale was the killer, was guilty, and should be severely punished,
regardless of his mental state. The extent of pretrial knowledge and publicity was probably comparable to that of the most notorious and serious
crimes of local scope.

Third, two surveys were conducted 16 months apart. The high con-
gruence of findings indicates that the results were reliable. Most often, we
examine the reliability within individual scales to see how well the items
hang together. These surveys indicate that the results came together consistently over time.

The final consideration is the attitude and emotional approach of the
attorneys and the trial consultant. In this case, the attorneys were intensely
professionally invested in getting the best possible disposition for Mr. Barksdale. In contrast, I understood that my role was a relatively small one. When
the court made its ruling against changing the site of the trial, my own reaction was that I understood that it was the court's business and prerogative.
Trial consultants do what they can and share what they can, as was true in
this context. As with all such situations, I did not interpret the results as a
reflection of my competence. Part of approaching such assessments objectively is to accept the court's decision objectively as well.

Part V

PUTTING IT TOGETHER

The concluding part integrates the content from the earlier chapters. It begins with Chapter 13, a case study of trial consultation in a capital murder case, one of considerably less visibility than the case described in Chapter 12. The allegations as described involve a young man charged with murder. The meetings and discussions with the defendant's attorneys about the approaches to the case are examined. The focal points of the trial consultation include the significance of having gruesome photographs shown to a jury and how the particular size (small stature) and interpersonal presentation (passive and compliant) of the defendant would influence preparation for the trial.

The civil case discussed in Chapter 14 illustrates the expanding role for trial consultation. The case involves eminent domain actions in which we consider the nature of government seizure of private property. The legal antecedents are described and then are reconciled with conceptualizations of likely juror attitudes.

This last part concludes with Chapter 15, which looks at the future of trial consultation. Those of us exposed to projections by the 21st century of personal jet-packs, magnetic levitation trains, and learning through virtual environments tend to be cautious about forecasting the future. A more realistic view is presented here, mostly extrapolations of emerging trends, including the likelihood of social networking playing a large role in jury selection, changes in the nature of survey methods, and the central role of universities in providing professional training.

Chapter 13

―――

TRIAL CONSULTATION IN A CAPITAL MURDER CASE

Integrating the Components of Trial Consultation

The case study in this chapter seeks to synthesize the elements of trial consultation work that have been considered separately. A capital murder charge was chosen because this kind of case galvanizes public attention, because it is an area in which trial consultants commonly work, and because the issues are literally a matter of life or death. The issues and criteria in such a case are somewhat different from those in civil cases, but major aspects of the methodology remain the same. In this illustrative case, we begin with a description of the facts and allegations of the case, examine the issues around the nature, impact, and possible prejudicial reactions to graphic photos of a bloody victim, and then discuss elements of the defendant. In particular, we examine his likely stimulus value in terms of the charges and his personal traits, and then look at how such a defendant is prepared for court testimony. We start with the allegations.

Charges of capital murder had been filed against a 20-year-old man and separately against his two codefendants. The defendant and his two companions were watching television and drinking heavily in a modest home that one of them rented. Three other young men with whom they were acquainted entered the house. An argument followed about the possession

171

and ownership of packages of illegal drugs, packages that had shifted from one group of men to the other. A brawl erupted, with the men in the home eventually using baseball bats in the fight. The three visitors to the house suffered blows to the head from the bats and, for two of these men, the blows led to death. The third visitor was injured and bloodied, but alive; he appeared to be unconscious and could be assumed to be dead. The victims were lifted into a van by the three assailants. The bodies were thrown from the car at an isolated country location. The one survivor eventually made his way to a road where he was picked up, then treated in a hospital and, after a while, released. The assailants left a number of clues that revealed to the police that they had been present at the site at which the two remaining bodies were found. The three young men were eventually located and were charged to be separately tried for murder. This case study describes the trial consultation with the attorneys for the youngest and shortest of the three.

THE TRIAL TEAM EXAMINES THE PHOTOS

Spread out over the defense attorneys' conference table were dozens of photographs of the three victims. As noted, two had died; the third man had recovered and adequately resumed his normal life of work and play. Displayed in vivid color, and taken at the site at which the three men had been thrown, these professionally taken photographs of the two deceased men showed smashed skulls, skin ripped away, purple bruises, and puddles of blood. An additional set of photographs had been taken of the survivor at the hospital. Tubes ran out of the man's skull, face, and mouth. With all of the tubing and visible injuries, he looked less like a man and more like a movie creature or a construction from a Stephen King novel. When the experienced investigator on the defense trial team turned away from the photos in disgust, it was a sign that when this evidence would be introduced, by itself it could evoke emotional reactions harmful to the defense.

After retiring from a career in federal law enforcement, this investigator had turned his considerable energies to his ranch and to working as an investigator for defense attorneys in capital murder cases. He had seen many death scenes and corpses and many forensic photographs. He had never before found himself disturbed by victim photos. These photos were to become a focal point of our jury selection for the defense.

Four of us looked carefully at the photos in the conference room: the two attorneys, the investigator, and I. Like many other attorneys' conference rooms, the one in which we met regularly had little natural light. This small law firm, located in the modest setting of a renovated older house, keeps the blinds closed, in part so that the bright Alabama sunlight does not make it difficult to look at individuals whose backs are to the window. Bent over the photographs in this subdued light, we discussed the impact of the gruesome images. We decided to consider them our first conceptual point for the selection of jurors and presentation of the defense. The following supported our working hypothesis, using the victim photos as the focal point.

Photograph Reactivity

To begin, we should note that judges routinely allow the admission of gruesome and graphic photographs into evidence. As Douglas, Lyon, and Ogloff (1997) point out, photographic evidence can help jurors to view the facts and details, to assess the accuracy of testimony and theories put before them, and to understand the intent of the offense. The overall rationale is that introduction of gruesome photos must be relevant and must serve a probative rather than a prejudicial purpose.[1] Furthermore, jurors are often instructed by the court not to be excessively influenced by their own emotional reactions to such photos. But does being exposed to gruesome evidence make a difference?

Bright and Goodman-Delahunty (2004) investigated this question by presenting gruesome verbal evidence to mock jurors. The mock jurors were given a 12-page trial transcript and were informed, in a nongruesome version, that the victim was stabbed in the chest. In a gruesome version, the victim was described as having been brutally tortured for more than 30 minutes, with cuts made to almost every part of her body, her face obliterated beyond recognition, and that an effort was made to cut off the victim's head after her death. Furthermore, one set of conditions presented a legally sufficient level of evidence for conviction, and in a matched set of conditions the level of evidence for conviction was legally insufficient. However, verdicts were not significantly related to level of sufficiency of evidence. Summing across both levels of evidence and looking only at verdicts, the overall conviction rate was 23.5%. Overall, in the nongruesome conditions, 13.9% of the jurors found the defendant guilty; in the gruesome conditions, 34.4% of the jurors indicated guilt. What is more compelling is what happened using a second dependent variable, subjective judgments of guilt, when the evidence was legally insufficient to sustain a conviction. In this condition the subjective conclusion of guilt ratings by jurors in regard to the gruesome condition was 57%, as compared with 37% in the nongruesome condition. Bright and Goodman-Delahunty (2004) concluded:

> Gruesome evidence, such as descriptions of torture and mutilation, can bias juror decision-making toward conviction. Gruesome information

---

[1]Douglas et al. (1997) did observe that "the legal system assumes that jurors likely will not be prejudiced by graphic evidentiary photographs" (p. 488).

appears to influence jurors' processing of individual items of evidence and to increase the inculpatory value that jurors ascribe to particular items of evidence. Increased subjective estimates of the guilt of the defendant may also occur when gruesome information is present. (p. 164)

In their study of gruesome photographs, Douglas et al. (1997) used a transcript of a first-degree murder trial consisting of 30 single-spaced pages along with four sets of photographic exhibits, including autopsy photos. None of the evidence convincingly placed the defendant at the scene of the murder or convincingly supported his alibi of being sick in bed all day. Few differences were found between black-and-white photos and color photos, the latter having been a prori assumed to be more emotion eliciting. Overall, 57% of the people in the color photograph condition found the defendant guilty, 50% in the black-and-white photo condition found him guilty, and 27% in the control condition found him guilty. Of equal interest was the pattern of self-reports by the jurors stating that they had acted impartially and, although emotionally affected personally by the photographs, they reported (inaccurately) that their judgments of guilt had not been affected. The authors' conclusions were that such gruesome photos are prejudicial, and not probative.

APPLICATION TO THE CASE STUDY

We hypothesized that some potential jurors would react to the inarguably gruesome and graphic photographs so severely that they might quickly conclude guilt. As a consequence, they would not listen as carefully as they might otherwise to case evidence or information that would support the innocence of the defendant. Thus, the aim was to strike members of the panel who would be reactive to the photos. For the group voir dire, we decided to ask jurors if it would present a problem to them to view and then consider in evidence a number of photos that showed faces and heads of dead persons with visible brain tissue, skull and face fragments, considerable blood, and tissue damage. We also asked if such photos would make it difficult for them to presume innocence before the rest of the evidence was presented in order to challenge the most reactive jurors for cause and tag all of the remaining possible peremptory strikes.

This working hypothesis was drawn both from the case and from the body of psychological knowledge of how people in general react to disturbing or gruesome visual information. In the published research studies, a range of responses has been seen within the context of the significant differences already noted. When we act as researchers, we look for significant differences between groups exposed to upsetting content and those exposed to some control condition. A shift of thinking is in order when applying this approach to jury selection. Now our interest is the ways in which individuals, rather than groups, may respond to the material. In the trial consultant role we try to consider the outliers, the extreme reactors, the people who are not going to be able to hear and process evidence. The task in this case was to identify potential jurors who would likely respond to the disturbing photos with internal distress or panic, combined with a personal, immediate, and intense need to do something (usually to the defendant) to calm their distress and relieve their sense of wrong in regard to such injuries.

VOIR DIRE QUESTIONS ABOUT THE PHOTOS

Prior to my involvement, a standard jury questionnaire that was at best modestly useful had been mailed to people subpoenaed for jury duty. As a result, for the voir dire we constructed questions and inquiries that usually would have been included in a supplemental juror questionnaire.

A primary issue was reaction to the photographs, so six voir dire questions were constructed on this topic. Because the minimal standard jury questionnaire had already been mailed to potential jurors and because the judge denied a motion for a SJQ, the voir dire questioning took on great significance. Deselection questions, as discussed in Chapter 9, were the only questions asked, to help identify unfavorable jurors while not revealing parallel information useful for the prosecution. These were the voir dire questions prepared to address the photographs:

"It is possible that photos will be introduced into evidence that will show dead and wounded men. These photos may portray severe injuries to the head, including a great deal of blood and gore. The photos may or may not strike some of you as horrible and awful to see. Sometimes people who have seen similar photographs found them disturbing.

1. "Raise your hands if you would be very disturbed and upset to see such photos. [The follow-up questions were addressed to people who raised their hands.] Explain. What effects would they have on you?
2. "Indicate by raising your hands if you avoid looking at television shows or movies that have much blood and gore. [Again, the follow-ups were addressed to people who raised their hands.] What shows or movies do you avoid? Why? What do you do to avoid them?
3. "If you have had occasions in your own life to see accidents or injuries with much blood and much damage to people's heads or

bodies, please raise your hands. Describe what you have seen and how you reacted. It is OK to talk about these events privately if you prefer not to talk about them in front of other people here.

4. "If looking at and thinking about photographs of bloody, injured, or dead people would be a truly serious problem for you, please raise your hands. Explain.

5. "There will be much related information presented in evidence and in testimony that jurors will be asked to listen to and weigh. Please indicate whether you have any sense, that for you personally, seeing horrific photographs or hearing about horrific events would distract you or get in the way of your being able to listen objectively and carefully to the evidence that will be presented. Explain."

DEFENDANT'S ROLE AS DIMINISHER OF HARM

Conceptualization of this jury selection grew both from the evidence to be presented and the theory of the case being formulated by the attorneys for both sides. Lonnie, the defendant, was regularly in the company of the two larger, older, tougher men. Lonnie was 5'4" tall, weighed about 120 pounds, and looked much younger than his age. When the three other young men came to the house, a peripheral issue erupted in regard to this defendant. Lonnie's two companions started to hit two of the other men in the head and body with baseball bats and told him to do the same to the remaining man. Both scared and obedient, according to his story, Lonnie did as ordered by his companions and with a bat hit the third man on the legs and then the head, "but not too hard." As the man went down, Lonnie whispered to the man to play dead, which he did. The considerable blood on his head and face helped him to maintain this pose. Later, when the three victims were thrown out of the van, Lonnie again sought to conceal from his companions that the man he had hit was alive. He succeeded. This aspect of the case led to the next aspect of the consultation plan.

A central issue to be pursued by the defense in the trial, and to inculcate in the thinking of the jurors, was that Lonnie had tried to minimize damage and harm at the time of the offense. Jurors who would be good for the prosecution might be likely to lump Lonnie together with the already convicted and sentenced other offenders, as a violent and unseemly criminal. The defense perspective was to avoid jurors who would react with a philosophy of "a pox on them all." As part of identifying these jurors, the defense team decided to inquire as to which members of the panel would rush to lump the three together and not consider Lonnie individually. The voir dire questions were phrased to bring out the working assumptions that all parties to a major crime are equally responsible and that efforts to protect one victim made no difference if someone was a party to the death of others. Closely allied to the notion of Lonnie as diminisher of harm was the next issue of Lonnie as afraid of his companions and acting as a result of their directions.

FEARFUL FOLLOWER

Lonnie stated that at the time of the fighting and subsequent disposal of bodies, he was scared to death and had little choice. He said to his attorneys that if he objected, his companions might well have killed him too. The evidence available to the defense on this issue was limited, and this point depended in part on taking Lonnie's word. Still, it logically fit. The leader and primary other offender was large, temperamental, had a history of violence, and seemed to be in control. Lonnie both admired and feared him, much as some sons are with strong-willed and temperamental fathers. Lonnie said that he was never more afraid in his life than during the beatings. Jurors who would be bad for the defense would be unsympathetic to Lonnie, holding that he was fully responsible for what he did. One element that might contribute to Lonnie's successfully being seen as both fearful and a follower was his slight build and youthful appearance.

Smallness

Three components made up the dimension of smallness.

• This was a physically small man who came across as interpersonally small as well. When heiress Patty Hearst was tried for murder more than three decades ago, her defense team dressed her in oversized clothing to emphasize how small and easily intimidated she was. The defense team assumed that it would be worth dressing Lonnie likewise for trial. Lonnie already looked nonthreatening, and the plan was for clothing just noticeably too large for him because it had the potential for making his frail and small physical being even more salient.

• He played a small part in control of the events. He was there, he did swing a baseball bat, and he did hit one person, the victim who survived. However, in the overall scenario, he had not assumed a leading role.

• He was emotionally small, in the sense that he was dependent on others for direction and approval. His ways of relating were childlike. No sense of inner strength or personal autonomy ever appeared in the interviews with him or in the reports of the killings and assault.

The implication of such smallness in selecting jurors was that it would be helpful to strike individuals who could not accept or personally appreciate what it means to be dependent and psychologically and physically small. These might be strong, assertive, relatively insensitive people who had not been picked on, bullied, or intimidated, or, if so, minimally and without associated emotional distress.

The smallness concept had different implications for Lonnie's presentation in court. He had two male attorneys, one of whom was much bigger than the other. A strategic decision was to place Lonnie close to and alongside the large attorney, thus emphasizing Lonnie's smallness.

PREPARING LONNIE FOR THE STAND

The next decision was whether to allow Lonnie to testify on his own behalf. He had no strong feelings either way about testifying. Much as he was with his companions in the offense, he was passive, nonassertive, and fully and unquestioningly willing to do what we instructed. Here are the summaries of the notes from my initial visit with him in jail and from my repeated efforts to assess what he would be like testifying on his own behalf.

1. Emotionally flat
2. Sentences run on and trail off
3. Neither clear in details nor organized
4. Presents as honest
5. Hides little or nothing
6. Personal style of speaking diminishes himself as a person and is not malleable

Lonnie came across as being without guile, speaking in a weak voice, but with sincerity. We repeatedly role played the direct examination and the cross-examination process. His attorneys took turns assuming the roles of prosecution and defense examiners. When Lonnie was stuck or ineffective, we modeled possible ways of answering that stayed true to his self-reports of what had happened. He could not incorporate the desired manner of responding. He never got a full grasp or mastery of the effective witness role in our dry runs to see how he would do.

Lonnie was barely adequate in response to the questions during the simulated direct examinations. He answered questions briefly, he sometimes stayed on topic, and he gave diffident, subdued answers in an uncertain tone of voice. In the simulated cross-examinations, Lonnie could not manage well. He gave in right away. Forceful questions brought capitulation. When his attorneys or I asked him tough questions, he melted.

"Yes, that might have happened," he sometimes replied.

"Perhaps that was what I was thinking," he agreed.

The same psychological processes that made him so passive and eager to please in his ordinary interactions made him a danger to himself on the stand. The trial team could not anticipate what he would agree to, because his style was to submit, especially if pressured. Ask him almost anything assertively, and he would go along with it. If Lonnie were on the stand, he might well replay the dynamics of what happened in that little house when the two men were killed and the third man injured. His manner was characterized by acquiescence to others and conformity to their desires and ideas. The decision about calling him to testify was debated at length by the trial team. The team wished he could testify, because his version of the events could be drawn only from him. However, the risks were substantial. Calling him to the stand might be too dangerous and result in losing the case. The trial team was conflicted, but the final inclination was that testimony by this defendant could lead to harmful and perhaps untruthful admissions and would not be in his best interest. We persevered and still prepared him to testify, assuming that we could decide to call him if the outcome looked bad as the trial progressed.

Without any decisive sense that he would be able to incorporate it sufficiently for the trial, a plan of psychological and behavioral witness preparation was developed, based on Lonnie's behaviors and deficits as a witness. We made the following suggestions to Lonnie during his meetings with the trial team and his testimony rehearsals at the jail.

1. *Sit up straight.* Lonnie slouched. The more difficult the questions that were asked, the more he slid down into his chair. He was able to remember to sit up straight for a while, but as soon as he became nervous, his spine shifted into a C-shape.

2. *End statements clearly.* Lonnie had a habit of speaking in incomplete sentences. He would be speaking, then hesitate, and then end his statements with "ah … " or "er … " and trail off into very soft vocalizations. We worked to have him speak, say what he needed to, and then stop.

3. *Answer only the question asked.* Lonnie had weaknesses in organizing his thoughts. When responding to questions, he would drift to unrelated content. We worked to keep him from volunteering information, which was most important on cross-examination.

4. *When answering questions, scan the room.* Particularly during narrative answers, Lonnie would look only at the person asking the question or look down toward the floor. Try to make eye contact with others in the courtroom, we instructed him. His poor eye contact habits were difficult to overcome.

5. *Keep arms uncrossed.* When at all tense, Lonnie wrapped his arms around his chest and sides. The arms presented a barrier between him and the audience. He was tense and he looked tense. The instruction was to try to stay somewhat relaxed or at least look less bound in a knot. As with many of the other preparation efforts, he was able to master this change for a while. Although he never looked at ease, he was able to relinquish the wraparound arms as an automatic pattern.

6. *Take a breath.* The tension showed in the form of his shallow, rapid breathing when mock-testifying. With shallow breathing, one gives shallow, unpersuasive replies to questions. The instruction was to take a slow, deep breath before answering each question, especially on cross-examination. This slower breathing would also give the defense attorneys a chance to object and would give him time to collect his thoughts. Rapid, shallow breathing reflects tension. Slower breathing can give the impression of being more authentic as a person and more truthful.

7. *Remember to hold your ground.* As noted, Lonnie had a tendency during cross-examination to give in to the questioner. We decided he needed a simple, accurate phrase that he could commit to memory, that would be part of his ready and natural vocabulary, and that would serve him well under cross. The phrase we chose was this: "I'm just telling you the truth as it happened."

8. *Keep answers selectively short on cross-examination.* Lonnie tended to agree when he was asked a question that began with "Isn't it true that … ?" He was taught to take his time and listen to the question. Then he was able to say, "Yes sir, I did" or "No, that is incorrect" when those responses fit. He found it harder to give narrative answers during cross-examination, but he did understand not to answer "yes" or "no" every time. He was occasionally able to use declarative statements.

9. *Fearful follower.* Because one of the theories of the case was the desirability of presenting the defendant as fearful and a follower of orders, we sought a simple phrase to capture that notion. Two phrases emerged. He was able to emphasize "I couldn't" and "I was afraid" in reply to questions about why he did not call the police, why he did not get help from other people, or why he did not do something to stop the other two men committing the assaults.

IDENTIFICATION WITH THE VICTIMS

In murder trials, as well as in many other kinds of criminal and civil actions, a persistent defense concern is the possible psychological overidentification of potential jurors with the victims. A question usually raised is to what extent potential jurors may be able to view the evidence objectively versus how much their perspective may be clouded because of their concern about and identification with the victims and their families. For that reason, supplemental jury questionnaires (SJQs) and voir dire questioning often explores this issue. In the present case, with no SJQ permitted, the inquiry was limited to voir dire questions. The next set of questions concerned overidentification with the victims and possible inattention to the defense arguments.

1. "Have any of you had family members or friends who were hurt in physical attacks? Please describe what happened."
2. "Have any of you personally been hurt in physical attacks? If so, indicate whether you can talk about it here or need to explain privately."
3. "There are many other reasons that a person can experience strong and emotional feelings about attacks on people. Indicate by raising your hand if this is true for you. (To responders:) Please tell us what these reasons might be for you."
4. "The courts will ask that jurors not only start by presuming that the defendant is innocent, but that they keep that presumption of innocence throughout the presentation of all of the evidence. Tell us now if there is *any* reason that such a presumption of innocence may not be fully true for you, in any way. (After responses:) Tell us now if there is a possibility that you may not start with assuming that the defendant is innocent in a case involving assaults by a number of people, with much blood having been spilled, and persons who were severely injured or killed as a result."
5. "It is impossible to ask about every possible situation or experience you have had that might be related to this case. Please indicate now if there is anything else *whatever* about you that might be related to this case or might influence your serving on this jury."

CONCLUSION

In their book *Psychological Consultation in the Courtroom*, Nietzel and Dillehay (1986) made an offbeat and almost incidental observation that has vividly remained with me. They observed that one of the main benefits of jury consultation was that it heightened the confidence of the attorneys, so that the attorneys would then be able to negotiate a settlement or a plea from a position of greater psychological and interpersonal strength. The idea seemed surrealistic at the time. I thought it should be the substance of what we do as trial consultants that should make the difference, and not some serendipitous expectation effect. At that time this confidence-as-major-product seemed like the equivalent of a placebo effect. I have since changed my mind.

This case was like many others, in the sense that both sides felt pressures that pushed and pulled toward a settlement or plea. Judges sometimes issue instructions that command the two sides to negotiate until a plea bargain is reached. Each side is concerned about the uncertainties of a trial with the possibility of severe adverse outcomes. Most attorneys do not like the anxiety and demands of the performance inherent in trials, although a few trial attorneys do relish that challenge. The defense attorneys in this case were able to approach the possible plea bargain with confidence. Part of their felt empowerment in the bargaining was a result of the schema we had developed for approaching the voir dire process and striking adverse jury members.

Nietzel and Dillehay might give major credit to the trial consultant for such confidence. Such an assignment of credit is difficult. Nevertheless, I have come to believe that good, substantive consultation can make attorneys more effective in bargaining. No empirical data exist to support or refute this conclusion. Indeed, it is difficult to imagine how a design could be constructed to test the question. The observations about improving attorneys' confidence are subjective, but they are consistent over time, drawn from the observations of other consultants and through many cases.

Chapter 14

————◆————

TRIAL CONSULTATION IN EMINENT DOMAIN CASES

The opportunities for and possible applications of trial consultation extend to almost every aspect of litigation that may culminate in a trial. This breadth of applications includes both criminal and civil law. As an illustration of the broad scope of trial consultation, that is, how far it can reach, we examine here one important area of civil litigation: eminent domain.

Trial consultation and psychological knowledge are not commonly employed in eminent domain cases. Few articles and little empirical knowledge in the behavioral sciences address this important and common aspect of civil law. This chapter provides a starting point for understanding trial consultation in this area and in civil actions in general. The basic principles are identified in terms of how consultants may conceptualize eminent domain actions and how specific psychological-legal constructs are developed for eminent domain and related cases.

EMINENT DOMAIN:
BACKGROUND AND LEGAL ISSUES

Eminent domain law is based on the legal premise that the government has the right to take ownership of property from citizens for public use or in the

An earlier version of this chapter appeared in a law review article I coauthored with Michael Griffin and Veronica Tetterton (Brodsky, Griffin, & Tetterton, 2005). Copyright 2005 by the *American Journal of Trial Advocacy*. Adapted by permission.

public interest without the consent of the citizens, but with proper or just compensation. The term *compensation* describes the transfer of title to the property from private ownership to the government. The last clause of the Fifth Amendment to the Constitution reads, "Nor shall private property be taken for public use, without just compensation." Often the property owner and the government agency are in agreement about the amount of compensation. A dispute may arise about the worth of the property because the government typically relies on the market value of a property, as advised by government-retained assessors, to determine just compensation. This market value basis for monetary awards has its limitations. It does not take into consideration the intrinsic or personal value of the property to the individual. It may neglect wide discrepancies in valuation. Another consideration is the means by which the government assesses and obtains the property. Epstein (1985) argues that courts are not likely to be accurate in determining just compensation because of restrictive valuation methods that are detrimental to the individual. Epstein asserts that assigning a monetary value to the land the government acquires presents an ethical and moral question rather than a legal one. The means by which the government values and acquires the land are often difficult to modify prior to condemnation of the property.

In *Bailey v. Myers* (2003) land was condemned for a private redevelopment program in Mesa, Arizona. Compensation was offered in the form of relocating a displaced shop owner to a portion of a store not far from the original property. The essential question was whether this condemnation of property was for public use or was an underhanded deal for private ownership. In seeking the balance between the public welfare and individual rights, the essential questions are whether the needs of the many outweigh the needs of the one and what actions can be taken by private landowners with stakes in the outcome.

Eminent domain proceedings have been portrayed by Steven Greenhut (2004) as theft by another name and increasingly used to take property from one private owner to give to another. Greenhut has described a reverse Robin Hood scenario, in which the government takes from the (relatively) poor and gives to the rich. He goes on to assert that eminent domain actions are often an "administrative evil" (p. 139), and that "this is how governments now routinely operate, taking property from small owners and giving them to big ones, and treating the victimized owners shabbily" (p. 144). His polemic book portrays these proceedings as not routine administrative actions, but rather as emotionally charged events of injustice and abuse.

Considerable public opinion moved toward the Greenhut view following the 5–4 U.S. Supreme Court decision in *Kelo v. City of New London* (2005). The issue was the effort of the city of New London, Connecticut, to use the power of eminent domain to condemn waterfront private property to be used for a private development that would bring taxes and jobs to the city. The New London plan called for construction of a state park, a hotel and conference center, 80–100 new residences, 66 apartments, and office and retail space. Of the 115 private properties condemned by the city, 15 owners refused to sell and 9 owners sued, including the lead plaintiff, Susette Kelo. The Supreme Court majority ruled in favor of the city of New London.[1] A firestorm of indignant public opinion erupted. Nadler and Diamond (2007) wrote that, following *Kelo*, "public reaction to the case was surprisingly strong and uniform across the political spectrum. An overwhelming majority of citizens were astonished and dismayed by the decision. At the same time, most legal scholars and practitioners viewed the decision as a logical product of established precedent." Furthermore, Nadler and Diamond examined the many public polls that followed the *Kelo* decision and observed that between 43 and 61% of citizens were opposed to any form of eminent domain actions. Following the Supreme Court decision, six of the nine *Kelo* property owners either sold to the city or had the decision deferred. Three property owners, including the named plaintiff Susette Kelo, with the support of the Connecticut governor, continued unsuccessfully to fight the decision after the condemnation action in mid-2006.[2]

In addition to the legal bases for property condemnation cases, many factors affect the proceedings and outcome of an eminent domain trial. Such factors include juror opinions of the property in question, sales of similar properties, offers made by others to buy the property, external valuations, and landowner's income (Massey, 1970). In their analysis of trial strategies and escalating costs in condemnation cases, Handy and May (2003) noted, "Condemnation cases have grown increasingly complex as clients have become more sophisticated, the marketplace more sophisticated and the range of tactics and tools available to the condemnation practitioner have increased" (p. 485). They further noted that many landowners have unrealistic expectations of what they can realize in terms of cost recovery. Powell (2006) has addressed the psychological component of attachment to one's property, observing that it is both costly and difficult to measure the loss of community and one's emotional attachment to a property. He noted, "Some property owners move from their community willingly with little

---

[1]As of the time of the present writing, the development plan has not proceeded. However, 42 states have passed or proposed legislation or constitutional amendments limiting eminent domain actions for economic redevelopment.

[2]Ms. Kelo received compensation of $442,155, which was $300,000 above the assessed property value, and her house was moved. According to a follow-up review at *lawprofessors.type-pad.com/property/2006/12/susette_kelos_h.html*, she sent the following 2006 holiday card to city officials and members of the city development authority: "Your houses, your homes, your family, your friends. May they live in misery that never ends. I curse you all. May you rot in hell. To each of you I send this spell."

remorse, while others experience feelings of sadness and anger while being forced to leave behind the many memories attached to their home and the community that provided a sense of safety, comfort and identity" (p. 215).

External valuations, the nature of the property at issue, and testimony by witnesses may influence jurors' or judges' perceptions and decision. Moreover, civil trials other than eminent domain trials have long utilized certain techniques to persuade jurors on just these dimensions. Public attention is often drawn to civil trials that involve product liability suits, asbestos exposure suits alleging asbestosis or lung cancer, personal injury cases, and class action suits involving race, work conditions, or sex discrimination; in intensity and impact on the lives of the citizens and litigants, these cases have similarities to eminent domain proceedings.

TRIAL CONSULTATION

In addition to the headline-grabbing eminent domain cases, there are a variety of almost invisible cases. These cases draw little attention, and yet they often can benefit from contributions by the trial consultant. Brodsky (2000) has observed ways in which change of venue and trial consultation may be understood in low-profile cases. In this chapter, we examine how trial consultation knowledge may apply to eminent domain actions and the resolution of varying appraisals of a condemned property. Attorneys may employ consultation advice and intervention actions well before the actual appraisal takes place. Novak, Blaesser, and Geselbracht (1994) recommend the defensive strategy of improvement of the land before any evaluation occurs. Property improvement is possible in situations where there is foreknowledge that the state will condemn the property. However, where there is little indication beforehand or it is too late to have property improved prior to appraisal, some may still find it timely to employ a trial consultant.

In her advice to attorneys for the use of jury consultants in property condemnation cases, Macpherson (2003) urges the study of potential jurors' unanticipated reactions to evidence as well as attention to their comprehension of documents and graphics. She further advises preparing for unanticipated reactions to outside influences. Macpherson points out three instances in eminent domain litigation when the expense of trial consultation is merited: when the land is taken for a controversial development, when the landowner is a well-known person, and when the dispute is well publicized.

Trial consultants and attorneys should assume that property condemnation actions can be just as emotional, just as personally difficult, and just as important as other fiercely contested civil cases. Broussard (2000) and

Powell (2006) have argued that eminent domain actions in urban revital-ization efforts may be associated with emotional injuries and with major social distress to displaced residents. Emotional injuries and social distress can stem from difficulty in finding a new residence, sentimental attachment to the property, and questionable usefulness of the property to the com-munity. Many aspects of eminent domain cases overlap with civil jury selec-tion in general. Thus, in those instances where retention of trial consultants is merited in eminent domain proceedings, strategies fall into two distinct categories, which are discussed in turn here: strategies that apply to bored, resentful, and negative jurors and strategies that apply to examining oppos-ing appraisers.

STRATEGIES AND ISSUES THAT APPLY TO PROPERTY CONDEMNATION ACTIONS

The Bored Juror

Eminent domain cases are often perceived as dull by potential jurors. The absence of the drama of crime scene reports and photos and the lack of explicit accounts of a serious injury or a violent crime, combined with the presence of detailed testimony about a technical topic, may make these cases appear to be lackluster affairs. Thus, in selecting jurors, one must con-sider proneness to boredom or need for stimulation. Research has shown a relationship between boredom proneness and demographic factors such as gender and ethnicity. Watt and Vondanovich (1992) reported that African American mock jurors were significantly more boredom prone as compared with their white counterparts. African American females demonstrated the highest levels of boredom proneness, followed by African American males, white males, and white females. Of course, for legal and ethical reasons, jurors should not be chosen on the basis of race. We posit that boredom-prone individuals should be considered for strikes by the side most likely to offer detailed, complex, and technical testimony. Questions should be included in the supplemental juror questionnaires, or asked during the voir dire, that assess for individual proneness to boredom. Items such as "It takes more stimulation to get me going than it does for most people" and "In situations where I have to wait, such as in a line or queue, I get restless" can be adapted from the Boredom Proneness Scale (Farmer & Sunberg, 1986). In contrast, individuals who readily and actively engage in complex mental activities may be considered for strikes by the side with the least technical evidence or with the weakest case. When trials include such technical and detailed information, one may ask questions about the need for cognition, including queries about how much the potential juror likes to think through problems, how much the person gains satisfaction from solving difficult puzzles, and so forth. The scientific foundation for such queries is found in the extensive literature on the need for cognition.

Seib and Vodanovich (1998) found there to be a direct relationship between proneness to boredom and need for cognition. Given this finding, need for cognition can be included as a salient factor. As noted earlier, individuals who have a high need for cognition are characterized by a natural inclination to approach mental activities with eagerness and meticulousness. These individuals organize, elaborate, and thoroughly evaluate information that they have been presented (Cacioppo & Petty, 1982). Conversely, those persons low in a need for cognition fail to derive enjoyment from thinking activities, instead gaining satisfaction from simpler mental tasks. During the course of a property condemnation trial, jurors are presented with appraisal information and technical expert testimony. Individuals with a lower need for cognition may utilize heuristics or other facile mental strategies to come to a conclusion. Thus, the need for cognition can be evaluated to identify potentially bored jurors who are ill suited to contend with the details of property appraisals.

The Resentful Juror

Eminent domain involves an assertion of state power, in the sense that property is acquired from landowners and turned over to government agencies or private developers for the economic benefit or social welfare of the community. Therefore, the kinds of jurors who may affiliate psychologically with the landowner may also hold a belief parallel to that of the landowner, that they have been oppressed or dominated, perhaps by a spouse, family member, supervisor, or society in general. Those who endorse such feelings may identify more closely with the property holder, and, therefore, be more appropriate for peremptory challenges by the government. Questionnaires or voir dire designed to measure this factor may include queries of a personal nature. Questions that may indicate resentment include variations on the following:

> "Do you feel that you are pressured to prove yourself constantly to your boss?"

or

> "Are you under the impression that people in the world are trying to keep you down?"

Of course, individuals vary in the degree to which they identify with the misfortune of others. Criminal offenders and narcissists have empathy deficits, which hinder them from having feelings of compassion or genuine sympathy toward their victims (Hanson, 2003). In eminent domain cases, it may also be useful to assess the perspective-taking abilities of individual jurors in order to infer ability or inability to appreciate the landowner's plight. Any deficit in empathy or lack of perspective about the landowner's plight may skew their judgment. Empathy can be assessed informally by attending to tone of voice and how potential jurors relate to each other. When trial consultants are retained, they may have access to measuring empathy though the Interpersonal Reactivity Index (IRI), a multidimensional instrument that provides measures of perspective taking, empathic concern, fantasy, and personal distress (Davis, 1980, 1983). Attorneys may find this instrument particularly useful to incorporate in jury questionnaires or voir dire questioning. The following items were adapted from the Perspective Taking and Empathic Concern scales. Perspective taking items include:

> "I believe that there are two sides to every question and I try to look at them both."
> "I find it easy to see things from other peoples' perspectives."

Empathic concern items include:

> "I would describe myself as a pretty soft-hearted person."
> "I find it easy to experience feelings of sympathy and compassion for unfortunate others."

In our observations, these and similar items taken from empirically derived scales allow attorneys and trial consultants to tap into subtle aspects of juror predispositions. More obvious attitudes and leanings are visible to both sets of attorneys; subtle and indirect questions provide a substantial advantage in weighing jury strikes.

JURY SELECTION

Jurors carry with them a variety of experiences and opinions that often apply to property condemnation. When considering the nuances of opinions about eminent domain proceedings, Macpherson (2003) identified four areas of useful inquiry in the jury selection process. She suggested that attorneys ask questions that get at a potential juror's views on (1) land development in the area, (2) a property owner's rights, (3) government compensation, and (4) land redistribution. Macpherson (2003, p. 138) provides these examples of open-ended voir dire questions that go to the core issues in the proceedings:

"Some people would like to see more development in this area and others are opposed to it. What is your view?

"How do you feel about the property owner's right to challenge what
the government will pay?

"Some people think property owners should not get as much for their
land when it's needed for a public project. What do you think?

"Tell me about any situation where you supported or opposed change
in land use because you were concerned about the effect on land
values."

These four voir dire inquiries tap into central and important content.
The first, third, and fourth questions fit into the category of *obvious* items,
described earlier, and have the limitation of providing information potentially useful to both the attorneys for the government and the landowner.
Nevertheless, such questions do open up the broad topic of attitudes related
to property condemnation. Only the second question, however, potentially
evokes responses about opinions that may serve to aid jury selection for
one side more than the other, in this instance the landowner-plaintiff. In the
same sense, the third question could be rephrased to identify jurors who
may be antagonistic to the plaintiff's position by stating, "Indicate whether
you agree that property owners should not get as much for their land when
it is needed for a public project, and why."

RULES OF THUMB FOR JURY SELECTION IN EMINENT DOMAIN PROCEEDINGS

On the basis of this review, and on the discussion in earlier chapters on jury
selection, five rules of thumb may be constructed.

1. *Identify potential jurors with strong loyalties to the state and with
felt financial responsibility for state or city expenditures.* One should not
assume that state employees or family members of state-employed workers
have a strong loyalty to the state. To the contrary, many state employees are
angry or disillusioned with the state. Attorneys for property owners should
not rush to strike these jurors. Of related importance is to identify people
who see land and timber owners as cheating the state out of taxes. One
should seek to strike people who feel personally and emotionally invested in
the state's fiscal well-being. A property condemnation trial may offer these
overinvested citizens a chance to "set things right" and help the state gain
resources for schools, roads, and health care. Overinvested citizens are of
high priority for striking.

2. *Identify the overfrugal.* Property condemnation cases revolve around amount of payment. Penny-pinchers may bring their frugal life attitudes into the trial and be reluctant to award a large amount. Consultants may choose to identify people who cut coupons for supermarkets, are upset if checkbooks do not balance to the penny, and find the idea of large payments for almost anything to be unthinkable. Attorneys for landowners do not want jurors who will project their own fiscal tightfistedness into decisions about awards.

3. *Identify the litigation indignant.* Many people are distressed by the large number of legal actions of all sorts that are initiated in American society. One should identify these people by asking about how intensely they favor tort reform and caps on damage amounts. They have the potential for transferring such beliefs to the present case and generalizing their negative views. These indignant citizens are relatively easy to find; they speak up loudly and strongly about their beliefs.

4. *Identify potentially desirable jurors who have the ability to stay focused despite the presentation of dull and complex facts.* This may be an instance when demographics, such as type of employment, may come into play. However, just because potential jurors are scientists or bookkeepers does not necessarily mean they will deal well with the information presented. One may seek cumulative data—for example, combining information about their jobs with their need for cognition and proneness to boredom.

5. *Identify potential jurors who can empathize with your case and client.* These potentially positive jurors have the ability to take other people's perspectives. Other promising jurors have worldviews that most closely match a client's situation. Attorneys for landowners hope that during a trial such jurors will understand and empathize with the landowner.

CASE CONCEPTUALIZATION

As in other trial work, case conceptualization is an important aspect in land condemnation cases. Some elements of case conceptualization in these cases differ from those in typical civil trials. First, there is the factor of potential rewards derived from land development. Although the land may be worth a fixed amount of money at the time of trial, the jurors are typically required to make a decision based on the value of the land at the time the state offered the original compensation. Expansion or redevelopment on the surrounding property occurring subsequent to the initial appraisal may not be admissible. The trial attorney should take into account any recent development when deciding which jurors to challenge. If the land has appreciated in value, it makes sense to have jurors who are familiar with the financial aspects of the surrounding area. These jurors will be aware of the recent development and may be more likely to value the land more highly than jurors who are not aware of the development. If the land has depreciated in value owing to rising crime rates, industrial dumping, or other reasons, one may want jurors who are not familiar with the area.

Characteristics of the Land Owner

An issue related to case conceptualization in property condemnation cases is the reputation or financial standing of the landowner. Landowners who are well known and respected in the community can have a significant impact on jurors. A jury may be less likely to be sympathetic to a family who owns considerable property and loses a portion of that land, as compared with a family whose small amount of land is taken in its entirety for state use. Other factors that come into play include determining whether to present to the jury topics such as the sentimental value of the land, usefulness and value of the remaining property, and previous litigation.

QUESTIONING THE OPPOSING APPRAISER

The development of cross-examination questions for opposing counsel's experts is an important part of trial advocacy in court cases, and land condemnation cases are no exception. Opposing counsel's experts may have years of appraisal experience as well as courtroom experience. In such instances, counsel might draw on independent expert help in finding ways to question the witnesses effectively and find flaws in their arguments, without appearing insensitive or rude to the witnesses. One cross-examination approach that was used in my expert witness training workshops for appraisers is to rely on generalizations such as:

> "Would you say it is a fair assumption that you have made mistakes sometimes throughout your years of experience?"

A question that gets at the same issue is:

> "Has there ever been a time where you have wished that you could go back and change an appraisal after the fact because you felt it was not quite appropriate?"

Neither of these questions would appear intrusive, but both questions may raise doubts about the expert's appraisal of the land in question.

Smith (2004) offers an example of an instance when land appraisal experts were held to a standard other than the *Frye* standard of general acceptance of the appraisal procedure. In the case of *State Road Transportation v. Falcon, Inc.*, the court adopted the *Rochelle* standard, which held that an appraiser's testimony can be admitted as long as it is not "totally inadequate or improper" (*Florida Department of Transportation v. Armadillo Partners, Inc.*, 849 So. 2d at 287, 2003). Although this *Rochelle* standard has not been widely adopted, there are potential ramifications for jury selection. When questioning an expert who has used methods that are adequate, but not largely accepted by a majority of appraisers, a number of strategic approaches become possible. One may raise questions about the opposing counsel's expert on the basis of the method of appraisal. There is a substantial scholarly literature on competing models for the estimation of real estate market values. Both smoothing and price-discovery models have advocates and limitations (Geltner, MacGregor, & Schwann, 2002), and the prepared attorney should draw on such technical writings.[3] This tactic presents an opportunity to question the credibility of the expert openly, yet diplomatically, before the jury. When successful, this approach serves to reduce the credibility of the opposing expert, simultaneously strengthening the testimony of the supporting expert. Furthermore, we have noted earlier that the effectiveness of expert testimony is a function of four interrelated factors: confidence, trustworthiness, likeability, and knowledge (Brodsky, 2004; Griffin et al., 2005). The cross-examination should identify explicit deficits or relative weaknesses within these four domains of testimony, and mobilize questions about the style and credibility of opposing expert appraisers.

CONCLUSION

Eminent domain cases often lack the sensationalism of high-profile civil and criminal cases. The literature on trial consultation as it relates to property condemnation cases is modest. Still, trial attorneys and trial consultants in property condemnation cases can draw on the principles that apply to this type of case. Questions related to jury selection seek to determine jurors' need for cognition and ability to take another's perspective. The techniques to be used in examining opposing experts are generalizable from other types of trials. Although juror characteristics like identification with the government, frugality, and indignation aroused by seemingly excessive litigation

---

[3]A discussion of the nature and scope of the literature on smoothing and price-discovery models goes beyond the reach of this chapter. However, Geltner et al. (2002) offer a readable description of the competing appraisal methods.

may be specific to eminent domain cases, pertinent knowledge from other applications may be imported to trials about property condemnation. This importing of knowledge may be supplemented in three ways. First, direct in-court observations of property condemnation trials can be conducted to develop an actuarial database of constructs and methods. Second, gaps in the legal-psychological literature need to be recognized. Third, the professional practice of trial consultation in eminent domain cases should be shaped and expanded.

Chapter 15

———

WHERE NEXT FOR TRIAL CONSULTING?

Emerging Trends and Limitations

Trial consulting is less than four decades old, and, indeed, the American Society of Trial Consultants (ASTC) is just 25 years old. This is a young field, especially as compared with the centuries-old professions of law, medicine, barbering, surveying, and sheepherding. In this chapter we depart from what is happening and look ahead to what is about to emerge, with awareness that the elements that make this profession so promising also put it at risk. The more trial consulting leads to favorable legal outcomes, the higher the public's expectations of consultants may become—and, in turn, the greater the risk of consultants being seen as substantially responsible for failures in verdicts because of such high expectations. In this chapter we look at emerging trends and technologies that promise to play increasing roles in trial consultation.

CELL PHONES AND TELEPHONE SURVEYS

When the early political protesters and activists against the Vietnam War were arrested and tried, the volunteer social scientists—they did not call themselves trial consultants at the time—depended primarily on telephone surveys. They called representative or random groups of citizens and gained nonobvious and helpful information about community attitudes, information that contributed to hung juries and acquittals in many of the most pub-

licized cases. A good description of the 1970s consultations is presented by
Saks (1976). Furthermore, telephone polling continues to be part of election
coverage and analyses by newspapers and cable television news stations.

Yet four social forces are moving the telephone to a more limited role.
First, the rise of telemarketing has made great numbers of citizens suspicious
of calls from strangers. If they don't know the caller, they do not answer.
This option has been facilitated by the second technological-social influence,
the availability of caller ID, with the accompanying screening of calls. Many
people screen and do not answer calls even from people they know because
of their mood, distractions, or being engaged in other tasks. Calls from
unknown parties have an even lower priority.

The third influence is the widespread use of cell phones. In the 2006
Pew Center Report on cell phone use and survey research, 48% of people
who had cell phones only were less than 30 years old. Among respondents
over 50 years old, 49% had landlines only. Markedly fewer of the individuals with cell phones only were married, had children, and owned homes. In
the Pew Center report, cell phone users were more difficult to survey, with
only 20% of people responding versus 30% of individuals with landlines.
The most important finding was that in surveys about political and social
issues, minimal differences were found between cell phone and landline
users. Nevertheless, one can project that this trend of cell phone use will
increase and that future surveys will have to address this issue.

I asked a class of 120 university students how many had landlines.
Fewer than a dozen answered affirmatively. All had cell phones. It is currently against the law to use autodialing to make survey phone calls to cell
phones, whereas it is not illegal to use autodialing to call landline phones.
This means that researchers choosing to include cell phone users in telephone surveys must hand-dial these numbers, which may take additional
time and effort. Moreover, when survey-based phone calls are made to
recipients who use cell phones, the recipients may have to pay for the calls,
a payment structure not permitted for surveys. Some researchers utilizing
cell phone users choose to offer small monetary incentives for participation,
which increases the cost of including these participants in research.[1]

The fourth influence is the desire for instant communication, including
communication by e-mail, computer instant messaging, and text messaging
via cell phones. All of these have become widespread modes of communication, often supplementing or supplanting the use of landline telephones and
"snail mail."

The implications for these sea changes are that standard approaches
to surveys for change of venue assessments and for delving into commu-

---

[1]A detailed discussion of this issue is included in the Pew Research Center for People and the
Press (2006) report.

nity attitudes will be increasingly scrutinized. A more truncated sample of available respondents may be found initially, a sample skewed toward older persons. At some point, telephone surveys of community attitudes may be of diminished value. Nevertheless, surveys are used so widely for political polling and other general societal questions that there is no hint of discarding the use of telephone surveys.

ONLINE COMMUNITIES AND SOCIAL NETWORKING SITES AS SOURCES OF INFORMATION FOR JURY SELECTION AND OTHER TASKS

The terms *online communities* and *social networking sites* refer to communities of people who have major social contacts online, and a variety of ways of relating, both personally and impersonally, occur through the Internet. These communities can be small, restrictive, and intimate, or large and variable in their intimacy. Wernowsky (2007) identified several ways in which MySpace and Facebook have been used in court, including as evidence of motive for both the defense and the prosecution in a murder trial, another in which a suspect was shown on his MySpace page with a large weapon like that used in a crime, and still another case in which there was confirmation of underage drinking in a defendant's MySpace photos. These online communities largely consist of persons under 35 years old, but sometimes a great deal of information can be elicited for this age group. A Miss New Jersey entrant in the Miss America pageant had potentially problematic risqué photos posted on her online community page. I recently saw a detailed and highly personal MySpace page for a judge. The information on the page indicated much about the judge's political, social, musical, and occupational outlooks.

A brief historical review may be in order to discuss online communities, an easy task because social networking online is so recent. MySpace was established in 2003, and only in late 2004 and 2005 did it become popular for teens. In contrast, Facebook started in 2004 as a Harvard University-only site, then allowed individuals with *.edu* accounts to join, then high school students, and in September 2006, it became open to the general public (Boyd, 2007). Boyd drew on her ethnographic research to conclude that major class divisions are associated with the use of MySpace versus Facebook. She wrote:

> The goodie two shoes, jocks, athletes, or other "good" kids are now going to Facebook. These kids tend to come from families who emphasize education and going to college. They are part of what we'd call hegemonic

society. They are primarily white, but not exclusively. They are in honors classes, looking forward to the prom, and live in a world dictated by after school activities.

She went on to conclude:

> MySpace is still home for Latino/Hispanic teens, immigrant teens, "burn-outs," "alternative kids," "art fags," punks, "emos," goths, "gangstas," queer kids, and other kids who didn't play into the dominant high school popularity paradigm. These are kids whose parents didn't go to college, who are expected to get a job when they finish high school.

When Levy (2007) asked the MySpace founders to comment on the Boyd report, the founders suggested reasonably that it was simplistic to characterize the 70 million MySpace users in any uniform way. By mid-2008, Facebook had more than 40 million United States users. We can project that some of the personal and impersonal information that does not have privacy barriers will persist and be available to the active and thorough searcher.

In her proposed approaches to using inquiries about social networking sites as part of the voir dire, Reed (2007) offers three suggestions. First, and probably most important, ascertain whether potential jurors blog, have photos or other information on the Internet, and whether they belong to any social networking site. If they answer affirmatively, then she suggests asking them where the site is located and whether anybody can find and see it without a user name, password, or invitation. Her second suggestion is to extend the usual warnings—about staying away from news media and avoiding discussions of the case with friends or family—to Internet communications of all sorts. Finally, Reed concludes that knowledge of participation in Internet sites, even without knowing the specific content, is by itself of value in assembling an overall understanding of a potential juror.

Here a question may be raised about the intrusion into the privacy of possible jurors when an attorney is seeking to access their online data. Is it legitimate to Google the names of members of the jury pool? Is it unreasonable to check out their websites or MySpace pages? Broda-Bahm (2007) has suggested that the reaction by jurors might be akin to the indignation of teens finding that parents have snooped into their Facebook pages and, I would add, the distress of teens in prior generations to find that others have read their diaries. The ethical and privacy issues remain to be resolved in a clear and definitive way. In the meantime, it is a reasonable projection that more trial consultants and attorneys will surely seek out every source of information that is in the public domain about plaintiffs, defendants, selected witnesses, and potential jurors. In the absence of compelling standards to the contrary, such searches may become routine practice in the future.

Nobody knows in advance what involvement he or she may have with trials or other litigation, and a new caveat applies: Never put online, or in any retrievable form, information about yourself that you would not be absolutely comfortable in revealing in a court of law. This caveat is likely to be ignored, if even known at all, by many of the millions of personally disclosing members of the online communities. Finally, as the use of social networking sites increases, there are certain limitations that will have to be addressed, such as falsified information and citizen resentment. Many individuals construct false identities or play with presenting themselves as being other than they really are. Furthermore, an emotional and angry backfire effect can be predicted when some members of a venire discover that attorneys or consultants have looked at their MySpace pages.

ZOOMERANG AND OTHER INTERNET SURVEY METHODS

Many research firms have flourished in the field of Internet market survey research, including Survey Monkey and RiddleMeThis. Zoomerang is one of the largest and most visible of these firms (see *www.Zoomerang.com* and Spragins, 2005/2006). Like other Internet-based firms, Zoomerang offers to people or companies conducting surveys more than 3 million opt-in participants drawn from national recruitment mailings and online recruitment, with extensive demographic data on the participants. It claims effective methods of maintaining its participant pools and motivating participation so that high response rates are attained. Online focus groups with available expert moderators are also offered. Somewhat similar services are offered by Confirmit, Stellarsurvey, Surveyshack, and Quancept. Zoomerang, in particular, has been used by some trial consultants to assess attitudes toward major public figures or the publicized offenses of a variety of groups (D. E. Cannon, personal communication, June 8, 2007).

Several advantages promise to increase the use of online surveys in trial consultation work, including the ease of use, the ability to gain access readily to many respondents, and the many citizens, often at work, who have available time to complete online surveys. These online methodologies can target particular demographic groups and geographical areas. Furthermore, as compared with telephone surveys, the cost per participant is usually much less. However, the limitations include all of the problems that exist in online self-disclosure. Participants may misrepresent themselves in regard to age, sex, geographical location, occupation, marital status, and other basic identifying information, as well as their opinions. Because they are volunteers, they may have nonobvious motives for giving false responses. Finally, these online firms have primarily developed their approaches in the interest of market research for commercial business ventures, which sometimes yields a markedly different perspective than the more legal and case-oriented perspective of trial consultation.

AUDIENCE RESPONSE SYSTEMS

In most universities a technology of audience response devices has been implemented, including clickers by which respondents indicate how much they agree or disagree, how much they understand, and other response options. The information on shadow juries, mock trials, and focus groups in this book has been intentionally skimpy, reflecting my own limitations in knowledge. However, for all of those activities, dialers or other audience response systems have been developed. Banks (2006) has pointed out that clickers, dialers, keypads, and other audience response systems (ARS) are in use in virtually every university and every department in higher education in the United States. There are some good reasons to believe that they have a role in both instruction and motivation. Miller, Ashar, and Getz (2003) have found that an ARS improves enthusiasm and attention, but not acquisition of knowledge, in health professionals.

In their use with shadow juries and mock trials as well as with focus groups, the ARS have the merit of being able to elicit immediately quantifiable responses and attitudes. When presented with sample arguments, testimony, and evidence, the participants can indicate evaluative responses in terms of negative and positive reactions, as well as much more content about intensity, interest, persuasion, and beliefs. Because ARS are so widely used in education, the transfer of technology and applications to trial consultation is not a great leap. In this field, as in the field of education, ARS are only as good as the stimulus questions and materials. Many focus groups already work in an intensive and qualitative small-group research process. It is not yet known whether a substantial gain is produced by the use of ARS.

UNIVERSITY-BASED GRADUATE TRAINING AND RESEARCH

Few graduate programs exist in which there is an explicit commitment to training trial consultants or to develop a systematic and useful body of knowledge about trial consulting. Most trial consultants have developed their career interests and knowledge after graduate school (and in a few cases, directly after undergraduate school), and then moved into this field. Others moonlighted and slipped trial consulting research and placements into graduate programs in communications or psychology that are not, per se, part of the field. A handful of graduate programs do have an emphasis on trial consulting; Florida International University offers a graduate course on the psychology of trial consultation. The University of Alabama has an emphasis on trial consultation within its graduate offerings in forensic psychology. The University of Nebraska, Lincoln, offers a trial consultation course periodically under the graduate course title "Topics in Law and Psychology." The psychology department at Boise State University has a faculty member who brings a major focus on witness preparation and polygraph testing. John Jay College offers a graduate course in the psychology of juries. The Alliant International University campuses in Fresno and Irvine, California, offer experiences and instruction related to trial consultation. A number of other universities have individual graduate courses and interested faculty available to students. There were 21 graduate programs in psychology–law listed in mid-2008 on the American Psychology–Law Society website (2008). In a number of these programs, faculty members both serve as trial consultants and conduct research on selected aspects of trial consultation, most often in jury selection.

The frequent academic path into trial consultation is via conducting dissertation research on a topic central to the tasks of trial consultants. For example, Mead (2007) did his PhD dissertation for Cappella University on public perceptions of preparing a criminal defendant, of expectations of the behaviors of criminal defendants, and of expert witness characteristics. Sarver (2008), for his PhD dissertation at Sam Houston State University, studied jury representativeness and concluded that women and those with no prior civil jury experience were most likely to be selected as jurors. Every year some dissertations on aspects of trial consultation appear, often conducted at universities with no major faculty expertise on the topic. It is not a rash prediction that in the future more programs, dissertations, courses, and faculty will have trial consultation as a major focus.

STANDARDIZED METHODS IN THE VOIR DIRE

In their essay on using social science research as part of trial consultation for the voir dire, Lecci, Snowden, and Morris (2004) presented three ways to standardize assessments of potential jurors. They argued for incorporating items from standardized scales into the voir dire, for using validated scales in their entirety in supplemental jury questionnaires, and for using standardized measures to assess the community at large.[2] Because so many attitudes of jurors may be case-specific, it seems unlikely that one or even a

---

[2]Some of these issues have been discussed in part in Chapters 3 and 9.

few standardized measures could be applicable. A more desirable goal is to develop and use standardized scales and items for specific offenses. Thus, embezzlement charges may call for one set of scales. Illegal dissemination of stock information and trading may call for a second set of scales. Charges of capital murder of a stranger in the context of a robbery committed while the accused was highly intoxicated may call for a third set of scales. In this context, Peck (2005) has developed a Corporate Litigation Bias Scale, a 24-item scale with 13 items that reflect a corporate bias and 11 items that reflect an individual plaintiff bias. The scale has some indications of validity for predicting corporate liability.

One future pathway is development of circumstance- and offense-specific standardized measures that can be reasonably relied upon in jury selection. The limitation is that the range of possible cases coming to court is much greater than the range of available instruments. Even though the books and other resources mentioned in Chapter 3 provide a number of instruments of some general use, the specific and idiosyncratic nature of case facts and trial issues means that there will be many times in which nonstandardized methods are utilized.

EVIDENCE-BASED PREPARATION OF EXPERT AND LAY TESTIMONY

With the development of evidence-based medicine and psychotherapy and the positive attention directed toward them, perhaps it is logical that expert testimony may move in the same direction. Kwartner and Boccaccini (2007) have proposed that effective courtroom testimony by expert witnesses should follow evidence-based principles. They analyzed 62 research studies in which there were experimental manipulations of either testimony or of characteristics of expert witnesses. Four principles emerged. The first was clarity of communication so that the experts can be easily understood. In contrast, highly technical and complex testimony is not effective, except when jurors are expecting technical testimony. The second principle was inclusion of clinical knowledge and experience in testimony, and avoidance of purely actuarial testimony. We should add that the combination of clinical and actuarial testimony also yielded high credibility. The third principle was case-specificity, as opposed to general education of the jury. Thus, interview data relating to the case were more persuasive than general literature reviews. The final principle was certainty, and the most persuasive experts showed high but not absolute certainty.

The implications of this thoughtful review may be divided into two categories: those relating to witness preparation and those relating to all trial consultation activity. It follows logically from the Kwartner and Boccaccini

(2007) review and principles that trial consultants should prepare expert witnesses toward clarity, clinical knowledge, case-specificity, and relative certainty in testimony. The broader implication is that trial consultants themselves should move toward evidence-based consultation. Early in this book I criticized the excessive reliance on intuition by trial consultants. As more data about differential effectiveness make their way into the professional literature, consultants should draw on those research findings to map out the preferred path for consultation actions and decisions. Of course, no unconditional and universal guidelines will emerge, any more than they apply mechanistically to psychotherapy. Nevertheless, enough literature, studies, dissertations, and books are being published that responsible consultants in the future may well and properly seat their work in the empirical literature about what works.

GETTING STARTED IN TRIAL CONSULTATION

Eric Mart (2006) has authored *Getting Started in Forensic Psychology* as part of the Prentice-Hall series of Getting Started books. The Getting Started books are of help to psychologists in various areas, but even including the Mart book, there are no substantial guides for developing and marketing a career in trial consultation. I suggest these four steps for individuals at the beginning phase of planning a career in the field.

First, start research and projects early in college and graduate school. Many trial consultants have used their independent university research, theses, and, as mentioned, dissertations to investigate particular aspects of jury selection, juror traits, scales for use in trial consulting, and other related topics. These research studies open doors for future contact and legitimize the researcher as a person with knowledge that may be applied to trial work. Sometimes these research projects help carve out an area of specialization.

Second, make working contacts with experienced trial consultants. Most experienced consultants are generous with their time and advice to aspiring colleagues. They can speak to the lesser known paths to practice and professionalism. Although attending annual meetings of the ASTC is a first choice for such networking, establishing local professional friendships may have the better prognosis for long-term benefits.

Third, seek out opportunities for observation and for doing, in small ways, what you want to do for a career. That is, immediately after graduate studies, consider offering gratis consultation to attorneys of your acquaintance. Seek to assist trial consultants in some of their routine tasks. Ask permission to sit in on their meetings with attorneys and to join them in the courtroom or focus groups.

Fourth, try to specialize. Although some trial consultants work in the entire range of consulting activities, it may be most productive to master a content area or two in depth. This specialization can also enhance your value in seeking a position with one of the few large trial consultation firms.

YOUR FEEDBACK

In my three books on testifying in court, I invited readers to share with me their own experiences and observations about what I wrote. There were a number of informed and thoughtful comments, and I subsequently incorporated the comments and corrections into later books and articles. I extend the same invitation to readers of this book: Let me know what you think. If there are aspects I missed altogether or misstated, I would be grateful for your thoughts. Write to me at *sbrodsky@bama.ua.edu.*

REFERENCES

Adorno, T. W., Frenkel-Brunswick, E., Levinson, D., & Sanford, R. N. (1950). *The authoritarian personality*. New York: Harper.

Altemeyer, B. (1981). *Right-wing authoritarianism*. Winnipeg: University of Manitoba Press.

Altemeyer, B. (1988). *Enemies of freedom: Understanding right-wing authoritarianism*. San Francisco: Jossey-Bass.

Ambady, N., Krabbenhoft, M. A., & Hogan, D. (2006). The 30-sec sale: Using thin-slice judgment to evaluate sales effectiveness. *Journal of Consumer Behavior, 16*, 4–13.

Ambady, N., & Rosenthal, R. (1993). Half a minute: Predicting teacher effectiveness from thin slices of nonverbal behavior and physical attractiveness. *Journal of Personality and Social Psychology, 64*, 431–441.

American Bar Association. (2007). *Criminal justice section standards*. Retrieved April 25, 2007, from *www.abanet.org/crimjust/standards/jurytrial_blk.html#1.4*.

American Psychology–Law Society. (2008). *Graduate programs: Clinical PhD/PsyD programs*. Available at *www.ap-ls.org/students/graduateIndex.html*.

American Society of Trial Consultants. (2008). *ASTC Professional Code*. Retrieved December 5, 2008, from *www.ASTCweb.org/public/article.cfm/ASTC-Professional-Code*.

Anderson, R. E. (Ed.). (2005). *Medical malpractice: A physician's sourcebook*. Totowa, NJ: Humana Press.

Associated Press. (2007, July 21). Quarter of state's drivers uninsured. *Tuscaloosa News*, pp. 1, 4.

Azimi, N. (2005). *The Queen boat/Egypt*. Retrieved January 3, 2007, from *www.case-web.org/assets/cases/case_6.pdf*.

Babcock, B. A. (1975). Voir dire: Preserving "its wonderful power." *Stanford Law Review, 27*, 545–554.

Bailey v. Myers, 76 P. 3d 898 (Ariz. Ct. App. 2003).

Banks, D. A. (Ed.). (2006). *Audience response systems in higher education: Applications and cases.* Hershey, PA: Information Sciences Processing.

Barnette, W. P. (2007). Ma, Ma, where's my Pa? On your jury, Ha, Ha, Ha!: A constitutional analysis of implied bias challenges for cause. *University of Detroit Mercy Law Review, 84,* 451–477.

Berra, Y. (1999). *The Yogi book: I didn't really say everything I said.* New York: Workman.

Berry, B. (2007). *Beauty bias: Discrimination and social power.* New York: Praeger.

Black, R. (1999). *Black's law: A criminal lawyer reveals his defense strategies in four cliffhanger cases.* New York: Simon & Schuster.

Boccaccini, M. T. (2002). What do we really know about witness preparation? *Behavioral Sciences and the Law, 20,* 161–189.

Boccaccini, M. T. (2004). Impact of witness preparation training on the use of targeted testimony delivery skills, perceived credibility, and evaluations of guilt. *Dissertation Abstracts International: Section B. The Sciences and Engineering, 64*(8-B), 4023.

Boccaccini, M. T., Gordon, T., & Brodsky, S. L. (2004). Effects of witness preparation on witness confidence and nervousness. *Journal of Forensic Psychology Practice, 3,* 39–51.

Boccaccini, M. T., Gordon, T., & Brodsky, S. L. (2005). Witness preparation training with real and simulated criminal defendants. *Behavioral Sciences and the Law, 23,* 659–687.

Bornstein, B. H. (1999). The ecological validity of jury simulations: Is the jury still out? *Law and Human Behavior, 23,* 75–91.

Bosek, E., Knickerbocker, A., & Muskus, T. (2000). Venue. In *Corpus jurus secundum: A contemporary statement of American law as derived from reported cases and legislation* (Vol. 92A, pp. 241–533). St. Paul, MN: West Group.

Boyd, D. (2007, June 24). Viewing American class divisions through Facebook and MySpace. *Apophenia Blog Essay.* Available at *www.danah.org/papers/essays/ClassDivisions.html.*

Bright, D. A., & Goodman-Delahunty, J. (2004). The influence of gruesome verbal evidence on mock juror verdicts. *Psychiatry, Psychology and Law, 11,* 154–166.

Broda-Bahm, K. (2007, July). *Online communities.* Posting on ASTCNet.

Brodsky, S. L. (1991). *Testifying in court: Guidelines and maxims for the expert witness.* Washington, DC: American Psychological Association.

Brodsky, S. L. (1999). *The expert expert witness: More maxims and guidelines for testifying in court.* Washington, DC: American Psychological Association.

Brodsky, S. L. (2000). Change of venue assessments in civil litigation. *Journal of Psychiatry and Law, 28,* 335–349.

Brodsky, S. L. (2004). *Coping with cross-examination and other pathways to effective testimony.* Washington, DC: American Psychological Association.

Brodsky, S. L., Griffin, M. P., & Tetterton, V. S. (2005). Trial consultation in eminent domain cases. *American Journal of Trial Advocacy, 29,* 153–166.

Brodsky, S. L., Knowles, R. I., Cotter, P. R., & Herring, G. H. (1991). Jury selection in malpractice suits: An investigation of attitudes toward malpractice and physicians. *International Journal of Law and Psychiatry, 14*, 215–222.

Brodsky, S. L., Sparrow, V. M., & Boccaccini, M. T. (1998). Racial inquiries in depositions and trials. *Journal of Psychiatry and Law, 26*, 533–545.

Broussard, K. (2000). Social consequences of eminent domain: Urban revitalization against the backdrop of the takings clause. *Law and Psychology Review, 24*, 99–114.

Cacioppo, J. T., & Petty, R. E. (1982). The need for cognition. *Journal of Personality and Social Psychology, 42*, 116–131.

Cacioppo, J. T., Petty, R. E., Feinstein, J., & Jarvis, B. (1996). Disposition differences in cognitive motivation: The life and times of individuals low versus high in need for cognition. *Psychological Bulletin, 119*, 197–253.

Cacioppo, J. T., Petty, R. E., & Kau. C. F. (1984). The efficient assessment of need for cognition. *Journal of Personality Assessment, 48*, 306–307.

Capps, J. S. (2002). Explaining punitiveness: Right-wing authoritarianism and social dominance. *North American Journal of Psychology, 4*, 263–278.

Chancer, L. (2005). *High-profile crimes: When legal cases become social causes.* Chicago: University of Chicago Press.

Chandra, R. K. (2004). The resident 80-hour work week: How has it affected surgical specialties? *Laryngoscope, 114*, 1394–1398.

Charmaz, K. (2006). *Constructing grounded theory: A practical guide through qualitative analysis.* Thousand Oaks, CA: Sage.

Corcoran, K., & Fischer, J. (2000). *Measures for clinical practice: A sourcebook (3rd ed.): Vol. 2. Adults.* New York: Free Press.

Christie, R. (1991). Authoritarianism and related constructs. In J. P. Robinson, P. R. Shaver, & L. S. Wrightsman (Eds.), *Measures of social psychological attitudes: Vol. 1. Measures of personality and social psychological attitudes* (pp. 501–571). San Diego, CA: Academic Press.

Cramer, R. J. (2005). *Predictors of expert witness credibility and jury sentencing: Juror personality and expert witness confidence.* Unpublished master's thesis, University of Alabama, Tuscaloosa.

Cramer, R. J., Brodsky, S. L., & DeCoster, J. (in press). Expert witness confidence and juror personality: Their impact on credibility and persuasion in the courtroom. *Journal of the American Academy of Psychiatry and the Law.*

Crocker, C. B., & Koveral, M. B. (2008, August). *Effects of watching juror rehabilitation on juror judgments.* Presented at the annual convention of the American Psychological Association, Boston.

Cruess, S. R., Johnston, S., & Cruess, R. L. (2004). "Profession": A working definition for medical educators. *Teaching and Learning in Medicine, 16*, 74–76.

Curtner, R., & Kassier, M. (2005). "Not in our town": Pretrial publicity, presumed prejudice, and change of venue in Alaska: Public opinion surveys as a tool to measure the impact of prejudicial pretrial publicity. *Alaska Law Review, 22*, 255–292.

Dacy, J. M., & Brodsky, S. L. (1992). Effects of therapist attire and gender. *Psychotherapy, 29*, 486–490.

Darrow, C. S. (1936/1981). Attorney for the defense. *Litigation, 7*, 41–46.

Davis, C. M., Barber, W. L., Bauserman, R., Schreer, G., & Davis, S. L. (Eds.). (1998). *Handbook of sexuality-related measures*. Thousand Oaks, CA: Sage.

Davis, M. H. (1980). A multidimensional approach to individual differences in empathy. *JSAS Catalog of Selected Documents in Psychology, 10*, 85.

Davis, M. H. (1983). Measuring individual differences in empathy: Evidence for a multi-dimensional approach. *Journal of Personality and Social Psychology, 44*, 113–126.

Dillard, J. P., Hunter, J. E., & Burgoon, M. (1984). Sequential-request persuasive strategies: Meta-analysis of foot-in-the-door and door-in-the-face. *Human Communication Research, 10*, 461–488.

Dimitrius, J., & Mazzerella, M. (1999). *Reading people: How to understand people and predict their behavior—anytime, anyplace*. New York: Ballantine.

Douglas, K. S., Lyon, D. R., & Ogloff, J. R. P. (1997). The impact of graphic photographic evidence on mock jurors' decisions in a murder trial: Probative or prejudicial? *Law and Human Behavior, 21*, 485–501.

Epstein, R. A. (1985). *Takings: Private property and the power of eminent domain*. Cambridge, MA: Harvard University Press.

Farmer, R., & Sundberg, N. D. (1986). Boredom proneness: The development and correlates of a new scale. *Journal of Personality Assessment, 50*, 4–17.

Faust, D., Guilmette, T. J., Hart, K. J., Arkes, H. R., Fishburne, F. J., & Davey, L. (1988). Neuropsychologists' training, experience, and judgment accuracy. *Archives of Clinical Neuropsychology, 3*, 145–163.

Federal rules of evidence, with evidence map, 2007–2008. St. Paul, MN: Thompson-West.

Fischer, J., & Corcoran, K. (2007). *Measures for clinical practice: A sourcebook* (4th ed.): *Vol. 1. Couples, families and children*. New York: Oxford University Press.

Fisher, W. (1989). *Human communication as narration: Toward a philosophy of reason, value and action*. Columbia: University of South Carolina Press.

Flamm, M. B. (1998). Medical malpractice and the physician defendant. In American College of Legal Medicine (Ed.), *Legal medicine* (4th ed.). St. Louis, MO: Mosby.

Fleischauer, E. (2004, January 12). Alleged Citydale police killer has long history of paranoia. *Decatur Daily*, p. xx. Retrieved April 26, 2007, from *www.officer.com/article/article.jsp?id=8537&siteSection=1*.

Florida Department of Transportation v. Armadillo Partners, Inc., 849 So. 2d at 287 (2003).

Frame, K. A. (2001). Cognitive processes underlying pretrial publicity effects. (Doctoral dissertation, Simon Fraser University, 2001). *Dissertation Abstracts International, 68*, 3871.

Friedman, S. R. (1992). Sixth Amendment. The right to an impartial jury: How extensive must voir dire questioning be? *Journal of Criminal Law and Criminology, 82*, 920–954.

Freidson, E. (1953). *Profession of medicine: A study of the sociology of applied knowledge*. Chicago: University of Chicago Press.

Fulero, S. M., & Penrod, S. D. (1990). Attorney jury selection folklore: What do they think and how can psychologists help? *Forensic Reports, 3*, 233–259.

Garb, H. N. (1989). Clinical judgment, clinical training, and professional experience. *Psychological Bulletin, 105*, 387–396.

Garb, H. N., & Boyle, P. A. (2003). Understanding why some clinicians use pseudoscientific methods: Findings from research on clinical judgment. In S. O. Lilienfeld, S. J. Lynn, & J. M. Lohr (Eds.), *Science and pseudoscience in clinical psychology* (pp. 17–38). New York: Guilford Press.

Garb, H. N., & Grove, W. M. (2005). On the merits of clinical judgment: Comment. *American Psychologist, 60*, 658–659.

Garcia, L. T., & Griffitt, W. (1978). Authoritarianism-situation interactions in the determination of punitiveness: Engaging authoritarian ideology. *Journal of Research in Personality, 12*, 469–478.

Geiser, R. L., & Newman, R. W. (1961). Psychology and the legal process: Opinion polls as evidence. *American Psychologist, 16*, 685–690.

Geltner, D., MacGregor, B. D., & Schwann, G. M. (2002). Appraisal smoothing and price discovery in real estate markets. *Urban Studies, 40*, 1047–1064.

Gleser, L. J., & Olkin, I. (1996). Models for estimating the number of unpublished studies. *Statistics in Medicine, 15*, 2493–2507.

Goodkind, T. (2005). *Chainfire*. New York: Tor.

Green, M. J. (1995). What (if anything) is wrong with residency overwork? *Annals of Internal Medicine, 123*, 512–517.

Greenberg, S. A., Feldman, S. R., & Brodsky, S. L. (1987). Exposing the expert. *Bar Bulletin, 5*, 1, 23, 28.

Greene, E., & Loftus, E. F. (1984). What's new in the news?: The influence of well-publicized news events on psychological research and courtroom trials. *Basic and Applied Psychology, 5*, 211–221.

Greenhut, S. (2004). *Abuse of power: How the government misuses eminent domain.* Santa Ana, CA: Seven Locks Press.

Griffin, M. P., Brodsky, S. L., Blackwood, H., Abboud, B., & Flanagan, C. B. (2005, March). *The development of credibility scales for witness research.* Paper presented at the meeting of the American Psychology–Law Society, La Jolla, CA.

Haidt, J., McCauley, C., & Rozin, P. (1994). Individual differences in sensitivity to disgust: A scale sampling seven domains of disgust elicitors. *Personality and Individual Differences. 16*, 701–713.

Hammond, S. (2004). The challenge of sex offender assessment: The case of Internet offenders. In M. C. Calder (Ed.), *Child sexual abuse and the Internet: Tackling the new frontier* (pp. 85–97). Dorset, UK: Russell House.

Handy, J. B., & May, M. E. (2003). Remedies for escalating costs in condemnation cases. (pp. 483–490). Prepared for ALI-ABA course on eminent domain and land valuation litigation, San Francisco, January 8–10, 2004.

Hans, V. P., & Jehle, A. (2003). Symposium: III. The jury in practice: Avoid bald men and people with green socks? Other ways to improve the voir dire process in jury selection. *Chicago–Kent Law Review, 78*, 1179–1198.

Hans, V. P., & Vidmar, N. (1982). Jury selection. In N. L. Kerr & R. M. Bray (Eds.), *The psychology of the courtroom*. New York: Academic Press.

Hanson, R. K. (2003). Empathy deficits of sexual offenders: A conceptual mode. *Journal of Sexual Aggression, 9,* 13–23.

Harney, D. M. (1973). *Medical malpractice*. Indianapolis: Allen Smith.

Herrin, J. (2003). The fall of Constantinople. *History Today, 53,* 12–17.

Hartwell, S. (2002). Classes and collections: How clinicians feel differently. *Clinical Law Review, 9,* 463–493.

Henderson, V., & Henshaw, P. (2007). *Image matters for men: How to dress for success*. New York: Hamlyn.

Heaven, P. C. L. (1985). Construction and validation of a measure of authoritarian personality. *Journal of Personality Assessment, 49,* 545–551.

Hunt, J. (2006). Police accounts of normal force. In V. E. Kappeler (Ed.), *The police and society* (3rd ed., pp. 339–357). Long Grove, IL: Waveland Press.

Hutson, M. (2007). Unnatural selection. *Psychology Today, 40*(2), 91–95.

Hyde, A., Howlett, E., Brady, D., & Drennan, J. (2005). The focus group method: Insights from focus group interviews on sexual health with adolescents. *Social Science and Medicine, 61,* 2588–2599.

Irvin v. Dowd, 366 U.S. 717 (1961).

Iyengar, S., & Greenhouse, J. B. (1988). Selection models and the file drawer problem. *Statistical Science, 3,* 109–136.

Jacobson v. United States, 502 U.S. 540 at 551 (1992).

Kalven, H., & Zeisel, H. (1966). *The American jury*. Boston: Little, Brown.

Kassin, S. M., & Wrightsman, L. S. (1983). The construction and validation of a juror bias scale. *Journal of Research in Personality, 17,* 423–442.

Keeter, S., Best, J., Dimock, M., & Craighill, P. (2004). *Consequences of reducing telephone survey nonresponse*. Paper presented at the annual meeting of the American Association for Public Opinion Research, Phoenix, AZ.

Keeter, S., Kennedy, C., Dimock, M., Best, J., & Craighill, P. (2006). Gauging the impact of nonresponse on estimates from a national RDD telephone survey. *Public Opinion Quarterly, 70,* 759–779.

Keller, P. A. (1995). How and when to conduct focus groups. In L. VandeCreek, S. Knapp, & T. L. Jackson (Eds.), *Innovations in clinical practice: A source book* (Vol. 14, pp. 383–391). Sarasota, FL: Professional Resource Press.

Kelly, G. A. (1955). *The psychology of personal constructs*. New York: Norton. (Reprinted by Routledge, London, 1991)

Kelo v. City of New London, 545 U.S. 469 (2005).

Kennedy, P. (1987). *The rise and fall of the great powers: Economic change and military conflict from 1500 to 2000*. New York: Random House.

Kerr, N. L., & Huang, J. Y. (1986). Jury verdicts: How much difference does one juror make? *Personality and Social Psychology Bulletin, 12,* 325–343.

Kilmartin, C. Y. (2006). *The masculine self* (3rd ed.). Cornwall-on-Hudson, NY: Price, Stern & Sloan.

Klockars, C. B. (1996). A theory of excessive force. In W. A. Geller & H. Toch

(Eds.), *Police violence: Understanding and controlling police abuse of force* (pp. 1–22). New Haven, CT: Yale University Press.

Klockars, C. B. (2006). The Dirty Harry problem. In V. E. Kappeler (Ed.), *The police and society* (3rd ed., pp. 403–420). Long Grove, IL: Waveland Press.

Korman, M. (Ed.). (1976). *Levels and patterns of professional training in psychology*. Washington, DC: American Psychological Association.

Krauss, D. A., & Sales, B. D. (2001). The effects of clinical and scientific expert testimony on juror decision making in capital sentencing. *Psychology, Public Policy, and Law, 7*, 267–310.

Kressel, N. J., & Kressel, D. F. (2002). *Stack and sway: The new science of trial consulting*. Boulder, CO: Westview.

Kurzban, R., & Weeden, J. (2005). HurryDate: Mate preferences in action. *Evolution and Human Behavior, 26*, 227–244.

Kwartner, P. P., & Boccaccini, M. T. (2007). Testifying in court: Evidenced-based recommendations for expert-witness testimony. In R. Jackson (Ed.), *Learning forensic assessment* (pp. 565–589). London: Routledge.

Larson, B. A., & Brodsky, S. L. (in press). When cross-examination offends: How men and women assess intrusive questioning of male and female expert witnesses. *Journal of Applied Social Psychology*.

Lecci, L., & Myers, B. (2002). Examining the construct validity of the original and revised JBS: A cross-validation of sample and method. *Law and Human Behavior, 26*, 455–463.

Lecci, L., Snowden, J., & Morris, D. (2004). Using social science research to inform and evaluate the contributions of trial consultants in the voir dire. *Journal of Forensic Psychology Practice, 4*, 67–78.

Levy, S. (2007, August 6). Social networking and class warfare. *Newsweek*, p. 16.

Lichtenstein, B. (2005). Domestic violence, sexual ownership, and HIV risk in women in the deep South. *Social Science and Medicine, 61*, 701–714.

Lieberman, J. D., & Sales, B. D. (2007). *Scientific jury selection*. Washington, DC: American Psychological Association.

Lisnek, P. M., & Cochran, J. (2003). *The hidden jury: And other secret tactics lawyers use to win*. Naperville, IL: Sourcebooks.

Longo, R. E., Brown, S. M., & Orcutt, D. P. (2002). Effects of Internet sexuality on children and adolescents. In A. Cooper (Ed.), *Sex and the Internet: A guidebook for clinicians* (pp. 87–95). New York: Brunner-Routledge.

Macpherson, S. (2003). *Use of jury consultants in a condemnation case. ALI-ABA course of study materials* (pp. 119–142). Prepared for ALI-ABA course on eminent domain and land valuation litigation, San Francisco, January 8–10, 2004.

Mart, E. (2006). *Getting started in forensic psychology practice: How to create a forensic specialty in your mental health practice*. Somerset, NJ: Wiley.

Martin, C. R. A. (1973). *Laws relating to medical malpractice*. London: Pitman Medical.

Martin, R. C., & Melvin, K. B. (1964). Fear responses of bobwhite quail (*Colinus virginianus*) to a model and a live red-tailed hawk (*Buteo janaicensis*). *Psychologische Forschung, 27,* 323–336.

Massey, D. T. (1970). *Rules of compensability and valuation evidence for highway land acquisition.* Washington, DC: Highway Research Board, National Research Council.

Mead, R. H. (2007). Jury perceptions, personality, and self-esteem. *Dissertation Abstracts International: Section B. The Sciences and Engineering, 68*(2-B), 1352.

Melton, B. F. (2001). *Aaron Burr: Conspiracy to treason.* New York: Wiley.

Melvin, K. B., Gramling, L. K., & Gardner, W. M. (1985). A scale to measure attitudes toward prisoners. *Criminal Justice and Behavior, 12,* 241–253.

Memon, A., & Shuman, D. W. (1998). Juror perception of experts in civil disputes: The role of race and gender. *Law and Psychology Review, 22,* 179–197.

Miller, H. G. (2001). *On trial: Lessons from a lifetime in the courtroom.* New York: ALM.

Miller, R. G., Ashar, B. H., & Getz, K. J. (2003). Evaluation of an audience response system for the continuing education of health professionals. *Journal of Continuing Education in the Health Professions, 23,* 109–115.

Miller, W. R. (2004). The phenomenon of quantum change. *Journal of Clinical Psychology, 60,* 453–460.

Mitchell, K. J., Wolak, J., & Finkelhor, D. (2005). Police posing as juveniles online to catch sex offenders: Is it working? *Sexual Abuse: Journal of Research and Treatment, 17,* 241–267.

Mize, G. E., Hannaford-Agor, P., & Waters, N. L. (2007). *The state of the states survey of jury improvement efforts: A compendium report.* Williamsburg, VA: National Center for State Courts.

Mohr, J. C. (2000). American medical malpractice litigation in historical perspective. *Journal of the American Medical Association, 283,* 1731–1737.

Molloy, J. T. (1996). *New women's dress for success.* New York: Grand Central.

Moran, G. (2004). Trial consultation: Why licensure is not necessary. *Journal of Forensic Psychology Practice, 1,* 77–85.

Moran, G., & Cutler, B. (1997). Bogus publicity items and the contingency between awareness and media-induced pretrial prejudice. *Law and Human Behavior, 21,* 339–344.

Morris, G. H., Haroun, A. M., & Naimark, D. (2004). Assessing competency competently: Toward a rational standard for competency-to-stand-trial assessments. *Journal of the American Academy of Psychiatry and Law, 32,* 231–245.

Mu'Min v. Virginia, 500 U.S. 315 (1991).

Myers, B., & Arena, M. P. (2001). Trial consultation: A new direction in applied psychology. *Professional Psychology: Research and Practice, 32,* 386–391.

Myers, B., & Lecci, L. (1998). Revising the factor structure of the Juror Bias Scale: A method for the empirical validation of theoretical constructs. *Law and Human Behavior, 22,* 239–256.

Nadler, J., Diamond, S. S., & Patton, M. M. (2007). Government takings of private property: *Kelo* and the perfect storm. In N. Persily, J. Citrin, & P. Egan (Eds.),

Public opinion and constitutional controversy (pp. 287–310). New York: Oxford University Press.

National Health Lawyers Association and American Medical Association. (1991). *Physician's survival guide: Legal pitfalls and solution.* Washington, DC, & Chicago: Author.

Neal, T. M. S. (2007). *Are men more credible than women?: Examining the credibility of expert witnesses as a function of eye contact behavior.* Unpublished master's thesis, University of Alabama, Tuscaloosa.

Neal, T. M. S., & Brodsky, S. L. (2008). Look into my eyes: Expert witness credibility as a function of eye contact behavior and gender. *Criminal Justice and Behavior, 35,* 1515–1526.

Nicholle, D., Turnbull, S., & Haldon, J. (2007). *The fall of Constantinople: The Ottoman conquest of Byzantium.* Oxford, UK: Osprey.

Nietzel, M. T., & Dillehay, R. C. (1986). *Psychological consultation in the courtroom.* New York: Pergamon Press.

Novak, T. I., Blaesser, B. W., & Geselbracht, T. F. (1994). Landowners need defensive strategies; when contesting condemnation cases, property owners should be well prepared to do battle in court with the government. *National Law Journal, 17,* B10.

O'Barr, W. (1982). *Linguistic evidence: Language, power and strategy in the courtroom.* New York: Academic Books.

O'Connor, A. (2006). Merchant of mercy, merchant of death: How values advocacy messages influence jury deliberations. *Journal of Applied Communication Research, 34,* 263–284.

O'Connor, M., & Mechanic, M. (2000, June). *A broader exploration of the role of gender in expert testimony.* Paper presented at the Meeting of the Society for Psychological Study of Social Issues, Ann Arbor, MI.

O'Neil, K. M., Patry, M. W., & Penrod, S. D. (2004). Exploring the effects of attitudes toward the death penalty on capital sentencing verdicts. *Psychology, Public Policy, and Law, 10,* 443–470.

Ortet-Fabregat, G., Perez, J., & Lewis, R. (1993). Measuring attitudes towards prisoners: A psychometric assessment. *Criminal justice and behavior, 20,* 190–198.

Osgood, C. E., Suci, G. J., & Tannenbaum, P. H. (1967). *The measurement of meaning.* Urbana: University of Illinois Press.

Peck, M. J. (2005). Construction of the Corporate Litigation Bias Scale (CLBS): Measuring civil juror attitudes toward corporate defendants and individual plaintiffs. *Dissertation Abstracts International: Section B. The Sciences and Engineering, 65*(11B), 609.

Pennington, N., & Hastie, R. (1992). Explaining the evidence: Tests of the story model for juror decision making. *Journal of Personality and Social Psychology, 62,* 189–206.

Perlin, M. (1994). *The jurisprudence of the insanity defense.* Raleigh: Carolina University Press.

Petsko, G. A. (2003). Everything I need to know about genomics, I learned from Yogi Berra. *Genome Biology, 4,* 102.

Pew Research Center for People and the Press. (2006, May 15). *The cell phone challenge to survey research: National polls not undermined by growing cell-only population*. Washington, DC: Author.

Philip, A. E. (1973). Assessing punitiveness with the Hostility and Direction of Hostility Questionnaire (HDHQ). *British Journal of Psychiatry, 123*, 435–439.

Plantia, J., Small, R., Fusco, S., Miller, M., & Perrault, R. (2008, August). *Investigating legal safeguards against prosecutorial misconduct in closing argument*. Paper presented at the annual convention of the American Psychological Association, Boston.

Posey, A., & Wrightsman, L. (2005). *Trial consulting*. New York: Oxford University Press.

Powell, J. T. (2006). The psychological cost of eminent domain takings and just compensation. *Law and Psychology Review, 30*, 215–227.

Price, P. C., & Stone, E. R. (2004). Intuitive evaluation of likelihood judgment producers: Evidence for a confidence heuristic. *Journal of behavioral decision making, 17*, 39–57.

Pulford, B., & Colman, A. M. (2005, April). *Testing the confidence heuristic: Are confidence communicators more persuasive?* Paper presented at the annual meeting of the British Psychological Society, Manchester, UK.

Ray, I. (1838). *A treatise on the medical jurisprudence of insanity*. Boston: Little, Brown.

Ray, J. J. (1984). The punitive personality. *Journal of Social Psychology, 125*, 329–333.

Reader's Digest. (1996). *Reader's Digest new fix-it-yourself manual: How to repair, clean, and maintain anything and everything in and around your home*. Pleasantville, NY: Author.

Reed, A. (2007, November 1). Jurors and social networking?: So what? *Deliberations: Law, news, and thoughts on juries and jury trials*. Available at *jurylaw.typepad.com/deliberations/2007/11/jurors-and-soci.html*.

Rehman, S. U., Neitert, P. J., Cope, D. W., & Kilpatrick, A. O. (2005). What to wear today?: Effect of doctor's attire on the trust and confidence of patients. *American Journal of Medicine, 118*, 1279–1286.

Rigby, K. (1987). An authority behavior inventory. *Journal of Personality Assessment, 51*, 615–625.

Robins, N. (1996). *The girl who died twice: Every patient's nightmare: The Libby Zion case and the hidden hazards of hospitals*. New York: Dell.

Robinson, J. P., Shaver, P. R., & Wrightsman, L. S. (Eds.). (1991). *Measures of personality and social psychological attitudes: Vol. 1. Measures of social psychological attitudes*. San Diego, CA: Academic Press.

Rodafinos, A., Vucevic, A., & Sideridis, G. D. (2005). The effectiveness of compliance techniques: Foot in the door versus door in the face. *Journal of Social Psychology, 145*, 237–239.

Rottman, D., Cantrell, M., Flango, R., Hansen, R., Moninger, C., & La Fountain, N. (2000). Table 41: Who conducts voir dire and the allocation of peremptory challenges. *State court organization, 1998*. Washington, DC: Bureau of

Justice Statistics. Retrieved June 25, 2007, from *www.ojp.usdoj.gov/bjs/pub/pdf/sco9806.pdf.*

Saks, M. J. (1976). The limits of scientific jury selection: Ethical and empirical. *Jurimetrics, 3,* 3–22.

Sales, B. D., & Shuman, D. W. (2005). *Experts in court: Reconciling law, science, and professional knowledge.* Washington, DC: American Psychological Association.

Sanbar, S. S., Annas, G. J., Grodin, M. A., & Wecht, C. H. (1998). Legal medicine and health law education. In American College of Legal Medicine (Ed.), *Legal medicine* (4th ed., pp. 3–20). St. Louis, MO: Mosby.

Sargent, M. J. (2004). Less thought, more punishment: Need for cognition predicts support for punitive responses to crime. *Personality and Social Psychology Bulletin, 30,* 1485–1493.

Sarver, R. A. (2008). Jury representativeness. *Dissertation Abstracts International: Section A. Humanities and Social Sciences, 68*(8-A), 3602.

Schmid, J. (2007, June). Presented in a symposium on persuasion and the use of story, annual meeting of the American Society of Trial Consultants, Long Beach, CA.

Scottberg, B., Yurcik, W., & Doss, D. (2002). Internet honeypots: Protection or entrapment? *Technology and Society,* (ISTAS '02). 2002 International Symposium on Technology and Society, 387–391.

Seib, H., & Vodanovich, S. (1998). Cognitive correlates of boredom proneness: The role of private self-consciousness and absorption. *Journal of Psychology: Interdisciplinary and Applied, 132,* 642–652.

Selzer, R. (2006). Scientific jury selection: Does it work? *Journal of Applied Social Psychology, 38,* 2417–2435.

Sinott-Armstrong, W. (1999). Entrapment in the net? *Ethics and Information Technology, 1,* 95–104.

Skitka, L. J., & Houston, D. A. (2001). When due process is of no consequence: Moral mandates and presumed defendant guilt or innocence. *Social Science Research, 14,* 305–326.

Slovenko, R. (1973). *Psychiatry and law.* Boston: Little, Brown.

Slovenko, R. (2002). *Psychiatry in law/Law in psychiatry.* London: Routledge.

Smith, J. (2004). Expert testimony in eminent domain proceedings: Oh Frye, where art thou? *Florida Law Review, 56,* 831–840.

Sommers, S. R., & Norton, M. L. (2007). Race-based judgments, race-neutral justifications: Experimental examination of peremptory use and the Batson challenge procedure. *Law and Human Behavior, 31,* 261–273.

Sorrells v. United States, 287 U.S. 435 (1932).

Spears, J. M (1975). Voir dire: Establishing minimum standards to facilitate the exercise of peremptory challenges. *Stanford Law Review, 27,* 1493–1526.

Spence, G. (2008, July 28). *Defrauding our nation's lawyers.* Gerry Spence's Blog. Retrieved August 4, 2008, from *gerryspence.wordpress.com/2008/07/28/defrauding-the-nation's-lawyers/.*

Spragins, E. (2005, December/2006, January). Ask them yourself. *FSB: Fortune Small Business,* p. 92.

Sprott, J. H. (1999). Are members of the public tough on crime?: The dimension of public "punitiveness." *Journal of Criminal Justice, 27*, 467–474.

Stancil, C. L. (2005, June 19). Accused police killer in court: Barksdale to get change of venue. *Decatur Daily*. Retrieved April 26, 2007, from *www.decaturdaily. com/decaturdaily/news/050610/court.shtml*.

Starr, P. (1982). *The social transformation of American medicine: The rise of a sovereign profession and the making of a vast industry*. New York: Basic Books.

St. John, W. (2004). *Rammer jammer yellow hammer*. New York: Three Rivers Press.

Stone, V. A., & Eswara, H. S. (1969). The likability and self-interest of the source in attitude change. *Journalism Quarterly, 46*, 61–68.

Strier, F. (1999). Whither trial consulting?: Issues and projections. *Law and Human Behavior, 23*, 93–115.

Strier, F. (2004). Why trial consultants should be licensed. *Journal of Forensic Psychology Practice, 1*, 69–76.

Studebaker, C. A., Robbennolt, J. K., Pathak-Sharma, M. K., & Penrod, S. D. (2000). Assessing pretrial publicity effects: Integrating content analytic results. *Law and Human Behavior, 24*, 317–337.

Sullivan, J., & Beech, A. (2004). Assessing Internet sex offenders. In M. C. Calder (Ed.), *Child sexual abuse and the Internet: Tackling the new frontier* (pp. 69–83). Dorset, UK: Russell House.

Swindler v. Lockhart, 495 U.S. 911 (1990).

Thomas, J., & McFayden, R. G. (1995). The confidence heuristic: A game-theoretic analysis. *Journal of Economic Psychology, 16*, 97–113.

Tiller, J., Schmidt, U., Shireen, A., & Treasure, J. (1995). Patterns of punitiveness in women with eating disorders. *International Journal of Eating Disorders, 17*, 365–371.

Toch, H. (1996). The violence-prone police officer. In W. A. Geller & H. Toch (Eds.), *Police violence: Understanding and controlling police abuse of force* (pp. 94–112). New Haven: Yale University Press.

Tooher, N. L. (2005). Trial consultants' role challenged as their influence expands. *Lawyers Weekly USA*. Retrieved August 29, 2005, from, .

Tversky, A., & Hahneman, D. (1984). Judgment under uncertainty: Heuristics and biases. *Science, 185*, 1124–1131.

Walsh, W. A., & Wolak, J. (2005). Nonforcible Internet-related sex crimes with adolescent victims: Prosecution issues and outcomes. *Child Maltreatment, 10*, 260–271.

Watt, T., & Vodanovich, S. (1992). An examination of race and gender differences in boredom proneness. *Journal of Social Behavior and Personality, 7*, 169–175.

Wedding, D., & Faust, D. (1989). Clinical judgment and decision making in neuropsychology. *Archives of Clinical Neuropsychology, 4*, 233–265.

Weiser, A., & Hargrave, J. (2001). *Judge the jury: Experience the power of reading people*. Dubuque, IA: Kendall/Hunt.

Wernowsky, K. (2007, July 19) Networking sites play new roles in legal battles; Milton man awaits fate after MySpace defense fails. *Pensacola News*.

Woodward, J. L. (1952). A scientific attempt to provide evidence for a decision on change of venue. *American Sociological Review, 17*, 447–452.

Worden, R. E. (1996). The causes of police brutality. In W. A. Geller & H. Toch (Eds.), *Police violence: Understanding and controlling police abuse of force* (pp. 23–51). New Haven, CT: Yale University Press.

Wyzga, D. (2007, June). Paper presented at a symposium on persuasion and the use of story. Annual meeting of the American Society of Trial Consultants, Long Beach, CA.

Zion vs. New York Hospital: Deadly dosage. (1995). CT1901. CourtTV Online Store. Available at *www.courttv.com/store/videos/great_deals/CT1091.html.*

Ziskin, J. (1995). *Coping with psychiatric and psychological testimony* (5th ed.). *Vol. 3. Practical guidelines, cross-examination and case illustrations.* Los Angeles: Law and Psychology Press.

Ziskin, J., & Faust, D. (1988). *Coping with psychiatric and psychological testimony:Practical guidelines, cross-examination, and case illustrations* (4th ed.): Vols. 1–3. Marina del Rey, CA: Law and Psychology Press.

INDEX

Page numbers followed by an *n* or *t* indicate notes or tables.